Georgetown University Round Table on Languages and Linguistics 1976

Semantics: Theory and Application

Clea Rameh

Editor

Georgetown University Press, Washington, D.C. 20057

BIBLIOGRAPHIC NOTICE

Since this series has been variously, and confusingly, cited as:
Georgetown University Monograph Series on Languages and Linguistics,
Monograph Series on Languages and Linguistics, Reports of the Annual
Round Table Meetings on Linguistics and Language Study, etc., begin-
ning with the 1973 volume, the title of the series was changed.

The new title of the series includes the year of a Round Table and
omits both the monograph number and the meeting number, thus:
Georgetown University Round Table on Languages and Linguistics
1976, with the regular abbreviation GURT 1976. Full bibliographical
references should show the form:

Lehmann, W. P. 1976. Diachronic semantics: 1976. In: George-
    town University Round Table on Languages and Linguistics 1976.
    Edited by Clea Rameh. Washington, D. C., Georgetown University
    Press. 1-13.

Library of Congress Catalog Card Number: 58-31607
ISBN 0-87840-111-3

CONTENTS

WELCOMING REMARKS

James E. Alatis
Dean, School of Languages and Linguistics   v

INTRODUCTION

Clea Rameh
Chairman, Georgetown University Round Table 1976   vii

SEMANTICS: SOME SYNCHRONIC AND DIACHRONIC ASPECTS

Chairman: Robert J. Di Pietro, Georgetown University

W. P. Lehmann
Diachronic semantics: 1976   1

SEMANTICS AND LINGUISTICS

Chairman: Rev. Walter A. Cook, S. J., Georgetown University

Jorge Hankamer
The semantic interpretation of anaphoric expressions   15

Ray Jackendoff
Toward a cognitively viable semantics   59

Geoffrey Leech
Metalanguage, pragmatics, and performatives   81

Barbara Hall Partee
Semantics and syntax: The search for constraints   99

iii

SEMANTICS AND OTHER DISCIPLINES

Chairman: R. Ross Macdonald, Georgetown University

Oswald Werner and Martin D. Topper
On the theoretical unity of ethnoscience lexicography
and ethnoscience ethnographies   111

Chuck Rieger
The representation and selection of commonsense knowledge
for natural language comprehension   145

Gilbert Harman
Logic and grammar   173

Alfonso Caramazza and Ellen Grober
Polysemy and the structure of the subjective lexicon   181

SEMANTICS AND LANGUAGE PEDAGOGY

Chairman: Maria Isabel Abreu, Georgetown University

Frances M. Aid
Semantics in Spanish language curricula   207

Milton M. Azevedo
Thematic meaning, word order, and
indefinite actor sentences in Portuguese   217

Christopher N. Candlin
Communicative language teaching and the debt to
pragmatics   237

Ragnhild Söderbergh
Learning to read between two and five: Some observations
on normal hearing and deaf children   257

WELCOMING REMARKS

JAMES E. ALATIS

Dean, School of Languages and Linguistics
Georgetown University

Good evening, ladies and gentlemen. It gives me much pleasure, indeed, to welcome you, on behalf of Georgetown University and its School of Languages and Linguistics, to this, the 27th Annual Georgetown University Round Table.

The theme of our conference this year is 'Semantics: Theory and Application.' The program will take an interdisciplinary approach to include the fields of anthropology, computer science, philosophy, and psychology. In keeping with this viewpoint, interest-group sessions were held this afternoon so that the Round Table could be responsive to as broad a range of participants as possible.

Here in the School of Languages and Linguistics we have tried to develop a program in which students understand linguistic theory in its application to the study of languages. In the past, the relationship of semantics to the study of linguistics was little understood and therefore neglected. Now, however, we are beginning to learn how important a field it is, and--once it is understood scientifically--the impact it will have on linguistics. Because we in the School of Languages and Linguistics believe that penetrating this field is important to the future of linguistics, we decided that semantics would be a most appropriate topic for this year's Round Table.

I am most impressed with the roster of speakers and know there is much we can learn from all of them. I want to take this opportunity to congratulate and thank Dr. Clea Rameh for her fine selection of participants and for her organizational skill and professional competence in preparing for this event.

In closing may I say that the School of Languages and Linguistics takes much pride in its twenty-seven years of sponsorship of these meetings, and extends its thanks to all of you who have come to participate and help us celebrate this twenty-seventh anniversary of the Georgetown University Round Table.

INTRODUCTION

For the last twenty-seven years, Georgetown University's Annual Round Table Meetings on Languages and Linguistics have brought together scholars in linguistics and related disciplines to report on their latest research and to discuss current problems. The present volume represents the proceedings of the Georgetown University Round Table on Languages and Linguistics 1976. The theme of the meeting was: 'Semantics: Theory and application'.

The fourteen papers of the plenary sessions attempted to discuss current developments in semantics and its relationships to theoretical linguistics, to applied linguistics, and to other related disciplines. Thus, the first plenary session discussed semantics from the viewpoints of synchronic and diachronic linguistics. The second plenary session discussed semantics from the viewpoints of generative grammar, interpretive semantics, pragmatics, and Montague grammar. The third session discussed semantics and its relationships with anthropology, with computer science, with philosophy, and with psychology. The fourth session discussed semantics and language teaching pedagogy. This included the discussion of semantics in relation to the teaching of specific languages and language skills: semantics and its relationship to Spanish language curricula, to the teaching of particular Portuguese structures, to the teaching of English for communication where the foreign language pedagogy stresses teaching for communication rather than the teaching of the foreign language structural code, and finally, to the teaching of early reading to normal hearing and deaf children.

Of these fourteen papers, the one by Dwight Bolinger, 'A case of lexical invariance: There', will appear as a chapter in his forthcoming book Meaning and Form, to be published by the Longman Group, Ltd., as part of the English Language Series under the editorship of Professor Randolph Quirk (University College, London). This paper does not appear in this volume.

In addition to these plenary sessions of the <u>Georgetown University Round Table on Languages and Linguistics 1976,</u> fourteen interest groups were organized. Each group was directed by a chairman responsible for the format of his particular group. The purpose of these groups was to provide an opportunity for as many scholars as possible to discuss topics of mutual concern and interest.

The topics and chairmen of these groups were the following: (1) TEFL: English for special purposes, James E. Alatis, Georgetown University; (2) Communication strategies and modern language teaching, Frederick Bosco, Georgetown University; (3) The semantics of tense and aspect in English, Walter A. Cook, S.J., Georgetown University; (4) Semantics, cognition, and the brain, William Orr Dingwall, University of Maryland; (5) Linguistics, psychoanalysis, and dynamics of language groups, Robert J. Di Pietro, Georgetown University; (6) Semantics and the teaching of English to speakers of other dialects, Ralph Fasold, Georgetown University; (7) Linguistics and early reading, Robert Lado, Georgetown University, and Theodore Andersson, University of Texas at Austin; (8) Semantics and computer science, R. Ross Macdonald, Georgetown University; (9) Literature for basic language skills, Marzieh Samii, Ferdowsi (Meshed) University, and David P. Harris, Georgetown University; (10) Acquiring meaning in a second culture, Muriel Saville-Troike, Georgetown University; (11) Historical semantics, Shaligram Shukla, Georgetown University; (12) Sign language, semantics, semiotics, William C. Stokoe, Gallaudet College; (13) Bilingual education, F. LeRoy Walser, Office of Bilingual Education, USOE; (14) Comprehension in reading, Stanley Wanat, Cornell University.

As chairman, I would like to express my thanks to my colleagues who generously assisted me with advice and suggestions, as well as to the chairmen of the plenary sessions and interest groups; to the students who volunteered their time and help; and to the staff of the School of Languages and Linguistics who were so helpful in all kinds of ways. But I would like to acknowledge particularly the interest and support of Professor James E. Alatis, Dean of the School of Languages and Linguistics, and the assistance of Professor William Orr Dingwall of the University of Maryland. I also want to thank Michelle S. Bourgeois, who supervised and coordinated details and arrangements, and Leslie V. Dery, Robert M. Barrett, and Barbara Bab, for their contribution to the smooth running of the conference.

Finally, I am grateful to Professor Richard J. O'Brien, S.J., for his valuable suggestions and expertise both during the planning of the conference and the editing of the papers; and to Miss Eleanor Waters for her careful work in editing and proofreading the copy.

Clea Rameh

DIACHRONIC SEMANTICS: 1976

W. P. LEHMANN

University of Texas at Austin

Abstract. Diachronic semantics has been a topic of considerable
attention, which has led to various generalizations about the history
of words and about changes in the semantic component of language.
Historical linguists have developed procedures for relating words
with items in a culture, so that etymology is well advanced, based
largely on philological investigation. Advances in the understanding
of semantic systems will come through analyses of semantic fields
or sets, such as kinship terms and terms for domesticated animals.
In the study of such sets homology is a promising technique for
identifying poorly understood elements. Important contributions
will continue from detailed analyses of texts.

It is a commonplace that historical linguistics would be impossible
if language had no distinct semantic component. If there were some
necessary relationship between a thing and its name, say a 'man of
distinguished courage or ability' and the word hero, we could not
succeed in reconstructing the history or etymology of a word, nor in
producing a history of language. The huge amount of publication in
diachronic semantics, which can only be fragmentarily represented
here, alone gives the lie to such a conclusion (cf. the references in
Ullmann 1966 and Nida 1975). As a matter of fact, if a thing and its
name were necessarily related, the name or word should not change;
in such a linguistic elysium there would be no history.

Historical linguistics must view semantics as a study aimed at
determining relationships between language and the outside world.
Distributive semantics, the undertaking in which the interrelationships
between words in a lexicon are studied, is, of course, not neglected;

1

the topic was treated by a distinguished historical linguist at an
earlier Georgetown University Round Table meeting, the eleventh
(Hoenigswald 1962). By studying its distribution, for example, one
can label OE mēce as 'sword'; but unless a historian of English can
identify mēce as referring to a long sword among the half dozen or
so other words for 'sword' in Old English, he will consider his task
unfinished. Historical semantics, then, is closely related to linguistic paleontology, the attempt to delineate a culture on the basis
of a language. A historical linguist seeks to determine the meaning
of a word or other linguistic element for its speakers--to relate
such elements in the course of their modifications with objects and
concepts in real life.

In his study of meaning a historical linguist may have one of
several central aims. He may seek to determine the meanings of
words and other elements of a language in the past. Or he may pur-
sue the change of meaning of such elements. Achievement of each
aim depends heavily on the state of semantic theory, on understanding of devices for marking meaning in language, and on adequate
texts.

Unless we have adequate texts, giving detailed documentation of an
element in language, we cannot reliably determine the history of that
element, whether of form or meaning. Such detailed documentation
is available for only a few elements in language. The word kodak is
one. We know how, when, and why George Eastman invented this
word, and the advantages he obtained from patenting it in 1888. But
we cannot be certain about many other recent elements, like (ice
cream) sundae or OK, or of culturally important words like hero.
No one would propose any longer, as did Socrates in Plato's dialogue
Cratylus, that hērōs 'hero' is derived from érōs 'love' because male
gods gave rise to heroes through love affairs with human women.
Rather, on the basis of comparison with forms in Greek dialects unknown to Socrates or Plato, hero is now derived from the same base
as is Latin servō 'maintain intact, preserve', later 'serve'. Since
the days of Plato a good deal has been learned about the formal systems
of language and about relationships between languages, much of it in
the nineteenth century. Socrates might have been startled by the proposal that the word for hero was related to the word for servant, but
with our knowledge of language and its changes we propose such relationships. For us this etymology of hero is acceptable because we
have observed that a sound change like that of s to h in Greek is
credible, and because we expect languages with a historical background
of OV structure to make derivatives through suffixation.

This etymology is also credible because of the procedures that have
been developed in the study of texts. These procedures were produced
by the discipline known as philology.

Philology is primarily concerned with the interpretation of texts. Yet philologists have long known that such interpretation is impossible without an understanding of the culture in which the texts were produced. In their attempts to understand such cultures, philologists are much like anthropologists or ethnologists. The two types of scholars differ primarily in the kinds of materials and times of cultures studied. Philologists deal with ancient cultures. While they use all available means to understand such cultures, their primary access is through texts. Anthropologists or ethnologists, on the other hand, have been primarily concerned with nonliterate peoples. Fortunately, the two groups of scholars are moving closer together, applying the common findings and techniques (cf. for example Schuyler 1976). We have, in short, a good understanding of the analysis and interpretation of texts, and of the formal components of language, that is to say, of phonology, morphology, and syntax.

Our understanding and treatment of the semantic component in historical linguistics, on the other hand, has been far more limited. If a word is phonologically unidentifiable, we have been able to do little about its history, even if we may seem to know its meaning. Proper nouns, or names, provide many examples. We cannot give with certainty the etymology of the names of Indra or Varuna, two of the leading gods of the Rigveda. In the nineteenth century it seemed attractive to relate the name Varuna to Latin Uranus, Greek Ouranós. But phonological difficulties rule out the relationship, even though the three gods have something to do with the sky and with the bringing of rain and fertility. Our control of semantic possibilities has been far too weak to overturn formal evidence.

As a result, etymologies proposed on the basis of meaning alone have not been accepted. There is no question about the reference for Germani 'Germans' from the time of its first occurrence in Latin texts. It designates indigenous peoples of western Europe, especially those to the right of the Rhine. But no one has produced an accepted etymology of the name, though many fanciful etymologies have been advanced. As all of us could illustrate, fanciful etymologies of names are well known among children and genealogists, who profit from them. One, not very gracious, was told me by an old member of the German community in St. Louis, which may have been wealthier and more numerous but was less prestigious than the French. Asked for the etymology of her name by a woman who wanted to be placed among the select French group, he pondered about the source of Dubendrick and then gave his verdict: 'ah Duben-dreck' --the Low German for 'dove-droppings'. In his callousness he was probably no more correct than she was in her hopes. But any of us can spin tales in this way with proper names, since they are often grossly modified phonologically and the semantic possibilities allow our imaginations great latitude.

Yet though the etymology of isolated words may be difficult to determine, and though semantic observations cannot overturn those based on phonology and morphology, we have achieved some understanding of historical semantics which will permit advances in the field. It has long been observed that there are universal processes in historical semantic change such as metaphor (cf. for example, Ullmann 1966). Further, many metaphors are anthropomorphic, leading to ever farther development from the initial concrete reference; the 'head' of a class may still be an organism, but not the 'head' of a construction. An understanding of this process enables us to determine the origin of such labels as article, as in definite article, from the term for a joint as in ankle or neck.

Besides such observations semantic laws have been proposed, such as Sperber's on metaphorical expansion. According to Sperber, a complex of ideas may be so strongly charged with feeling that if it causes one word to extend its sphere and change its meaning, other words belonging to the same emotional complex will shift their meaning (Ullmann 1966:240; Sperber 1923:67). In support of his law Sperber cited labels for weapons, which soldiers in the First World War transferred to other spheres, such as females--or vice versa, as in the term 'Big Bertha' for a huge howitzer. Linguists provide further evidence for the law, though their emotions seem to be fired by spheres like folklore, which yields metaphors like pied-piping, or spheres like nature, which yields metaphors like node, branching, and so on. Besides metaphors, other widely observed processes of semantic change, such as those associated with taboo and synaesthesia, are cited in every elementary handbook on historical linguistics, in this way illustrating the assurance with which they are viewed.

Comparable assurance may be observed regarding general conclusions based on semantic characteristics. We find, for example, synonymy or near synonymy in those portions of a lexicon which include concepts of importance in a culture. Lexical differentiation resulting in synonyms or near synonyms is made to specify distinctions among such concepts. Among well-known examples are the many words in Eskimo for 'snow', which can be matched in a country like Norway where skiing is a common pursuit, or the many terms in Arabic for 'camel', which can be matched for 'horse' among our equestrians. Those of us who prefer more rapid transportation at the sacrifice of contact with the organic have numerous terms for the rarely used words automobile and airplane. By examining clumps of words with similar meaning in a language accordingly, we can draw some conclusions about its semantic system, and about the accompanying social system. As a historical example, the many words for 'sword' in Old English and for 'ruler' indicate the prominence of concern with warfare and societal hierarchy among its speakers. To provide current examples, we can look into descriptions of languages and associated cultures made by anthropologists, such as Malinowski's Coral Gardens and Their Magic; the language of the Trobriand Islanders has many terms for land and gardens, discussed by Malinowski with frequent commentary like 'almost synonymous expressions' (1935: 80).

When, on the other hand, we find polysemy, we conclude that the words in question have high frequency of use. The frequency of the NE verb get with its many meanings provides an illustration, as do adjectives like good and fine, nouns like front, period, seat, thing, and so on. Observing the many meanings of OE mōd 'mind, spirit, heart, courage, pride, arrogance', we would assume that it had high frequency in Old English; similarly, helm 'protection, cover, helmet, lord, protector'. The converse is not true. Though god is highly frequent in New English and Old English, it does not have a remarkable range of meanings. Yet by noting words of broad range, such as many prepositions, we obtain further insights into a semantic system.

Moreover, the occurrence of homonyms suggests that phonological changes have brought about the equivalence of sound. The English words [tuw] may serve as illustration. In the numeral, the bilabial sound [w] was lost before a high back vowel leading to homophony with the adverb and the preposition. We would posit a similar explanation for OE āeht 'property' and āeht 'pursuit', for NE elder in reference to a human and to a shrub, where the d is excrescent. For the Middle English speaker, Judas hanged himself on an eller, not on an elder.

These three semantic situations--prominent synonymy, prominent polysemy, and prominent homonymy in selected areas--can then lead us to insights concerning the semantic structure and the semantic developments in a language. We may observe that these insights depend on a structural view of the semantic component. However badly the term 'structural' has been manhandled in some recent linguistic treatises, it is clear that many of our advances in understanding the semantic and phonological components of language, to say nothing of the syntactic component, have come and will continue to come from regarding language and its components and subcomponents as structures, rather than as masses of isolated and independent elements. The increasing attention to the semantic component from a structural point of view permits us to begin to characterize the semantic system of a language rather than merely to give the history of individual words, as is done in etymological dictionaries.

The most notable instance of the structural view in semantics is Joost Trier's 'field theory'. By Trier's approach structural sets of the lexical component are identified and interpreted. The best known and most widely studied sets are kinship terms and color terms.

Anthropological linguists have identified and labeled characteristic patterns of such sets. The field of color terms may, for example, be based on degrees of shade or variations in hue. The current English set of color terms is based on hue; that of Old English may not have been, but like the Old Irish set may have been based on degrees of shade (R. P. M. Lehmann 1969). Such suggestions remain to be substantiated by historical linguists.

Sets of kinship terms may vary, in accordance with the views of relationship in a given culture. If, for example, terms for 'grandfather' and 'maternal uncle' are equivalent or parallel, as in Latin avus 'grandfather' and avunculus 'maternal uncle' as compared with patruus 'paternal uncle', the kinship system is patterned like a widely studied and identified variant of this semantic field; such a system has been labeled Omaha (cf. Friedrich 1966).

Identification of these and other fields, and characterization of specific fields, has provided an improved understanding of the semantic systems of languages in the past as well as the structure of the field of kinship terms in languages of interest to historical linguists. If, for example, a historical linguist were to find that in a reconstructed language the terms for maternal uncle and grandfather are similar, he would without further ado draw specific conclusions about the entire kinship system. The same procedures have been applied to other related sets, such as names for trees, labels for drinking terms, and so on.

Application of such understanding calls our attention to problems which indicate modifications that have taken place in a given language. For example, in the early Germanic dialects we find a number of kinship terms, which we must posit for Proto-Germanic as well, beside inherited terms. In the interests of simplicity I cite only the Gothic terms; magus 'boy, son' is a near synonym of the inherited sunus. Like mawi 'girl, daughter', a near synonym of dauhtar, and megs 'son-in-law', it carries the connotation of a family member related through marriage. These terms are also used for male and female servants in some of the Germanic dialects. As I have pointed out elsewhere (1968:15), the Gothic term magus is used in the sense of son only in Luke 2.48, when Mary addresses her son Jesus. To translate expressions referring to Jesus such as 'son of David', the inherited term sunus is used. The new terms then seem to carry the connotation of maternal descendants. In keeping with the observation that synonyms and near-synonyms reflect distinctions in a culture, we may conclude that these words point to a concern for refining the kinship designations in Proto-Germanic. Why this distinction was introduced, and how it reflects the family structure of 500 B.C. and later, is another problem. Presumably, the Germanic semantic system for kinship, and its social system, underwent modifications, probably as a result of outside influences.

The study of such modifications is now one of the major tasks in historical linguistics. We must set out to determine how the elements in a semantic system are modified as that system changes. The situation may well be comparable to that in syntax. Notable advances in our understanding of language have resulted in the past decade from observation of interrelated changes in syntax. When the position of the object (O) with regard to its verb (V) is changed, other characteristic syntactic patterns also undergo modification. German provides an instructive example. After OV order was established for subordinate clauses around A. D. 1500, other OV characteristics came to be introduced. Among these are postpositions. An example is entgegen, which unlike NE against is placed after its object. In Middle English, by contrast, the postposition emel 'between', which was taken over from Old Norse i millum, developed into a preposition before it was lost. We can determine the time of introduction of the German postpositions; they are attested several centuries after the establishment of the OV clause order. At the same time the German participial modifier construction became widespread, giving German a preposed modifying clause comparable to the preposed relative construction of OV languages (Lehmann 1971).

Investigation of the western Indo-European dialects has disclosed in a similar way the gradual modification of syntactic constructions towards VO patterning. English, for example, which manifests numerous OV characteristics in its earliest records, has been developing towards such VO patterns as postposed genitives. During the past millennium the proportion of genitive constructions has changed from approximately 90 percent of the preposed type, like John's horse, to 90 or more percent of the postposed type, like the horse of the Smith girls (Fries 1940). We still maintain preposed adjectives, except when these are modified as in the horse frightened by the car, lagging in this way behind the Romance languages in the shift from OV to VO structure. Investigations of syntactic shifts have also been carried out for non-Indo-European languages, especially in the recent Santa Barbara conferences (Li 1975, 1976).

These investigations lead to the conclusion that the syntactic component of language includes many constructions which are intimately related. When the key construction, that is, the position of the object with regard to its verb, is modified, other constructions are affected (Lehmann 1973). These observations have led to a wealth of new insights, and are pointing to problems which must be further investigated.

Historical linguists need to examine semantic sets in the same way. It is important to determine how changes take place in such sets, and what causes them. If the linguistic changes are brought about by changes in the culture, we will have a clearer understanding of the relationships between language and the outside world. Moreover, if semantic changes are carried out with no effect on the syntactic or phonological components, our understanding of the relationships between these three large components of grammar will be deepened.

The Germanic etyma of Gothic magus, mawi, and megs may well have been introduced to flesh out the elements desired in an Omaha system (Friedrich 1966:30). But for an understanding of changes in semantic sets we must deal with historic rather than prehistoric languages. Detailed studies should be carried out, for example, on the changes in the English kinship system. We have abandoned the Old English terms for both paternal uncle fædera and maternal uncle eam, adding instead the borrowing uncle. By Middle English times fædera was completely lost, and eam was used for maternal and paternal uncle, also for 'ancestor' and 'nephew'. Similarly, we have introduced one word for paternal and maternal aunt, replacing OE faðu and mōdrie. The reduction in the system is obvious, but when and why did it take place? As in syntactic study, we need to be concerned primarily with the categories rather than with the surface elements, noting that the Omaha kinship system has been broken down. Studies are now needed on a large scale to disclose how such semantic sets are modified in language. For kinship systems, linguists might begin with investigations of changes in the western Indo-European languages, though all documented languages must be studied in this way.

Germanic is used here as an example because considerable attention has been given to it. The results of these studies may clarify some of the problems which historical semantics should attempt to solve. These problems involve understanding the social and cultural system with which a language is associated as well as the semantic system, on the grounds mentioned earlier, that if we cannot posit satisfactory relationships between reconstructed words and the outside world, the results are bland and academic. As archeological evidence becomes more abundant and more secure, the terms which are widely cited in the standard handbooks will gain additional credence and they, in turn, will amplify conclusions from archeological finds.

The secure terms for such animals as the horse, cow, pig, and dog assure us of the set of domesticated animals in Proto-Germanic times, as the lack of terms for cat suggests its absence--conclusions supported by archeological evidence. Other linguistic evidence is in greater need of archeological supplementation, such as the term sheep and its cognates, found only in the West Germanic languages, in contrast with Gothic lamb and North Germanic sauðr, current Norwegian sau. Presumably, the terms for 'sheep' should not be assumed among

the set of domesticated animal terms in early Germanic, for the
animal may not have been adaptable to the Germanic territory until
the first millennium before our era, when some of the northern
forests had been cleared. When dealing with the Indo-European set
of terms for domesticated animals, we may make similar inferences
about the word for 'goat', and also about late acquaintance with goats
in Indo-European culture, on the basis of the diversity of terms: aja
in Sanskrit, aîks in Greek, capra in Latin, goat and its cognates in
English, Gothic, and North Germanic, in contrast with Ziege in High
German. By one hypothesis the consonants were metathesized in
Proto-Germanic, indicating awkwardness about the term, somewhat
comparable to our remodeling of orangutang or the apparent modification of Greek eléphas, eléphantos in Gothic ulbandus, meaning
'camel' (cf. Specht 1947, esp. 32-35).

Besides noting the terms, we should study the semantic sets of
designations for such animals, much like the kinship sets. A
semantic set for the long domesticated animals has five categories
in English: a generic name, such as horse, cattle, swine, dog; a
name for the female, such as mare, cow, sow, bitch; a name for the
male, such as stallion, bull, boar, but simply dog; a name for the
young, such as colt, calf, shoat, and pup; a name for the castrated
male, such as gelding, steer, barrow. It is instructive to observe
that sheep and chicken have developed such sets in English; goat has
not, even after several millennia, nor have duck and goose and donkey,
not to speak of well-known animals like elephants or camels. The
wild animals which come close are deer, with buck, doe, and fawn;
rabbit, with the same terms, except for the young; and swan, with
pen, cob, and cygnet. Besides observing the presence of such sets,
we must note their changes. The set for sheep or swine may not be
known to many speakers of English today, except for crossword
puzzle buffs. As with kinship sets, there are ample possibilities for
exploring semantic change.

Other Germanic terms provide problems of identification. It is
obvious, for example, that pottery and clay receptacles were prominent in the late neolithic age and thereafter; a culture may even be
designated by the kinds of pots it designs, such as 'corded-ware'.
We have many names in Germanic for pottery: pot itself is probably
from PIE budno- 'swelled out shape'; Danish gryde, related to NE
grit, is possibly a pot made of soft stone; NE crock was apparently
a small earthenware vessel; OE grēofa, presumably a roasting pan;
OHG hafan, presumably a storage vessel; NHG Topf, a shell-like
vessel (Buck 1949:341). These and other terms we would like to
associate with specific types of pots or vessels dug up by archeolo-
gists. One assumes that each type had a specific designation, and
that the names that have come down to us referred to specific shapes

or types. When we compare the even more numerous terms in the well-documented Ancient Egyptian, we find that the terms have been identified and related to specific receptacles. One hopes for such achievement in the early Indo-European dialects, including Germanic, to refine the meanings of terms and also to advance our understanding of the languages and their cultures. But how can we advance to such understanding?

We may move towards an answer through a technique adopted from biology that has been proposed recently to identify the meanings of poorly understood elements in a semantic set. The technique is called homology. Though probably known most widely from the works of Lévi-Strauss (e. g. 1966:93), homology is nicely illustrated in a recent article by Leonard R. Palmer (1974:11-19). I use his definition of it: 'Two or more terms constitute an homology when they exhibit semantic similarities and occur in a particular site of a semantic structure' (1974:12). As an example he gives the English term captain and the German Hauptmann. The semantic similarity they exhibit has to do with the relationship of each to words meaning 'head'; and both occur in the site of words for officers between lieutenant and major. The technique will not solve problems magically in historical semantics. Palmer's own study is published as a homological 'sketch' because in his words: 'twenty years of desultory research into the terminology of land-tenure have convinced me that a lifetime is not long enough for its completion' (1974:12). Nevertheless, Palmer makes an important identification. He proposes that Old Indic arya-, the term taken by some nineteenth century scholars to refer to the original speakers of Indic languages, and later debased, belonged to a homological set with brāhman and vaiśya: arya designated the warrior nobility with landed property. Adapted then to use as an ethnic term, it was replaced by the term ksatriya-.

Whether or not Palmer's views on Indic land tenure are accepted, the procedures illustrate a remarkable gain for historical semantic studies. As Palmer indicates, in dealing with 'homological structures the units compared are not sound-meaning units but purely semantic units' (1974:18). Homologies then are proposed to solve the old problem of determining the position of an element from its meaning alone, without involving its formal characteristics. The procedure can be used because semantic elements are dealt with in sets--in Trier's term, fields or subfields. To the extent that the use of homologies can be refined, historical semantics will have a tool comparable to those of historical phonology, historical morphology, and historical syntax.

Homological studies have also been carried out by Watkins, in clarifying terms used in Old Irish and Latin law and religion. Comparing these then with Hittite legal terms, Watkins has proposed a similar set of terms, and of activities, for the Indo-European culture of 3000 B.C. (e.g. Watkins 1973:370).

Yet homology will not solve all the problems of historical semantics, such as those that one faces in dealing with names. For names infrequently belong to such structural sets, as, for example, Essex, Sussex, and Wessex. Moreover, even in sets one must have some identification. One would like to apply the technique to the Germanic names for pottery, which to my knowledge have not been aligned with the actual finds. Until this is done, the words are somewhat like the words of a language for which we know the pronunciation and something of their relationship with other words, but not their references to specific objects in the outside world. Yet to apply the technique of homology, one or more of the names needs to be associated with well-known types of pottery. Such association, and further identification based on homology, would be a highly welcome contribution to Germanic studies.

Yet while historical linguists muster their courage to reach such difficult objectives, they must continue with the established procedures, such as those described and exemplified by Émile Benveniste.

Benveniste reviewed the procedures some twenty years ago, and subsequently exemplified them brilliantly in several collections of essays which are still too little known, even though they are now available in English (1954:251-64; 1966; 1969). The basic principle he proposes is as follows: 'the meaning of a linguistic form is defined by the types of association therefrom' (1954:249). In illustrating the application of the principle, Benveniste discusses such words as Greek tréphō, which is commonly used in the sense 'rear, bring up (children)', but also has the sense 'curdle (milk)'. Two homophones might be assumed. Benveniste, however, concludes from examining the 'totality of its uses' that the verb basically meant: 'to encourage the development of that which is subject to growth'--whether children or milk. The semantic problem then is to be found in English, not Greek. Semantic elements in this way are to be studied in the system in which they are found. In such study 'distinctive features' are to be identified, as has again been proposed by transformational linguists, and widely pursued in subsequent semantic studies (Benveniste 1954: 264).

Such study leads to illumination of the contemporary culture as well as the semantic system. One of Benveniste's most striking essays concerns the word civilization. Like other -ization words, e.g. fertilization, civilization might be expected to mean 'act of civilizing' rather than an achieved state, as it indeed did in some of its earliest uses around 1760--when it is first attested in English and also in French. According to Boswell, Samuel Johnson objected to it, preferring civility. Similarly, nouns in -ation used in the

Declaration of Independence also refer to acts rather than states, e. g. usurpation, migration, naturalization, and also population. The focus on 'state' in civilization interests Benveniste not only for the semantic change but also because it reflects 'changes in the traditional concept of man and society'. The earlier conception of the 'current state of man in society', expressed by civilité--a static term--was being modified to the conception of a 'universal and gradual development' among the optimistic thinkers of the Enlightenment, who included the men of influence in the formation of our country. Such study and the study of a few dozen other essential words may then in Benveniste's phrase illuminate 'the whole history of modern thought and the principal intellectual achievements' of the Western world (1966:336).

Diachronic semantics should in this way seek also to illuminate the 'history of thought' and the 'intellectual achievements' of any age. Language provides access to these. Our knowledge of the language may be less extensive than it is of French and English two hundred years ago, which even with their relatively full documentation left problems for Benveniste. But with increased understanding of semantic systems, and of the processes involved in semantic change, historical linguists can proceed to surer and more ample conclusions about semantic systems and their change than were possible in the past. Languages will then be more fully described, as well as the societies and cultures in which they were used.

REFERENCES

Benveniste, Émile. 1954. Semantic problems in reconstruction. Word 10. 249-264.

_____. 1966. Problèmes de linguistique générale. Paris, Gallimard. Translated as Problems in general linguistics, by Mary Elizabeth Meek. Coral Gables, University of Miami, 1971.

_____. 1969. Le vocabulaire des institutions indo-européennes. Paris, Minuit. Translated as Indo-European language and society, by Elizabeth Palmer. London, Faber and Faber, 1973.

Buck, Carl Darling. 1949. A dictionary of selected synonyms in the principal Indo-European languages. Chicago, The University of Chicago Press.

Friedrich, Paul. 1966. Proto-Indo-European kinship. Ethnology 5. 1-36.

Fries, Charles C. 1940. On the development of the structural use of word-order in Modern English. Lg. 16. 199-208.

Hoenigswald, Henry M. 1962. Synchronic and diachronic aspects of distributional meaning. In: Georgetown University Round Table on Languages and Linguistics 1962. Edited by Bernard Choseed. Washington, D. C., Georgetown University Press. 21-28.

Leech, Geoffrey. 1974. Semantics. Hammondsworth, Penguin.

Lehmann, R. P. M. 1969. Color usage in Irish. In: Studies in language, literature, and culture of the Middle Ages and later. Edited by E. Bagby Atwood and Archibald A. Hill. Austin, University of Texas. 73-79.

Lehmann, W. P. 1968. The Proto-Germanic words inherited from Proto-Indo-European which reflect the social and economic status of the speakers. Zeitschrift für Mundartforschung 1968. 1-25.

_____. 1971. On the rise of SOV patterns in New High German. In: Grammatik Kybernetik Kommunikation. Edited by K. G. Schweisthal. Bonn, Dümmler. 19-24.

_____. 1973. A structural principle of language and its implications. Lg. 49. 47-66.

Lévi-Strauss, Claude. 1966. The savage mind. Chicago, The University of Chicago Press.

Li, Charles N., ed. 1975. Word order and word order change. Austin, University of Texas Press.

_____. 1976. Subject and topic. New York, Academic Press.

Malinowski, Bronislaw. 1935. Coral gardens and their magic. II. London, Allen and Unwin.

Nida, Eugene A. 1975. Exploring semantic structures. München, Fink.

Palmer, Leonard R. 1974. Arya-. A homological sketch. In: Antiquitates Indogermanicae. Edited by Manfred Mayrhofer et al. Innsbruck, Institut für Sprachwissenschaft. 11-19.

Schuyler, Robert L. 1976. Review of Reconstructing complex societies. Edited by Charlotte B. Moore. Cambridge, Mass., American Schools of Oriental Research, 1974. Science 191. 1039-41.

Specht, Franz. 1947. Der Ursprung der Indogermanischen Deklination. Göttingen, Vandenhoeck and Ruprecht.

Sperber, Hans. 1923. 2nd ed. 1930. Einführung in die Bedeutungslehre. Bonn and Leipzig, Schroeder.

Trier, Joost. 1931. Der deutsche Wortschatz im Sinnbezirk des Verstandes: die Geschichte eines sprachlichen Feldes. Heidelberg, Winter.

Ullmann, Stephen. 1964. Semantics. An introduction to the science of meaning. Oxford, Blackwell.

_____. 1966. Semantic universals. In: Universals of language. Edited by Joseph H. Greenberg. Cambridge, Mass., MIT Press. 217-262.

Watkins, Calvert. 1973. Latin ador, Hittite ḫat- again. In: Indo-European studies ii. Edited by Calvert Watkins. Cambridge, Mass., Harvard University, Department of Linguistics. 367-378.

THE SEMANTIC INTERPRETATION OF ANAPHORIC EXPRESSIONS

JORGE HANKAMER

Harvard University

Abstract. The linguistic literature contains two major and diametrically opposed proposals for the semantic interpretation of
anaphoric expressions. The 'classical' transformational approach
has all anaphors derived from underlying full representations by a
deletion or substitution process; these underlying forms then receive
their interpretations by the same means as any ordinary expressions
(classically, by rules of semantic interpretation operating off of deep
structures). A strict interpretive approach such as that developed in
Jackendoff (1972), Wasow (1972) treats anaphoric expressions as
underlyingly present and meaningless dummies which are assigned
semantic interpretations by special rules at some superficial level
in syntactic derivations.

Arguments on purely syntactic grounds have been brought forth
against both of these extreme positions, and it is argued in a recent
paper (Hankamer and Sag 1976, to appear) that neither can be maintained as a theory of anaphora in general. Rather, it is necessary to
adopt a mixed theory which treats one class of anaphoric expressions
(which we call 'surface' anaphors) as derived by deletion, and another
class (which we call 'deep' anaphors) as underlyingly present in syntactic representations.

The present paper briefly recapitulates the arguments which lead
to this conclusion and then considers the implications of this result
for the theory of semantic interpretation of anaphoric expressions.
It is shown herein that none of the arguments against the transformational treatment of certain kinds of anaphora constitute arguments for the assignment of interpretation at a superficial level of

structure, but only for the presence of the anaphor at a deep level. Further, it is shown that the semantic interpretation of deep anaphors must in general be assigned at some essentially nonsyntactic level, so that in the theory which we are forced to adopt, no anaphors are assigned semantic interpretation by interpretive rules operating at a superficial level in derivations.

0. Introduction. One of the most prominent universal features of natural language is the device of anaphora. In most general terms, an anaphor is an expression which has no fixed semantic interpretation of its own, but rather may be assigned (by some regular grammatical process) any of an infinite number of interpretations varying with and determined by context. The following are examples of sentences containing anaphoric expressions:

(1a) Though <u>my uncle</u> trains <u>tigers</u>, he fears <u>them</u>.
(1b) Sue was riding the small <u>donkey</u>, and Al was riding the big <u>one</u>.
(1c) I tried to <u>get the animal to eat the hay</u>, but I couldn't $\emptyset$.
(1d) They say <u>she's fat now</u>, but I don't believe <u>it</u>.

In each of the examples given, the anaphoric expression (indicated by the single underscore) is associated with a semantic interpretation identical to that of some nonanaphoric segment of the discourse (the 'antecedent' of the anaphor). [1] In the examples, the antecedent is indicated by a double underscore.

There have been two major and diametrically opposed proposals for the semantic interpretation of anaphoric expressions. The 'classical' transformational approach has all anaphors derived from underlying full representations by a deletion or substitution process; these underlying forms then receive their interpretations by the same means as any ordinary expressions (classically, by rules of semantic interpretation operating off of deep structures). The anaphors are thus related to their semantic representations through the transformational derivation.

The alternative approach is the interpretive one developed, for example, in Jackendoff (1972), Wasow (1972), and others. According to this approach, anaphoric expressions are not derived from more explicit full representations at all, but are present in underlying structures in essentially their surface form. These anaphoric items are assumed to have no semantic interpretation at the level of underlying representation; they are assigned semantic interpretations by means of special rules at some superficial level in syntactic derivations.

Arguments on purely syntactic grounds have been brought forth against both of these extreme positions, and it is argued in a recent paper (Hankamer and Sag 1976) that neither can be maintained as a theory of anaphora in general. Rather it is necessary to adopt a mixed theory which treats one class of anaphoric expressions (which we call 'surface' anaphors) as derived by deletion, and another class (which we call 'deep' anaphors) as underlyingly present in syntactic representations.

This result has interesting consequences for the theory of semantic interpretation, which we pointed out in Hankamer and Sag (1976); unfortunately, however, the nature of the positions we rejected and of the position we assumed with regard to the semantic interpretation of anaphoric expressions was not made sufficiently clear in that paper, because it was not clear to the authors. The present paper is intended to rectify the inadequacy of the earlier one.

I will first briefly recapitulate the syntactic arguments which lead to the conclusion that there are two fundamentally different means of generating anaphors, and then consider more carefully than in the earlier paper the implications of these syntactic results, together with some semantic observations, for the theory of semantic interpretation of anaphoric expressions.

The claim advanced in Hankamer and Sag (1976), which I believe is still tenable, is that surface anaphors are derived and interpreted as in the classical theory, i. e. by a deletion rule operating at a superficial stage in derivations, with no special interpretive rule being involved; and that deep anaphors are inserted into underlying syntactic representations and assigned interpretations at the deep level. The constraint on backwards anaphora was asserted to be an interpretation filter on anaphoric relations in surface structure.

In the present paper I examine several specific alternative theories, each incorporating in some form the claim that semantic interpretations are assigned to anaphoric expressions at the level of surface structure. I attempt to formulate precisely a statement of what it means, in each of these theories, for a rule of semantic interpretation to apply at a given level of structure, and I show that under the only interpretation of this notion which is viable in the face of the facts, the resulting interpretive theory is indistinguishable from the position taken in Hankamer and Sag (1976), or at least from the position we intended to take. Since some confusion may well have resulted from the impreciseness with which that position was formulated, I am going to propose a different (and theoretically more neutral) statement of the semantic interpretation of deep anaphors, and specify exactly what I take to be excluded on the basis of the facts considered in reaching that position. The proposal is that the assignment of semantic interpretation to deep anaphors does not take place at any level of syntactic structure at all, but rather consists in an operation defined on semantic representations.

Finally, I discuss the implications of the investigation for the theory of semantic interpretation. The most prominent result of the study of anaphoric interpretation is that any theory of anaphora must make use of a power to refer to the relation between a surface constituent in syntactic representation and the portion of semantic representation associated with that constituent. This relation, which I call the C-R (constituent-reading) relation, is assumed by all interpretive approaches, I believe, but so far as I know has never been explicitly argued for. It is certainly by no means a priori obvious that reference to this relation should be possible; in fact, standard transformational theory (as developed in Chomsky 1965, for example) expressly excludes it. The fact that it has been tacitly assumed for many years by many linguists should in no way diminish the value of, or the necessity for, a careful demonstration that it is in fact necessary.

I also show that, given the C-R relation, it is possible to define the notion 'anaphoric relation' in such a way that this notion can be referred to independently of the processes which generate or interpret anaphoric expressions. Thus, I show that the Backwards Anaphora Constraint can be stated, as Hankamer and Sag (1976) argue that it must be, as a surface constraint on the position of anaphors with respect to their antecedents, rather than as a condition on the rules of derivation or interpretation.

1. Deep and surface anaphors

1.0 In this section I sketch the syntactic arguments which lead to the conclusion that some anaphors are derived by a syntactic rule of deletion (or equivalent device), while others are underlyingly present in syntactic representations, and establish the salient properties of the two kinds of anaphoric processes.

It will be useful to bear in mind the assumptions of the two extreme positions which are argued against:

The Classical Transformational Theory

(a) All anaphoric expressions are derived from fully specified underlying forms by rules of deletion or replacement.
(b) These syntactic processes take place at a relatively superficial level in derivations.
(c) The Backwards Anaphora Constraint (BAC) is stated as a condition on the application of the deletion or substitution rules.

The Interpretive Theory

(a) All anaphors are present in underlying representations, and have no semantic interpretation at that point.
(b) Anaphoric expressions are assigned semantic interpretations by means of interpretive rules at a superficial level in derivations.
(c) The BAC is stated as a condition on the application of the interpretive rules.

1.1 The arguments for surface-derived anaphors[2]

1.1.1 According to the interpretive theory, no anaphoric expressions are derived by deletion or substitution from underlying full forms. For one class of anaphoric processes, however, there is evidence that sentences containing the anaphoric expressions in question must at some stage have representations in which the segment corresponding to the (superficially null) anaphoric expression is syntactically complex.

The class of anaphoric processes for which such evidence is available includes Sluicing (Ross 1969b), VP Deletion (Ross 1969b, Grinder and Postal 1971), Sentential so anaphora (Hankamer and Sag 1976), and ellipsis processes[3] such as Gapping (Hankamer 1973). To provide some substance for the ensuing discussion, and to illustrate the nature of the arguments, I sketch one of them here; the reader should refer to the works cited for the full range of evidence.

The following argument is due to Ross (1969b), who presented it as an argument that null VP anaphors are derived from underlying full VP's by a deletion process. [4]

(2a) We looked to see if the thing in the net was a crab, and it was $\emptyset$.
(2b) We looked to see if the thing in the net was a crab, and it was a crab.

(3a) We looked to see if there was a crab in the net, and there was $\emptyset$.
(3b) We looked to see if there was a crab in the net, and there was a crab in the net.

In example (2a), the deletion theory would say that the null anaphor following was is the result of a deletion operation (VP Deletion), deriving (2a) from the full form (2b). The interpretive theory against

which Ross was arguing would say that (2a) and (2b) are not transformationally related; the truncated clause <u>it was</u> would underlyingly
have essentially its surface form.

Ross points out that such a theory cannot account for sentences
like (3a), where the subject is an item which otherwise appears only
as the result of a transformation defined on a full clause. The deletion
theory derives this sentence straightforwardly from (3b), in which the
conditions for <u>There</u> Insertion have been met and it has applied.

Further, Ross notes that in examples like (3a) agreement is determined by an NP which does not appear in the surface form of the
truncated clause:

(4a) We looked to see if there were crabs in the net, and there
      were. [*was]
(4b) We looked to see if there were crabs in the net, and there
      were [*was] crabs in the net.

Once again the derivation is straightforward under a deletion analysis,
since the agreement can be determined in the full form of the clause
(4b) before deletion takes place. The interpretive theory must introduce some ad hoc mechanism, other than the normal agreement rule,
to account for agreement in such cases.

The essence of the argument, which is common to all of the arguments in the references cited, is that some property of the surviving
structure is determined by something which is not overtly present in
the surface representation of the anaphoric segment; the deletion
analysis accounts for this by positing an underlying structure in which
the superficially null segment has a syntactically more complex representation. Crucially, certain syntactic processes (in the case cited,
<u>There</u> Insertion and Agreement) take place in the derivation of the
sentence before the deletion takes place. Thus the evidence indicates that such anaphors are superficially derived.

1.1.2 Wasow's interpretive theory. Wasow (1972) proposes a
modification of the interpretive theory which is designed to evade
the counterarguments of the class exemplified in the last section and
developed in the references cited there. Since the crucial failure
of the original interpretive theory is the absence of a syntactically
complex representation at any level for the null anaphors, he proposes
to assume an underlying syntactic representation for sentences containing null anaphors which is in every respect like the underlying
representation for full sentences, except that lexical items have not
been inserted under certain nodes. These representations are thus

syntactically fully specified, but the phonological and semantic features of the empty nodes are undetermined at the level of underlying structure.

Thus, the underlying representation for a sentence like (3a) would differ from that of (3b) only in that the lexical items a, crab, in, the, net are not inserted:

(5)

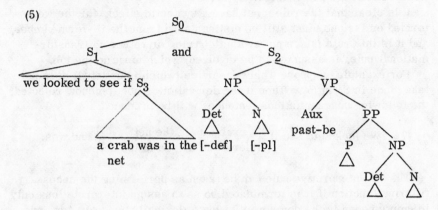

It is assumed that all syntactic features (such as ± plural, ± definite) are properties of the terminal nodes before lexical insertion. I have indicated this for the subject NP of S_2, where it is crucial; other syntactic features have been omitted. Now, There Insertion and Agreement can take place in S_2, since everything necessary for their application is present in the representation, and the result is (6):

(6)

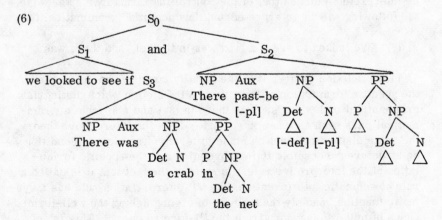

From this point on, nothing interesting happens syntactically. At some superficial point (presumably surface structure) an interpretive rule applies which assigns semantic features to the empty nodes, by reference to the semantic features of corresponding nodes in the controlling clause.

Wasow is quite inexplicit about the exact mechanism of this assignment of semantic interpretation, and the implications of particular assumptions as to how it is done will be considered in section 2 of this paper. For the moment I will leave aside the semantic effect of the interpretive rule and consider its syntactic effect.

It is clear that the rule must have a syntactic effect, for the well-formed omissions must still be distinguished from the ill-formed ones, and it is this rule (since no 'syntactic' rule, or rather no transformational rule, is assumed to be involved) which must do the job.

For example, suppose <u>There</u> Insertion (which is optional) does not take place in S_2 in (5). Then if the derivation is not somehow rejected, the following ungrammatical sentences will be produced:

(7) *We looked to see if $\begin{Bmatrix} \text{a crab was in the net} \\ \text{there was a crab in the net} \end{Bmatrix}$ and was.

The VP Interpretive rule can be taken as performing the necessary filtering function if it is formulated so as to assign interpretations only to empty nodes in the domain following a (lexically present) Aux, and to require that all such nodes be empty up to the right VP boundary; and it is assumed that a structure to which this rule cannot assign an interpretation (and no other can either) is rejected as semantically uninterpretable.

Further, the VP interpretation rule must be so formulated as to be inapplicable unless the superficial syntactic shape of the structure to be interpreted matches that of the controlling structure. Otherwise, the following will be interpreted and thus accorded grammaticality:

(8) *We looked to see if a frog was in the net, and there was.

In the deletion theory, it is the identity condition on deletion and the specific formulation of the rule of VP Deletion which distinguish grammatical omissions such as those in (3a) and (4a) from ungrammatical ones such as those in (7) and (8). In the interpretive theory, the same distinction must be made in terms of an identity condition on structures accessible to interpretation and the specific formulation of the interpretive rule. In spite of the fact that it is called a rule of semantic interpretation, the VP interpretation rule has a syntactic function, namely the function of distinguishing the well-formed cases of null VP anaphora from the ill-formed ones. [5] This is, of course, exactly the syntactic function of the rule of VP deletion in a deletion theory.

Syntactically, the interpretive theory proposed by Wasow is at best[6] a notational variant of the deletion theory. The VP interpretation rule has a syntactic entry condition identical to that of VP Deletion, it is defined at the same syntactic level as VP Deletion, and its syntactic effect is exactly the same as that of VP Deletion: both rules filter derivations at that point, specifying by exactly the same structural conditions what class of omissions is allowed and what class is disallowed.

To be more explicit, the syntactic effect of the VP interpretation rule is to pass (as 'interpretable', which in this case means 'grammatical') all structures which satisfy the conditions of a certain structural template, and to reject (fail to interpret) all others. This is exactly what the syntactic rule of VP Deletion does; it passes (as permissible deletions) pairs of representations which satisfy exactly the same template, and rejects (as impermissible deletions) all others.

I conclude that syntactically the only difference between Wasow's theory and the classical deletion theory for VP anaphora is notational; if there is a difference between the two theories, it must be in the claims made about how semantic interpretations are assigned to null VP anaphors. Since there is no syntactic difference, and since the classical theory posits no special devices at all for the interpretation of such null anaphors, it would appear to be crucial for Wasow to provide some argument on semantic grounds in favor of the interpretive approach. The question whether such arguments exist is taken up in section 2.[7]

The foregoing discussion could be replicated for the other anaphoric processes mentioned at the beginning of this section. In each case there are unchallenged arguments showing that sentences containing the null anaphors in question must have a representation more complete than the apparent surface representation. The deletion approach accommodates this by deriving the anaphoric expressions from full forms, thus giving them a surface null representation and an underlying full representation; Wasow's approach gives the anaphoric segment a full syntactic representation simultaneous with its anaphorized representation, by distinguishing at the same level between full and empty nodes. In no case is there a syntactic difference between the two approaches, and both agree for these processes in giving the anaphors a syntactically complex representation and determining wellformedness of the anaphorized structure at a superficial level in syntactic derivations. Following the terminology established in Hankamer and Sag (1976), I call such anaphors 'surface' anaphors.

1.2 The arguments for deep anaphors. We have seen that for one class of anaphors at least, there is evidence that they are derived by a superficial syntactic process equivalent to deletion under identity.[8] There is another class of anaphors, however, for which it is quite clear that they are not syntactically complex in the same way at any level of derivation. The most familiar members of this class are the personal pronouns, and the arguments that such anaphors are not derived from more complex underlying forms are well known (cf. Dougherty 1969, Bach 1970, Bresnan 1970, Kayne 1971, Wasow 1975). These arguments are reviewed in Hankamer and Sag (1976).

Since the focus of the present paper is on sentential anaphora, I illustrate the arguments for the underlying presence of such anaphors (called 'deep' anaphors) as unanalyzable units, not derived from more complex sources, for the case of sentential it anaphora. The arguments which follow all indicate that sentential it (hereafter S-it) is present as a pro-form in underlying representations, and is not derived from a clause by a transformational rule of S-pronominalization (or if it is, it is derived by a unique 'precyclic' transformation, with the consequence that there is no chance of demonstrating its existence).

1.2.1 Lakoff's argument. The oldest and best known of these arguments is due to George Lakoff (1968), and was presented as an argument that the transformational rule of S-pronominalization (which Lakoff assumed to exist) was precyclic.

(9) Sally was believed by John to have been proven to be
     rich, but Harry didn't believe it.

Sentence (9) has a reading where it is interpreted to mean 'Sally was rich'. Under the assumption that it is derived from an underlying full clause under identity with an antecedent clause elsewhere in the structure, Lakoff argued that the transformation effecting this substitution would have to apply precyclically. If the transformation were cyclic or postcyclic, one would expect to derive sentences like (10) (where the antecedent clause remains intact at least until the top cycle) or (11) (where S-pronominalization has not applied), but sentences like (9) should not be derivable because there is no clause at either the stage of the top cycle or postcyclically which could serve as the antecedent for pronominalization of the target clause.

(10) John believed that it had been proven that Sally was rich,
      but Harry didn't believe it.
(11) Sally was believed by John to have been proven to be
      rich, but Harry didn't believe that Sally was rich.

The argument is impeccable, given the assumption that S-it is derived by a transformation and that if a transformation is neither cyclic nor postcyclic, it must be precyclic. To say that S-it is inserted precyclically, however, is tantamount to saying that it is present underlyingly, unless some other precyclic transformational operation is found which must precede S-pronominalization. Not only has no such interaction been found, but no evidence has ever been found that would indicate that any other precyclic rules even exist.

Syntactically, then, Lakoff's argument is an argument against a theory which derives S-it from full clauses at a superficial stage in derivations, under identity with an antecedent clause, and is consequently an argument against the classical transformational approach to anaphora. The syntactic difficulty disappears, of course, if there is no transformation of S-pronominalization.

1.2.2 Bresnan's argument. An argument of a quite different sort is due to Bresnan (1971). In response to Grinder and Postal (1971), who suggest on the basis of their 'missing antecedent' argument that all identity-of-sense anaphora involve deletion, she points out that S-it does not seem to permit missing antecedent readings:

(12) Mack wasn't knocked out with a left hook, but Rocky was, and it was thrown by a lefty.

(13) *Mack wasn't knocked out with a left hook, but it happened to Rocky, and it was thrown by a lefty.

In (12), as Grinder and Postal note, the pronoun it refers to a left hook that knocked Rocky out; but there is no overt antecedent for this pronoun in the surface form of the sentence. The overt NP a left hook which appears in the first clause cannot be the antecedent, because if the intervening anaphoric clause is omitted, the result is ungrammatical (on the intended reading):

(14) *Mack wasn't knocked out with a left hook, and it was thrown by a lefty.

The antecedent for it in (12) must be a NP which is not overt in the surface structure of the sentence, but is present in the more complex representation underlying the null VP-anaphor:

(15) Mack wasn't knocked out with a left hook, but Rocky was knocked out with a left hook, and it was thrown by a lefty.

This is one of the arguments for the superficial derivation of null VP anaphors from underlying full forms.

Bresnan's observation was that the same capacity to contain non-overt antecedents for pronouns is not exhibited by S-it, witness the badness of (13) (on a reading where the second it refers to the left hook that got Rocky). If the S-it anaphor were assumed to be derived from a full sentential source, we would expect the missing antecedent reading to be just as good in (13) as it is in (12). Bresnan observes correctly that it is not, and concludes that S-it are not transformationally derived.

1.2.3 Witten's argument. The following argument is a modified version of one of several arguments given in Witten (1971) to show that S-it anaphors are not derived by a (nonprecyclic) transformation. Given the following two assumptions:

(a) Extraposition applies only to sentential subjects:

(16) It surprised me that he was incompetent.
(17) *It surprised me his incompetence.

(b) Extraposition is cyclic. This is now a fairly secure assumption, cf. Jacobson and Neubauer (to appear) and Hankamer (in preparation).

Then a superficial (cyclic or postcyclic) derivation of sentential pronouns will not prevent the generation (by extraposition on the cycle and subsequent S-pronominalization of the extraposed clause) of the following ungrammatical sentence:

(18) *That he was incompetent soon became clear, and it
       didn't surprise me it.

If sentential pronouns are present in underlying structures the ungrammatical sentence will not be derived; it will automatically be blocked by the observed restriction on extraposition, which cannot extrapose ordinary NP's.

1.2.4 An argument due to Kuno. Pinkham and Zaenen (1976) (see also Iwakura 1976) note the existence of the following constraint:

The Pinkham-Zaenen Effect: No constituent may be extracted across a sentential subject.

This constraint is proposed to account for the ungrammaticality of sentences like (19):

(19)   *Who do you think that for Sue to kiss a gorilla would
         surprise?

I have used an example with a <u>for-to</u> clause because they are generally
possible in the same contexts:

(20)   I think that for Sue to kiss a gorilla would surprise no one.

Susumu Kuno (personal communication) has pointed out that if sentential pronouns are not in place before the extractions which are
sensitive to this constraint take place, the constraint will block grammatical sentences like the following:

(21)   If Sue kissed a gorilla, who do you think it would surprise?

The grammaticality of (21) is an automatic consequence of the
theory that sentential pro-forms are present in underlying representations, rather than being derived from full clauses at some superficial stage.

1.2.5 Summary. The arguments I have sketched constitute only a
small sample of the arguments which can be brought forth to show that
some anaphors (pronouns in particular) are present in underlying
representations and not superficially derived. Many of these arguments have been presented in the form of an ordering 'paradox' which
results from the assumption that pronouns are derived by a cyclic or
postcyclic transformation from full NP's or clauses; the general
structure of the argument is to pick out a property that distinguishes
pronouns from the corresponding nonpronominal forms, and to show
that some rule must have access to this distinction at a stage in derivations earlier than that at which it would appear according to the
classical theory of transformational derivation of pronouns. [9]
     Considering only the question of syntactic derivation, as I have
done in this section, it is clear from the evidence that there are two
distinct kinds of anaphors, one kind which is present in underlying
representations and simplex throughout the derivation, and another
kind which is derived from a complex source at a superficial stage in
derivations. The former kind, the deep anaphors, are internally syntactically inert and insensitive to superficial discrepancies in the
shape of their antecedents, while the latter, the surface anaphors,
are syntactically active internally and are sensitive to superficial
syntactic properties of their antecedents. The latter difference is
directly observable in the contrasts exhibited here:

(22a) The report said that Sue fed the geese, but Joe did.
(22b) The report said that Sue fed the geese, but Joe did it.

(23a) *The report said that the geese were fed by Sue, but Joe did.
(23b) The report said that the geese were fed by Sue, but Joe did it.

These contrasts follow immediately from a theory which says that deep anaphors like it are present in underlying structures and un-affected by surface variations in the shape of their antecedents, whereas surface anaphors like the null VP anaphor in (22a) and (23a) are derived by a superficial deletion rule requiring superficial identity between antecedent and deleted segment.

I take it as established that syntactically there are two kinds of anaphoric processes, deriving deep and surface anaphors with the syntactic properties outlined in this section. In the following section I consider the assignment of semantic interpretations to anaphoric expressions of the two types.

2. The interpretation of anaphors. In the preceding section I reviewed the syntactic evidence for the superficial derivation of surface anaphors and for the deep generation of deep anaphors. One might assume that we have thus accepted the classical transformational theory for surface anaphors, and the interpretive theory for deep anaphors, but this would be an error. The question of how an anaphor receives its interpretation is independent of the question of how it is derived; it should be noted that the transformational and interpretive approaches as outlined in the introduction to the last section involve separate and independent assumptions about the generation of ana-phoric expressions and the assignment of interpretations to them. In this section I take up the question of how anaphoric expressions receive interpretation, and in particular I consider and reject a theory (which I believe to be a fair reconstruction of the intention of Wasow 1972) which says that the interpretation of anaphoric expressions can be accounted for by interpretive rules defined on surface syntactic representations.

2.1 The absence of arguments for superficial interpretation of anaphors

2.1.0 The interpretive theory as outlined in the introduction to the last section incorporates three distinct assumptions: (a) that anaphors are deeply derived; (b) that anaphors are superficially interpreted; and (c) that the BAC is a condition on the application of the rules which assign interpretation to anaphors. These assumptions are independent and each one needs to be independently motivated, even if the approach is confined to a subclass of anaphors.

We have accepted (a), for a subclass of anaphoric expressions, on the basis of a considerable body of evidence. The question now is whether there is any evidence for superficial interpretation, either for deep anaphors or for surface anaphors. So far as I know, no evidence has ever been brought forth to support the claim that any anaphors are superficially interpreted; the only arguments for assumption (b) are based on the acceptance of assumption (c), and that assumption has generally been simply taken for granted in these arguments. In this subsection I discuss the nonexistence of direct arguments for superficial interpretation, and in the following subsection I discuss the argument which assumes (c). In the subsequent subsections I show that any interpretive approach which incorporates assumption (b) requires devices which remove the basis for assumption (c), and consequently, the only argument for (b) vanishes. The positive result of this investigation is that the devices mentioned are shown to be necessary, under any theory of interpretation of anaphoric expressions. I conclude that there is no basis for assuming that any anaphors are assigned interpretation at a superficial level in syntactic derivations (in any transparent sense of this phrase), but nevertheless that one of the fundamental assumptions of interpretive theory is correct, namely, that there must be access to the relation between a surface constituent and its 'reading', or corresponding portion of semantic representation.

2.1.1 I consider first the surface anaphors. Under the classical transformational analysis, they are derived from full forms, and the full forms are assigned interpretations by whatever devices assign interpretations to nonanaphoric expressions. In other words, no special interpretive device is required for these anaphors.

Under the analysis proposed by Wasow, surface anaphors involve the application (at the surface) of a rule which has two effects: to distinguish the syntactically well-formed cases of such anaphora from everything else, and to assign an interpretation to the empty structures assumed under this analysis. What Wasow fails to do, however, is to provide any argument that the structures underlying surface anaphors cannot have semantic features at the underlying level (allowing straightforward semantic interpretation by ordinary means, as in the classical theory).

In short, he proposes an alternative analysis which is syntactically nondistinct from the transformational analysis, and provides no argument for the claim that semantic interpretation is done superficially, nor against the transformational assumption that it is accomplished by the ordinary devices of interpretation (whatever they are). Wasow, in fact, confines his attention to the syntactic effect of the VP anaphora rule, saying nothing about how interpretation is to be accomplished by such a rule. [10] The question of how and whether such a rule might work will be taken up in the next subsection.

2.1.2 As for deep anaphors, there has been considerable argument (and by now substantial agreement) on their syntactic derivation, but virtually no argument regarding the question of how they receive semantic interpretation. As noted earlier, the question whether deep anaphors are superficially derived is independent of the question whether they are superficially interpreted. The independence of these questions has not generally been recognized, because the motivation for the double assumption in interpretive theory (that anaphors are deeply derived and superficially interpreted) has not generally been made very clear. [11]

Jackendoff (1972) does advance as an argument for his interpretive treatment of pronouns, reflexives, and null subjects the following claim: that the interpretive analysis allows all three processes to be regarded as cyclic, thus allowing them to be ordered adjacent to each other in the cycle, and consequently allowing partial similarities in their entry conditions to be captured by some kind of abbreviatory convention.

I think it is clear that this is no argument at all. The unsupported assumption is that the only way to capture partial similarities in conditions on rules is by means of an abbreviatory convention which can only be applied if the rules are 'adjacent'. This is unjustified, as (a) it is easy to invent abbreviatory devices which do not require adjacency, and (b) it is clear that exactly such devices are required, since there are many known instances of constraints common to a class of rules defined by some property having nothing to do with ordering. Point (a) is fortunate and (b) is not surprising, given the fact that there is no evidence for a linear order of rules in the cycle at all.

I conclude that on the basis of what we know so far, there is no real evidence against a theory which in effect derives deep anaphors by precyclic deletion and surface anaphors by postcyclic deletion, and has no special rules for the assignment of interpretation to anaphors, their interpretations being assigned by whatever processes assign interpretations to ordinary sentences without anaphors in them. [12]

2.2 The only argument for superficial interpretation. In the discussion so far of the syntactic and semantic properties of deep and surface anaphora, I have stayed away from the most prominent property of anaphora in general: the well-known restrictions on backwards anaphora. These restrictions are rather complex, and certainly not adequately described by the familiar Precede/Command Constraint (due in various forms to Ross 1967, Langacker 1969):

The Backwards Anaphora Constraint (BAC):
An anaphor may not both precede and command its antecedent.

This statement nevertheless captures the essence of the constraint, and is accurate enough for the present purpose. Two observations about the nature of this constraint are relevant to the subsequent discussion:

(a) The BAC applies at a superficial level of structure. [13]
(b) The BAC is a constraint on all anaphoric processes; in particular, it applies to both deep and surface anaphora.

Both the classical transformational theory and the interpretive theory incorporate the assumption that the BAC is a constraint on the rule involved in the derivation/interpretation of an anaphor. In the transformational theory, the deletion transformations are assumed to apply subject to the BAC: i.e. the BAC acts as a condition on the application of the deletion rule. In the interpretive theory, the BAC is again considered to act as a condition on the application of the rule, in this case the interpretive rule assigning semantic interpretation to the anaphor; since the filtering function of the interpretive rule has a syntactic effect, the BAC is again a condition on the syntactic derivation of anaphoric expressions.

Since the BAC is (no matter how interpreted) defined on surface configurations, it is straightforward in the transformational analysis to regard it as a condition on the application of the deletion rules, which (it has been shown) themselves operate at the surface level. On the other hand, it is impossible to maintain the assumption that the BAC is a constraint on the syntactic rule which creates a deep anaphor, since it has been shown that these anaphors are created at a deep level, and the BAC applies, even for deep anaphora, at the surface level. This is shown (for S-it anaphora) by examples like the following:

(24a) For John [to marry a gorilla]$_i$ would make it$_i$ easier for Bill.

(24b) *It would make it$_i$ easier for Bill for John [to marry a gorilla].

The anaphoric relations indicated by the indices are impossible in (24b) because the BAC is violated. The difference between (24a) and (24b) is the superficial order difference resulting from the cyclic operation of Extraposition.

Wasow (1972) claims that this constitutes an argument against the transformational approach to anaphora and in favor of an interpretive approach, because in the interpretive framework which he proposes all anaphors are interpreted at a superficial level, and consequently, the BAC can be assumed to be a constraint on the application of the interpretive rules. The application of the BAC to deep and surface anaphora alike can thus be accounted for in a simple and unified fashion.

2.3 A simple conception of the notion of surface interpretation. Wasow is quite inexplicit about the nature of the interpretive rules which are to provide semantic interpretations for anaphors at the level of surface structure. In this and the following subsections, I examine a series of reconstructions of what could be meant by the notion 'surface structure interpretation' and show that the only viable one is a terminological variant of the theory proposed in Hankamer and Sag (1976), where interpretation is at deep structure. (That theory is, of course, thereby also shown to be a terminological variant of 'surface structure interpretation', suitably reconstructed.) It is also shown (in section 2.5) that once the Surface Interpretive approach is reconstructed so that it is viable, Wasow's argument for surface interpretation of anaphors disappears.

Reconstruction #1

I assume throughout that rules of semantic interpretation are taken to have the form A:B, where A is an entry condition defined in terms of some level or levels of representation, and B is an operation effecting some change in semantic representation. The interpretation of the rule is that if, at the stage (or stages) of representation of a given sentence on which the entry condition is defined, it is satisfied, the operation B is performed, modifying the semantic representation of the sentence in the specified way.

We thus have two things to make explicit about the nature of interpretation rules in a given theory: what the assumed limitations on entry conditions are, and what the assumed limitations on operations are. The interpretive theories to be considered here have in common that they assume the entry conditions for rules assigning interpretations to anaphoric expressions to be limited to surface structures; that is, the entry conditions for such rules can make reference only to information that is present in the surface structure representation of a sentence.

In the first reconstruction of surface-interpretive theory, which is offered as one possible interpretation of Wasow's proposal (cf. Wasow 1972:98), the following assumptions are made:

(a) The entry condition for a rule assigning interpretations to anaphoric expressions is a structural condition defined on surface structure.

(b) The operation which such a rule performs is to copy the semantic features of the antecedent nodes into the corresponding empty nodes in the surface structure.

This might appear to be a reasonable thing to mean by saying that the interpretation of anaphors 'takes place at the surface'. Such a proposal leads to absurd consequences, however.

Consider first a case of surface anaphora (VP Deletion). According to Wasow's theory, the null segment is represented in the surface as a structure with empty nodes:

(25) Sally seems to be tough to beat at tennis, but Jill doesn't [ΔΔΔΔΔΔΔΔ] .

[I have not represented the structure of the null segment, but it is assumed to have some.]

If, as this theory assumes, all the interpretive rule does is to associate each Δ with the reading of the corresponding constituent, the anaphoric structure will by no means be provided with an 'interpretation'; it is well known that the semantic representation of a clause is not determinable from the surface structure plus the semantic features of the individual lexical items (some of the lexical items in this structure probably do not even have semantic features); the semantic representation cannot in general be determined without access to the underlying syntactic representation. [14]

Consider secondly a case of deep sentential anaphora (S-it):

(26) They say that Sally is expected to be tough for John to beat at tennis, and it doesn't surprise me at all.

One reading for the it is that of the clause-complement to say. We have shown that such it's are deep pronouns, and do not have complex representations as clauses at any syntactically significant stage in the derivation. Here the interpretive rule must assign a reading to it, on the basis of information present in the surface representation of the antecedent clause. But again the required information (the semantic representation of the clause Sally is expected to be tough for John to

<u>beat at tennis</u>) is not present in the surface representation; and to say
that the semantic interpretation rule for S-<u>it</u> anaphora reconstructs
this reading on the basis of information present in the surface structure is absurd; such a rule would have to be able to unravel the syntax
of the clause, undo all the cyclic transformations which have chopped
and spread parts of underlyingly unified clauses all over the place,
and reconstruct the underlying relations. It would in effect (and it is
not clear that this is possible) have to incorporate all of English syntax, backwards.

It is clear that this simple conception, in which not only the entry
condition of the rule but its entire input is in surface structure and its
effect is simply to insert semantic features (determined on the basis
of information present in surface structure) into empty nodes of anaphoric expressions, can be rejected without further ado.

2.4 A more sophisticated conception of surface interpretation

2.4.0 I do not believe that the approach to surface interpretation
outlined in the last section is what Wasow had in mind, and I doubt
that any interpretivist will admit to even having considered such a
theory; nevertheless, I think it has been instructive to examine it,
because it points out quite clearly where crucial innovations must
be made.

In this section I outline a reconstruction of the notion 'surface
interpretation rule' which is probably closer to Wasow's intention
(see Wasow 1972:167), and which is not so clearly absurd as the first
reconstruction. It involves, however, a radical change in the conception of what kinds of information are accessible to such rules.

It is clear that an interpretive rule, even if it is defined on surface
structures (i.e. its entry condition is formulated in terms of conditions on surface structure), must have direct access to information
present in the semantic representation[15] (and to information regarding the relation between semantic representation and surface structure). This is noted explicitly in Jackendoff (1972:269-70) and is implicit in some of Wasow's discussion (Wasow 1972:167). The reconstruction I offer here incorporates these features in a particular way;
there are doubtless other ways to construct such a theory which incorporate essentially the same features.

Reconstruction #2

(a) As before, the entry condition for a rule assigning inter-
     pretations to anaphoric expressions is a structural condi-
     tion defined on surface structure.

Schematically, the entry condition for an interpretive rule will have the form

$$X \ A \ Y \ B \ Z^{16}$$

where B is the anaphoric segment (either a deep anaphor such as S-it or a structure full of deltas) and there are certain syntactic conditions on the variables and on the form of A and B.

(b) If the entry condition is met (i.e. if the segments A and B in the surface representation of a given sentence are in a shape and structural configuration appropriate for the application of the rule), the rule can refer directly to the reading of A (the portion of the semantic representation of the sentence which is associated with A) and copy it into the position in the greater semantic representation associated with B.

Thus conceived, a surface interpretation rule is one which, given an anaphoric expression in surface structure,

(a) locates an appropriate antecedent in surface structure,
(b) looks up the reading associated with that antecedent,
(c) copies the reading of the antecedent into the delta position in semantic representation associated with the anaphor.

In the remainder of this section, I show that while the proposed conception of how a surface interpretation rule operates removes the absurdity of the first reconstruction, and allows the formulation of interpretive rules which can deal with some of the problems discussed in Hankamer and Sag (1976), it is still necessary to recognize a fundamental distinction in semantic as well as syntactic behavior between deep and surface anaphora, and the interpretive theory as reconstructed is still not viable.

2.4.1 Deep anaphora

2.4.1.1 For S-it anaphora, the revised conception of the nature of a surface semantic interpretation rule allows the objections of the last section to be set aside. The rule now no longer needs to be able to determine from information present in the surface representation of a clause what its semantic representation is, since the semantic representation is assumed to be directly available.

The operation of the rule now, in a case like that of example (26), is as follows:

(a) Entry condition of rule, defined on surface representation:

$$X \ S_p \ Y \ it_q \ Z \ ^{16}$$

(b) Semantic representation of sentence which satisfies (a):

$$X \ S_p' \ Y \ \Delta_q \ Z \ ^{17}$$

(c) Effect of the rule: in the semantic representation, Δ is replaced by S'.

Thus in sentence (26), which satisfies the entry condition for the rule, the reading of the antecedent clause <u>Sally is expected to be tough for John to beat at tennis</u> will be associated with the anaphor <u>it</u>. This association operates independently of the ordinary rules of amalgamation and what not which assign interpretations to clauses on the basis of their structure and the lexical items contained in them.

Another objection which can be set aside, in a somewhat less straightforward manner, is the argument based on scope opacity presented in Hankamer and Sag (1976).

2.4.1.2 The scope opacity of deep anaphors. Postal (1974), in a discussion of the ambiguity of sentences like (27), noticed that the ambiguity disappears in (28):

(27) Jack believes that Sally is older than she is.
(28) Jack believes that Sally is older than she is, but Joan doesn't believe it.

In (28), unlike (27), the only possible reading is such that Jack believes a contradiction (that Sally's age exceeds her age) and Joan does not believe that contradiction.

Postal notes also that a similar effect is observed when a quantifier binds a pronoun inside a complement of <u>believe</u>, and a sentential <u>it</u> is anaphoric to the <u>believe</u>-complement:

(29) Each one of us believes that he is sane.
(30) Each one of us believes that he is sane, but Arthur doesn't believe it.

In (29) there are two readings, one in which the pronoun <u>he</u> is bound by the quantifier <u>each</u>, and another in which it is not (in the latter case <u>he</u>

is taken as referring to some particular person, e. g. Max, Dick, or Arthur). In (30), however, where it is anaphoric to the believe-complement, only the unbound reading is possible. The sentence cannot have the reading where each person except Arthur attributes sanity to himself. [18]

It was claimed, perhaps over-hastily, in Hankamer and Sag (1976) that these examples constitute evidence that sentential it anaphors receive interpretation at a syntactically deep level. The reasoning was as follows: if we assume that it is assigned the reading of its antecedent at the deep-structure level, before the lowering rule applies which (according to Postal's analysis) gives (27) its noncontradictory reading, then the only reading it can ever receive is the contradictory one, since under Postal's analysis the sentence on the noncontradictory reading has an underlying structure in which there is no clause which could serve as the antecedent for it:

(31) More x [Jack believes [Sally is x old]] y [Sally is y old]

Under this analysis the clause Sally is older than she is does not exist in the underlying representation. On the contradictory reading there is such a clause:

(32) Jack believes [More x [Sally is x old] y [Sally is y old]]

It was assumed that any interpretive process applying at a level of derivation later than the application of the lowering rules would not have access to this distinction.

What was not made explicit in Hankamer and Sag (1976) was that this argument assumes the rather strict interpretation of the notion 'surface interpretation rule' outlined in section 2.3. It was assumed that to say that a rule of semantic interpretation applies at the level of surface structure means that the rule has access only to information present in the surface representation. With this understanding of the notion of surface level interpretation, it is obvious that a distinction such as that between the two readings of (27) will not be available.

Taking the revised reconstruction of what a surface interpretation rule can do, this argument no longer has the same force. Under this reconstruction, one could say, for example, that the rule for interpreting S-it anaphors operates as outlined in section 2.4.1.1, and that on the noncontradictory reading of (27) the surface clause (than) she is is associated with the open sentence 'Sally is x old' in the semantic representation. Such a rule can now account for the observed loss of ambiguity in (28).

On the noncontradictory reading of the first clause, a sentence like (28) must have a semantic representation something like the following, before the it interpretation rule applies:

(33) More x [Jack believes [Sally is x old]] y [Sally is y old]
but Not [I believe Δ]

where Δ represents the as yet unspecified semantic value of the surface it. A rule operating as sketched would first locate the clause in surface structure which is to serve as the antecedent, in this case the complement of the first believe; it would then determine what portion of the semantic representation corresponds to this surface clause, which in this case is 'Sally is x old', and copy this into the position occupied by Δ in the semantic representation.

The result, of course, will be a representation in which the variable x, which should be bound by a quantifier, is in a location where it is not bound at all (having been copied into a domain which is outside the scope of the quantifier originally binding it), and the semantic representation is senseless. One could say that such representations do not conform to a well-formedness condition on semantic representations (to the effect that unbound variables may not be left lying around) and that is why the reading is rejected.

This account seems reasonable, and it extends automatically to the other cases cited. It also has the virtue that it is not dependent on any assumptions about the syntactic deep structures of sentences like (27) and (29). What is crucial is that the constituent-reading relationship be available, and so defined that a surface clause is associated with an open sentence in semantic representation on the noncontradictory readings of such examples.

2.4.2 Surface anaphora. While the observations represented in (27)-(30) do not provide an argument against a surface-level interpretation of sentential it under reconstruction #2, there is a related set of observations which, taken together with these, does provide an argument against the analysis of surface anaphora such as null VP anaphora as an interpretive process, unless it is an interpretive process of an entirely different kind.

It was observed in Hankamer and Sag (1976) that whereas deep anaphors like S-it are opaque to externally bound variables as exemplified in examples (27)-(30), surface anaphors are not. The VP Deletion analogue of (28) is ambiguous:

(34) Jack believes that Sally is older than she is, but Joan doesn't.

This fact follows directly from the theory of Hankamer and Sag (1976), according to which surface anaphors are derived by a superficial syntactic deletion process, insensitive to deep syntactic relations and to semantic representation. [19] Example (34) is derived straightforwardly from the source (35), which itself has the relevant ambiguity, which is preserved under deletion: [20]

(35) Jack believes that Sally is older than she is, but Joan doesn't believe that Sally is older than she is.

An interpretive analysis along the lines of that sketched for S-_it_ anaphora, however, is in trouble:

(36) More x [Jack believes [Sally is x old]] y [Sally is y old]
     but Not [Joan Δ [$\Delta\Delta\Delta\Delta$]]

This would be the semantic representation before null VP interpretation corresponding to the surface representation of (34). Now if we proceed as above, copying into the Δ positions the portions of the semantic representation corresponding to the antecedent segments, we get exactly the same result as before:

(37) More x [Jack believes [Sally is x old]] y [Sally is y old]
     but Not [Joan believes [Sally is x old]

The resulting semantic representation is the same as in the case of S-_it_ anaphora, and the same principles appealed to in that case would reject this semantic representation as senseless; but the fact to be explained is that the noncontradictory reading is not blocked in (34).

I see no way out, except to say that the VP interpretation rule does a great deal more than copy portions of semantic representation into delta positions. It would have to copy essentially the whole quantificational structure, totally rebuilding the semantic representation of the clause containing the null VP anaphor. [21]

There are two things to be said about this. The first is that it treats as a surprising, cumbersome, and unexplained property of certain anaphoric rules something which follows straightforwardly from the claim that the anaphors are derived by deletion; the second is that it leaves unexplained the correlation between sensitivity to structural identity of configuration (noted in section 1.2.5) and insensitivity to semantic coherence on the part of deep anaphora.

In conclusion, although the facts regarding the interpretations of anaphors in sentences involving bound variables do not, as Sag and Hankamer thought, provide an argument against the interpretation of

deep anaphors at the surface level, they do provide an argument
against a surface-interpretive approach to all anaphora. The contrast between (28) and (34) provides evidence in favor of a deletion
analysis of null VP anaphors over an interpretive one, and under any
kind of analysis for a fundamental difference between deep and surface
anaphora, in their semantic characteristics as well as in their syntactic characteristics.

2.5 The only viable conception of surface interpretation. In this
section, finally, I will show that even the revised conception of surface
interpretation developed in the last section must be abandoned, for the
case of S-it anaphora. Consider again the example, due originally to
G. Lakoff, discussed in section 1.2.1:

(9) Sally was believed by John to have been proven to be rich,
     but Harry didn't believe it.

It is clear that there are sentences in which the S-it anaphor is
interpreted as semantically equivalent to an antecedent clause which
is intact in deep structure but broken up and scattered in surface structure as a result of the action of cyclic transformations.

Under reconstruction #2, a semantic interpretation rule defined on
the surface syntactic representation has an entry condition in the form
of a structural condition, which must be met by the surface representation of a sentence if the rule is to be allowed to apply. In particular,
the rule for interpretation of S-it anaphors must locate an antecedent
clause in surface structure in the appropriate configurational relationship to the anaphor. The Lakoff examples show, however, that it is
impossible to devise such a condition for S-it anaphora, because in
surface structure there is not necessarily any such clause, even
though the anaphor is interpreted as anaphoric to one. The fact is that
in the general case not only does no such clause necessarily exist in
surface structure, no such clause necessarily exists at any syntactic
level above the deepest. There is no way that the structural condition
of an interpretive rule can be formulated so as to pick out, on the
basis of an inspection of the surface representation of a sentence like
(9), the pieces Sally . . . be rich as the remains of a once intact
clause.

I believe this applies the coup de grace to interpretive theory of
anaphora, reconstruction #2. There is no way to state the rule of
S-it anaphora as an interpretive rule with an entry condition defined
on surface representations. There is, however, a seemingly trivial
modification which we could make in reconstruction #2 which would
evade this death blow: instead of saying that a surface semantic
interpretation rule has an entry condition stated in terms of surface

syntactic representation, we could turn things around and say that
its entry condition is stated on semantic representations (which would
make such rules look more familiar, since then their entry conditions
would be stated on the very representations which they alter, just like
syntactic transformations). The entry condition for the S-it rule
would then be that in the semantic representation of the sentence
there be a clause-reading and a clause-Δ (where a clause-Δ is the
thing in semantic representations associated with a sentential it).
The operation would still be simply to copy the clause-reading into
the Δ. Oddly enough, if we simply state the rule this way and if we
have the relations between semantic readings and surface elements
which we needed anyway, the treatment of the Lakoff sentences is
trivial: our rule gets to apply if its entry condition is met and if in
surface representation the elements corresponding to the reading to
be copied are not preceded and commanded by the pronoun.

We now have a rule whose entry condition and effect are defined
on semantic representations, though it is subject to a constraint on
its application stated in terms of the surface configuration of the elements associated with the semantic elements on which it operates.
One could, by an appropriate terminological maneuver, make this
out as a rule of surface interpretation; it is difficult to see what the
point of this would be.

Reconstruction #2 embodied the assumption that an interpretive
rule would be taken as applying at a point in the syntactic derivation,
its applicability being determined, as in the case of syntactic transformations, by a structural condition on syntactic representations at
that stage. Note that if it is assumed that interpretive rules are defined as in reconstruction #2, it is possible to regard S-it interpretation as a rule defined at the level of deep structure, but not as a
rule defined at the level of surface structure. Surface anaphora rules
like VP deletion, however, whether formulated as deletions or as
interpretation rules, must have entry conditions formulated in terms
of surface structures; we have seen that a null VP anaphor does not
necessarily correspond to a unit either in deep structure or in
semantic representation, and it is in fact impossible, by inspection
of a deep or semantic representation, to pick out those parts which
will correspond to a surface 'VP'.

For the case of deep anaphors, then, we have an account which is
indistinguishable from the one adopted in Sag and Hankamer (1976b),
where it was proposed that the semantic interpretation of deep anaphors is accomplished at the level of deep structure. It now seems
foolhardy to claim that these anaphors are interpreted 'at' any syntactic level of structure, since any adequate account of their interpretation requires reference to the constituent-reading (C-R) relation,

and since readings are determined in part by deep-structure properties, making any such account necessarily global in nature as far as
its relation to syntactic representations is concerned.

Wasow's argument. We may now ask the question, where does
Wasow's argument stand? Recall that the only reason ever proposed
for treating anaphora by means of rules of interpretation operating
at the level of surface structure was that in such a framework the
BAC could be stated as a unified condition on the application of all
anaphora rules. We see now that the entry conditions for deep and
surface anaphora rules, if they are stated on syntactic representations at all, must be stated at entirely different levels even if the
rules are rules of interpretation.

Fortunately for all of us, it is not necessary, once we have access
to the C-R relation, to state the BAC as a condition on the application
of anaphoric rules. In the next and final section I discuss the nature
of the BAC in the light of what we have found, and show that it can
be defined in terms of the C-R relation in such a way that it acts as
a general constraint on all anaphoric processes, regardless of the
manner of derivation or interpretation of the anaphor.

Once it is seen that such a formulation of the BAC is possible, of
course, Wasow's argument disappears. There is no reason whatever
to assume that any anaphors are assigned interpretations at the level
of surface structure.

3. The Backwards Anaphora Constraint and the notion 'anaphoric
relation'

3.0 So far as I know, every theory of anaphora in generative terms
has incorporated the assumption that the BAC must be stated as a
part of the entry condition on the rule (whether deletion or
interpretation) which is assumed to be crucially involved in the
derivation/interpretation of the anaphor. We see from the results
of the preceding section that this assumption must be given up.

We are forced to give up this assumption because, we have discovered, there are two radically different kinds of anaphoric processes, and there is no way to formulate the rules involved so that
their entry conditions are stated in terms of the same kinds of
representations; in particular, the deep anaphora rules cannot in
general have entry conditions defined on surface structures, where
the BAC must be stated.

The problem thus posed is actually deeper than the statement of
the BAC: the problem is, if there are such radically different means
of generating and interpreting anaphors, why do we have the notion
'anaphoric process' at all? We must have it, of course, and not just

because we always thought we did; the fact that all anaphoric processes are subject to the BAC shows that the notion is a necessary
one, and an adequate linguistic theory must somehow provide an
explicit characterization of it, in terms of the more primitive notions
of the theory.

If it had been possible to maintain the classical transformational
theory, for example, we could say that the notion 'anaphoric process'
is reconstructed in the theory as deletion under identity, and the BAC
would be a constraint on entry to all such deletions. Wasow's argument was essentially that since that particular reconstruction is impossible, we should choose a theory which allows the reconstruction
of the notion 'anaphoric process' as interpretation of semantically
unfilled nodes, with the BAC a condition on entry to the rules which
effect such interpretation. Since the BAC is a surface structure
condition, such a theory would require that the interpretation rules
apply at the level of surface structure. We have found this reconstruction, too, to be untenable.

If anaphoric processes are not all deletion processes controlled
by identity, and they are not all interpretive processes assigning
readings to pro-forms, then what do they have in common? Why
have they all been recognized as the same thing, and called by the
same name, in advance of any analysis?

3.1 What is an anaphoric relation? The fact is that, pretheoreti-
cally, we have a pretty clear idea what anaphora is, and what it means
for a particular item to be 'anaphoric to' another. An anaphor is
anaphoric to (in anaphoric relation with) that linguistic segment from
which we reconstruct, by whatever means, the intended reading of the
anaphor.

If the means of associating an anaphor with its interpretation were
in all cases the same, we could simply reconstruct the notion
'anaphoric relation' in terms of those processes; since it is not, we
must apparently reconstruct the notion directly. If we ask what
notions are needed to do so, it turns out that they are notions which
we have found to be necessary anyhow, the crucial one being the
notion 'reading of a (particular) surface constituent'.

In somewhat more formal terms, we can define the notion 'anaphoric relation' as follows:

Definition of anaphoric relation[22]

Given surface segments A and B (in a sentence or discourse)
B is anaphoric to (in anaphoric relation with) A if:

(a) A and B are disjoint
(b) the reading of B and the reading of A have identical subparts
(c) when A is varied both readings vary, but when B is varied the reading of A remains constant.

Clauses (b) and (c) are designed to make explicit the notion that the reading of the anaphor (B) depends on the reading of the antecedent (A).' The simplest such relation would be one where the reading of B is identical to the reading of A; such a case is the relation between a sentential it and its antecedent. Note that a linguistic segment need not be continuous; in example (9) (sections 1.2.1 and 2.5) the discontinuous segment Sally . . . be rich is a segment and has a reading. If this segment is varied (for example, to read Sally . . . be pregnant) the reading of it in the same sentence varies too (if indeed it is anaphoric to this particular antecedent); but if the segment it is varied (to, for example, that Paris is in Texas) the reading of Sally . . . be rich is not affected in the least.

Less simple semantic relations serving as the basis for anaphoric relations are discussed further on; but one reason for the rather circumspect wording of the proposed definition can be seen immediately, when we consider a case of surface anaphora such as VP deletion. In the general case it does not really make sense to say that the null segment 'has a reading'; often the surface null segment corresponds to nothing coherent in semantic representation at all, as in examples like (25) and (34), repeated here:

(25) Sally seems to be tough to beat at tennis, but Jill doesn't.

(34) Jack believes that Sally is older than she is, but Joan doesn't.

With the proposed definition, we can say that the whole clause Jill/Joan doesn't is anaphoric to the antecedent clause. It is thus unnecessary to posit a sequence of null segments in surface structure, each having an anaphoric relation to some part of the antecedent structure.

3.2 The Backwards Anaphora Constraint. Given the notion of anaphoric relation, which we see is definable in terms of the C-R relation, we can now state the BAC as a constraint on anaphoric relations in surface structure:

The Backwards Anaphora Constraint
If B is in anaphoric relation with A, B may not precede and command A in surface structure.

This is strikingly familiar; it is exactly the pretheoretical statement that I used to introduce the constraint in section 2. 2, and it is, in fact, the form in which the constraint is generally stated when one talks loosely about anaphora. My contention is simply that this is exactly the form in which the BAC must be incorporated into linguistic theory: as a direct limitation on anaphoric relations, and not as a condition on the application of the rules which create anaphoric relations.

We now have a statement of the BAC which is independent of the mode of derivation or interpretation of an anaphor. No matter how an anaphoric relation is created, according to this principle, the anaphor and antecedent must conform to certain limitations on their configurational relationship in surface structure.

The fact that such a constraint is statable (in particular, it is statable within any theory which proposes to account for deep anaphora by means of interpretive rules) is sufficient to destroy Wasow's one argument for treating anaphoric processes as surface rules of interpretation. If the BAC can be stated as proposed, then it is no longer necessary for rules creating anaphoric relations to be of the same type, or apply at the same level of structure.

3.3 Further implications of the rule-independent statement of the BAC. To examine all the consequences of regarding the BAC as rule-independent would require volumes; I point out, however, several particular points where the BAC as I have formulated it, together with the definition of anaphoric relation which I propose, lead to exactly the right predictions and consequently receive empirical support.

Consider first the celebrated example of Ross (1969a), from which he attempted to argue that Pronominalization was a cyclic obligatory transformation:

(38) *$\emptyset_i$ realizing that Oscar$_i$ was unpopular disturbed him$_i$.

Ross's explanation for the ungrammaticality of this sentence (with the indicated coreference relations) depended on the assumption that the BAC was part of the entry condition for pronominalization. Under this assumption, together with the assumption that on each cycle, pronominalization is obligatory when possible, (38) will not be derived because on the cycle of the clause containing realizing, the subject of the embedded clause will be obligatorily pronominalized, the backwards-and-upwards pronominalization of the subject of realizing being blocked by the BAC. If we do not make these assumptions, Ross says, nothing prevents backward control of (deletion of) the subject of realizing from the third NP (him in (38)), and forward control of pronominalization from Oscar to him, producing the impossible sentence.

The idea that pronominalization can be regarded as a cyclic transformation has long since been discredited; in particular, any attempt
to regard the BAC as a cyclic constraint must be abandoned, in the
face of arguments such as those in Postal (1970, 1971), among others.

Ross's explanation then is lost, along with his argument for the
cyclicity of pronominalization; which means we need another explanation for the ungrammaticality of (38), on the intended reading. Indeed, we have one: the ungrammaticality of (38) on the intended reading follows immediately from the BAC as stated in the last section.

Example (38) has Oscar and the null subject of realizing (attempting
to be) in the anaphoric relation, but the BAC is violated. It does not
matter how this anaphoric relation is established, it is ill-formed
according to the BAC and is rejected. The rule-free formulation of
the BAC thus provides a direct explanation for the badness of (38),
which a rule-bound BAC could not do.

Second, the rule-free BAC accounts for the following facts, which
so far as I know have not been discussed before:

(39) ?John$_i$ thinks the award will go to John$_i$.

It is generally claimed that pronominalization is obligatory for one of
two coreferent NP's within a sentence, if the coreference is pre-
supposed and not stipulated. In certain cases, however, the boundary
between presupposition and stipulation is blurred or something, and
sentences with two nonpronominal coreferent NP's are not too bad.
Now, if a sentence like (39) is placed in a context where there is an
instance of John$_i$ in previous discourse, optional discourse pronominalization can yield (40):

(40) I was talking to John$_i$ . . .
      he$_i$ thinks the award will go to him$_i$.

It can leave things alone, with the same slight oddness as before:

(41) ?I was talking to John$_i$ . . .
      John$_i$ thinks the award will go to John$_i$.

And, of course, the second of the two John$_i$'s within the sentence in
question may be pronominalized:

(42) I was talking to John$_i$ . . .
      John$_i$ thinks the award will go to him$_i$.

What is impossible is for discourse pronominalization to control pronominalization of just the first John$_i$, leaving the second one intact:

(43) *I was talking to John$_i$ . . .
he$_i$ thinks the award will go to John$_i$.

The situation is similar to the case of Ross's example. With a rule-bound version of the BAC it is impossible to account for the difference in badness between (41) and (43), unless one makes the unmotivated assumption that discourse pronominalization, if it applies, must apply across the board. The facts follow directly from the rule-free version of the BAC, however; no matter how it gets that way, (43) contains an anaphoric relation forbidden by the BAC.

3.4 The generality of anaphoric relations and the BAC. Under the definition proposed in section 3.1, many expressions which are not generally thought of as anaphors participate in anaphoric relations. (But cf. Dougherty 1969, Wasow 1972.) For example, consider the expression someone else, as in

(44) John$_i$ thinks Sue is seeing someone else$_i$.

The indices indicate not coreference but distinctness; the sentence is interpreted as meaning that John thinks that Sue is seeing someone who is not John. As with all anaphoric expressions, of course, the expression can be controlled from outside the sentence, giving it a different reading; but in the absence of such outside control, the reading of someone else is dependent on the reading of the antecedent John in the relevant way.

According to the proposed definition, this is an anaphoric relation. We consequently predict that such relations will be subject to the BAC. Indeed, they are:

(45) The fact that someone else$_i$ is seeing Sue bothers John$_i$.
(46) *Someone else$_i$ thinks Sue is seeing John$_i$.

Example (45) shows that someone else can precede the NP it indicates distinctness from, as long as it does not command that NP. Example (46) shows that the relation is blocked if someone else both precedes and commands the NP. The sentence is grammatical, but not on a reading where someone else means 'some person other than John'. Someone else is, in fact, an anaphoric expression, and as such is subject to the BAC. Many examples of this kind of anaphora involving not identity but some other regular relation between readings of anaphor and antecedent can be observed. So far as I know, they all obey the BAC.

Notice also that the relations between epithets and their antecedents, no matter how they are assigned, are quite predictably subject to the BAC. Similarly, for other cases of incomplete semantic identity:

(47a) If Jackson$_i$ ever looks the other way, I'll steal the bastard's$_i$ watch.

(47b) If the bastard$_i$ ever looks the other way, I'll steal Jackson's$_i$ watch.

(47c) *I'll steal the bastard's$_i$ watch if Jackson$_i$ ever looks the other way.

(48a) Jackson might lend us his horse$_i$, if he wasn't in love with the thing$_i$/the creature$_i$/the animal$_i$.

(48b) If he wasn't in love with the thing$_i$/the creature$_i$/the animal$_i$, Jackson might lend us his horse$_i$.

(48c) *We might be able to borrow the thing$_i$/the creature$_i$/ the animal$_i$, if Jackson wasn't in love with his horse$_i$.

3.5 Summary. In this section I have proposed a formulation of the BAC as a condition on anaphoric relations in surface structure. I have presented independent evidence for the correctness of this formulation (in the form of predictions made by it which are borne out) and I have finished with some very limited discussion of the implications of this view for the general theory of anaphoric relations.

The most important consequence of this proposal, however, is that it renders null and void all arguments about the ordering or level of application of particular anaphoric processes based on the assumption that the BAC is an entry condition on anaphoric rules. This goes not only for many of the 'ordering paradox' arguments which were directed against the transformational account of pronominalization, but also for Ross's argument for the cyclicity of pronominalization, and for arguments such as those of Jackendoff (1972) and Wasow (1972) attempting to locate interpretive rules of anaphora at particular levels of syntactic derivation on the basis of the same assumption.

The result, I believe, is that there is no argument remaining to support the claim that any anaphoric expression is interpreted at a superficial level in syntactic derivations. For surface anaphors, there appears to be no reason whatever to assume that anything happens except simple deletion, with no special interpretive device required at all. [23] For deep anaphora, there appears to be no reason to associate the assignment of interpretation to any particular stage in syntactic derivations. It can be taken as a strictly semantic operation, as suggested in section 2.5, or, so far as I can tell, it

could still be analyzed as a precyclic deletion. But there is no interpretation of anaphoric expressions at the syntactic level of surface
structure.

4. Summary and conclusion. This paper, in spite of the considerable amount of space which it devoted to quite abstract and sometimes nonempirical questions, is basically a paper about the real
nature of anaphora. The conclusion, that we may and must talk about
the anaphoric relation between an anaphor and its antecedent, may
seem obvious and even trivial, especially in view of the fact that we
always have talked that way, at least in private. Yet I think it is a
far from trivial conclusion, just as the conclusion that we may and,
in fact, must talk of passive sentences as the passives of corresponding active sentences was a far from trivial conclusion. It seems that
our science is still in a state where much of its progress consists in
discovering what we already knew.

I recapitulate the main points, with some commentary:

(1) Sentential it anaphora and null VP anaphora represent radically
different means of establishing an anaphoric relation. Each is representative of a larger class of anaphoric processes with similar properties, which are called 'deep' and 'surface' anaphora.

One reason for selecting these two processes for comparison is
that the semantic complexity of the anaphors in each case yields insights into the nature of anaphoric interpretation which are not available from an examination of semantically less complex anaphors,
such as ordinary pronouns.

(2) Surface anaphors are derived by deletion at a superficial stage
in derivations, or by a device only notationally distinct from deletion.
This deletion is controlled by an antecedent structure under the condition of superficial identity.

(3) Deep anaphors are internally inert syntactically, i.e. they
give no evidence of being derived by deletion from a more complex
underlying form. They are inserted or derived precyclically.

(4) There are no arguments that any anaphor is assigned interpretation at a syntactically superficial level. A careful reconstruction
of what it means for an interpretive rule to apply 'at level X' leads
to the conclusion that deep anaphors receive interpretation at the
deep level, if at any syntactic level at all. [24]

In the case of deep anaphora, however, it seems wrongheaded to
attribute the assignment of interpretation to such anaphors to any
syntactic level at all. What is clear is that two conditions must be
satisfied in order for a deep anaphor to be interpreted as anaphoric
to a particular segment: the segment in question must correspond to

a semantic unit, and the segment must not be preceded and commanded by the pronoun in surface structure. The second condition is accounted for by the BAC as formulated in section 3, and the first may be guaranteed in any one of several ways. A possibility, suggested by the pragmatic controllability of such anaphors (cf. Hankamer and Sag 1976), i.e. the fact that they can occur in certain situational contexts with no linguistic antecedent at all, is that there is no rule of interpretation for such anaphors, other than the pragmatic one which only says 'look for a plausible reading'.

(5) Any viable interpretive account would require the C-R relation, i.e. the association of a particular portion of semantic representation with particular constituents in surface structure. Any account requires the notion 'anaphoric relation', which is definable in terms of the C-R relation.

(6) Given the notion 'anaphoric relation', the BAC can be stated as a surface constraint on anaphoric relations. With the BAC thus stated in a manner which makes it independent of the rules deriving or assigning interpretations to anaphors, Wasow's one argument for superficial interpretation of anaphoric expressions vanishes.

The resulting general picture is that there is at most one rule of semantic interpretation which specifically assigns interpretations to anaphors, and that rule either says 'look anywhere in the semantic representation (or in some representation of nonlinguistic context) for a reading of the appropriate type (clause-reading for S-$\underline{it}$, NP-reading for a definite NP-pronoun, etc.) and copy it into the Δ position associated with the anaphor' or it says 'put any reading whatever in the Δ position corresponding to the anaphor, subject to the pragmatic constraint that it is recoverable (either from elsewhere in the semantic representation or from nonlinguistic context)'. [25]

This is not a very exciting result, but perhaps we should look elsewhere for our excitement. There never was any good reason for believing that there existed any special interpretive rules for anaphors associated with any particular level of syntactic structure, and if there are no such rules they can hardly have any interesting properties. I hope that this paper will have served not only to illuminate somewhat the nature of anaphora but also to clarify what is and can be claimed by particular theories of anaphora, particularly those which pretend to assign interpretations to anaphoric expressions at the level of surface structure.

NOTES

I would like to thank Thomas Wasow for comments and suggestions.

1. For a subclass of these anaphoric expressions, it is not required that an overt linguistic antecedent be present in discourse; it is sufficient for the interpretation of the anaphor to be recoverable from the nonlinguistic context. Sentence (i), for example, can be said felicitously in the presence of a strikingly slim girl, without any previous discourse:

(i) They say she used to be fat, but I don't believe it.

This use of an anaphoric expression in the absence of a linguistic antecedent is traditionally separated from anaphora and referred to by another term, such as deixis or exophora. I do not follow this tradition here, but continue the usage established in Hankamer and Sag (1976) where the distinction is preserved as that between linguistically controlled and pragmatically controlled anaphora.

2. There are some indications that the operation of the rules discussed in this section is not strictly at the 'surface': certain very superficial processes may apply after these deletions have taken place. Nevertheless, in relation to major transformational processes such as cyclic movements, the anaphoric deletions are strictly superficial, and I refer to them for simplicity of exposition as 'surface' processes.

3. I restrict the term ellipsis to those anaphoric processes which delete segments under identity with corresponding segments in a controlling clause, and where the location of the deletion is not marked by an adjacent constant term. See Hankamer (1971) for some discussion of the properties of this class of rules.

4. I have changed Ross's example to avoid a complication irrelevant to the present discussion.

5. Taken literally, Wasow's theory claims that (7), (8) are syntactically well formed, being rejected only because they cannot be assigned a semantic interpretation. It is clear that if one says this, the distinction between semantic and syntactic ill-formedness has disappeared, and that Wasow has introduced nothing more than a change in terminology. I do not follow this usage, but retain a more traditional terminology in considering (7), (8) to be syntactically ill formed. In these (traditional) terms, interpretive rules which have a filtering function, such as Wasow's VP interpretation, are syntactic as well as semantic rules.

6. I say 'at best' because there is a place or two where Wasow's theory might make different claims from a deletion theory, if he is not careful. If, for example, there are any insertion rules (which is unfortunately difficult to prove) and no principle is invented or discovered which would prevent them from applying to empty structures,

things like the following will be syntactically derived (up to the point of application of the VP interpretation rule):

(i) Max told me that he would bring me a frog from that pond where there are such big ones, but I don't believe he will there.

(From There Insertion among the empty nodes in the region following will; I have not represented the empty nodes.)

(ii) I believe it is clear that the Greeks will invade Cuba, but Joe doesn't it.

(From Extraposition operating within the null complement of the right clause.)

These structures can be filtered out (as semantically 'uninterpretable') as long as the VP interpretation rule is only allowed to interpret segments containing nothing but empty nodes (even when the non-empty ones have no semantic value at all). The point is that it must have exactly the properties of a transformation of deletion under identity.

7. I ignore several suggestions which Wasow advances diffidently as possibly providing evidence for his proposal, because in no case is it clear how the facts he cites could constitute an argument in favor of it. He has one argument which can be taken seriously, and that is examined carefully in section 2.

8. In absolutely neutral terms, 'the syntactic well-formedness of sentences containing these anaphors is determined by rules sensitive to a match between the syntactic shape of the anaphorized segment and that of an antecedent segment at a superficial level'.

9. For simplicity, I have restricted the discussion in this paper to a few types of anaphoric processes, and in particular in the case of deep anaphora, have discussed only pronominal deep anaphora. It should not be concluded, however, that the deep/surface distinction among anaphoric processes correlates exactly with the distinction between pronominal anaphora and null anaphora. As is demonstrated in Hankamer and Sag (1976), there are cases of null deep anaphora, and at least apparent cases of pronominal surface anaphora.

10. There are more explicit proposals in Chomsky (1975a, b) and Williams (1976), but these proposals involve semantic interpretation defined on 'surface structures' which are redefined so as to include global reference to deep relations of constituents.

11. The one exception is Wasow (1972); cf. discussion in next subsection.

12. This position, so far as I can see, is empirically nondistinct from that taken in Hankamer and Sag (1976), which assumes deep anaphors to be inserted by lexical insertion rules, with a special interpretive rule for deep anaphora operating at the deep level. It is only necessary to say that precyclic deletion/insertion operations can operate under pragmatic control, whereas the Hankamer/Sag proposal says that deep anaphors may be interpreted under pragmatic control.

13. Essentially surface structure. There do exist a few syntactic processes which apply subsequent to the application of the BAC, notably Clefting and Yiddish Movement, but the relation of these processes to other syntactic processes is very poorly understood. In general, any transformation involving movement, whether cyclic or noncyclic, will affect anaphoric relations in that the possibilities for backwards anaphora are determined by the derived structure after movement.

Ross (1969a) argued that the BAC should be regarded as applying cyclically (as a condition on a cyclic rule of pronominalization) and Jackendoff (1972) attempts to maintain this assumption. I believe the arguments of Postal (1970, 1971) render this assumption untenable.

14. In a theory which defines 'surface structure' as containing a record (encoded in bound 'traces') of the movements and relations of all NP's throughout the derivation, as in Chomsky (1975a, b), Williams (1976), it is, of course, possible to say that the interpretation of deep anaphors happens at 'surface structure'. This theory adopts a new use of the term 'surface structure' to mean what used to be meant by surface structure plus a great deal of global information. I am using the term 'surface structure' in the traditional way.

15. Another possibility is to say that the semantic interpretation rules have access to information present in deep structures. This is the position taken in Chomsky (1975a, b), Williams (1976) (with terminological confusions removed).

16. Some 'directionless' notation must be invented for the representation of anaphora rules, since the order of A and B may be reversed, as long as the BAC is not violated. This is easily done: let the superscript [16] appended to a structural description mean that the order of symbols is irrelevant, except that if the two constant terms are reversed, the first (in the modified order) may not command the second.

17. The indices p and q are there to represent the relation 'corresponds to' between a portion of semantic representation and a constituent in surface structure. S_p^i is the reading assigned to S_p by the ordinary rules of semantic interpretation. The superscript [17] appended to a representation such as that in (b) indicates that the order of elements in the representation has significance only as specified in the conventions for interpreting such representations.

18. A related case was noticed by Witten (1971). He observed that there is an ambiguity in (i) (as to whether <u>several girls</u> is interpreted as specific or not), which disappears in (ii):

(i) Bill believes that Tom has seduced several girls,
(ii) . . . and I believe it too.

In (i), it is possible to read the sentence as meaning 'there are several girls such that Bill believes that Tom has seduced them' (the 'specific' reading) or as meaning 'Bill believes that there are several girls such that Tom has seduced them' (the 'nonspecific' reading). In (ii) only the second reading is possible. Note that the translations make explicit the fact that on the forbidden reading, but not on the permitted one, there is a variable within the <u>believe</u>-complement which is bound by a quantifier outside the <u>believe</u>-complement.

19. In a paper which came to my hands too late for me to make substantial changes in the present paper, Williams (1976) discusses facts which indicate that the claim in the text is wrong. Sag (personal communication) has independently observed such facts, and refers me to Sag (in preparation). Williams notes a contrast between the ambiguity preserved in an example like (34) and lost in (i):

(i) Jack believes that Sally is older than she is, but Joan doesn't believe she is.

Here only the contradictory reading comes through. Williams describes these facts, but does not explain them, within the framework of an interpretive model (but one of considerably greater power than a surface-interpretive model). His description is equivalent to saying that a variable within a null VP anaphor may be interpreted as bound by a quantifier which has scope over both it and the antecedent clause, or by a quantifier within the same simplex clause as the VP anaphor, but not by a quantifier in a higher clause which does not have scope over the antecedent clause as well.

It is difficult to assess the full impact of these and related observations for the general theory of anaphora; it is clear, however, that the Hankamer-Sag theory (= the classical deletion theory for surface anaphora) is too simple. If VP deletion were blind deletion, insensitive to any properties of semantic representation, we would have to expect (i) to be ambiguous, just like its source (and just like (34), derived from the same source).

Furthermore, I fear that a constraint like that which we must recognize in these cases, no matter what theory we have, may also account for the difference between S-<u>it</u> anaphora and null VP anaphora, attributed in the text (and in Hankamer and Sag 1976) to the deep/

surface distinction. Since the S-it anaphors are semantically clauses themselves, variables embedded within them would always be one clause level further down from a potential controlling quantifier than in the corresponding VP anaphor.

20. One might wonder why (35) itself is only two ways ambiguous, not four ways. The mind is severely wrenched if one attempts to read such a sentence with the contradictory reading in one clause and the noncontradictory reading in the other. There appears to be a parallelism constraint on semantic representations in such cases.

21. This is, in fact, proposed in Williams (1976).

22. A definition identical in intent and only slightly different in wording may be found in Wasow (1972:8). Wasow also makes use of the notion 'anaphoric relation', thus defined, in the statement of his 'transitivity condition' (1972:19).

23. But see note 19.

24. Thrainsson (1976), on the basis of quite different arguments than those considered in this paper, draws a similar conclusion regarding the interpretation of referential pronouns and reflexives. He shows that certain distributional regularities holding universally (it seems) between pronouns and reflexives cannot be accounted for in a theory which does not assume that the coreference relations are specified underlyingly, or at least available for reference by the rules specifying the distributions of pronouns and reflexives, rather than being introduced by an interpretive rule.

25. Lasnik (1976) suggests essentially this for the interpretation of personal pronouns.

REFERENCES

Bach, E. 1970. Problominalization. Linguistic Inquiry 1.1.

Bresnan, J. 1970. An argument against pronominalization. Linguistic Inquiry 1.1.

_____. 1971. Note on the notion 'identity of sense anaphora'. Linguistic Inquiry 2.4.

Chomsky, N. 1965. Aspects of the theory of syntax. Cambridge, Mass., The MIT Press.

_____. 1975a. Reflections on language. New York, Random House.

_____. 1975b. Conditions on rules of grammar. Unpublished mimeo, MIT.

Dougherty, R. 1969. An interpretive theory of pronominal reference. Foundations of Language 5.488–508.

Fiengo, R. 1974. Semantic conditions on surface structure. Unpublished doctoral dissertation, MIT.

Grinder, J. and P. Postal. 1971. Missing antecedents. Linguistic Inquiry 2.3.

Hankamer, J. 1971. Constraints on deletion in syntax. Unpublished doctoral dissertation, Yale University.

_____. 1973. Unacceptable ambiguity. Linguistic Inquiry 4.1.

_____. (In preparation). On the cyclicity of extraposition.

_____ and I. Sag. 1976. Deep and surface anaphora. To appear in Linguistic Inquiry 7.3.

Iwakura, K. 1976. Another constraint on sentential subjects. To appear in Linguistic Inquiry 7.4.

Jackendoff, R. 1972. Semantic interpretation in generative grammar. Cambridge, Mass., The MIT Press.

Jacobson, P. and P. Neubauer. Rule cyclicity: Evidence from the intervention constraint. To appear in Linguistic Inquiry.

Kayne, R. 1971. A pronominalization paradox in French. Linguistic Inquiry 2.2.

Lakoff, G. 1968. Deep surface grammar. Ditto, Indiana University Linguistics Club.

Langacker, R. 1969. Pronominalization and the chain of command. In: Modern studies in English: Readings in transformational grammar. Edited by D. Reibel and S. Schane. Englewood Cliffs, N.J., Prentice-Hall.

Lasnik, H. 1976. Remarks on coreference. To appear in Linguistic Analysis 2.1.

Pinkham, J. and A. Zaenen. 1976. The discovery of another island. To appear in: Harvard studies in syntax and semantics, vol. II. Edited by J. Hankamer and J. Aissen. Cambridge, Mass., Harvard University.

Postal, P. 1970. On coreferential complement subject deletion. Linguistic Inquiry 1.4.

_____. 1971. Crossover phenomena. New York, Holt, Rinehart and Winston.

_____. 1972. Some further limitations on interpretive theories of anaphora. Linguistic Inquiry 3.3.

_____. 1974. On certain ambiguities. Linguistic Inquiry 4.3.

Ross, J. 1967. Constraints on variables in syntax. Unpublished doctoral dissertation, MIT; ditto, Indiana University Linguistics Club.

_____. 1969a. On the cyclic nature of pronominalization. In: Modern studies in English. Edited by D. Reibel and S. Schane. Englewood Cliffs, N.J., Prentice-Hall.

_____. 1969b. Guess who. In: Papers from the Fifth Regional Meeting, Chicago Linguistic Society.

Sag, I. (In preparation). Deletion and logical form. Doctoral dissertation, MIT.

Sag, I. and J. Hankamer. 1976. Syntactically vs. pragmatically controlled anaphora. To appear in: Proceedings of the Third Conference on New Ways of Analyzing Variation, etc., Georgetown University.

Thrainsson, H. 1976. Some arguments against the interpretive theory of pronouns and reflexives. To appear in: Harvard studies in syntax and semantics, vol. II. Edited by J. Hankamer and J. Aissen. Cambridge, Mass., Harvard University.

Wasow, T. 1972. Anaphoric relations in English. Unpublished doctoral dissertation, MIT.

_____. 1975. Anaphoric pronouns and bound variables. Language 51.2.

Williams, E. 1976. Discourse grammar. Unpublished paper, University of Massachusetts, Amherst.

Witten, E. 1971. A transderivational constraint on anaphora. Unpublished paper.

TOWARD A COGNITIVELY VIABLE SEMANTICS

RAY JACKENDOFF

Brandeis University

Abstract. It is argued that semantic theory has the same goal as
syntactic theory, namely, the explication of the child's ability to learn
a language. This implies that a semantic representation should reflect on the nature of conceptualization. The theory of thematic relations is presented briefly; one of its most important features, cross-
field generalization, is shown to reflect an aspect of language and of
cognition that has not played a role in other semantic theories.

I would like to sketch out a partial theory of the meanings of verbs.
This theory grew out of Jeffrey Gruber's (1965) semantic analysis and
out of the lexicalist approach to syntax discussed by Chomsky (1972),
Emonds (1970), Bresnan (1972, 1973), Jackendoff (1972, forthcoming),
and others. The theory is presented in much more detail in Jackendoff (1976). The lexicalist approach claims that an autonomous syntactic component of the grammar is responsible for determining the
set of structural descriptions of sentences. Many semantic relationships among sentences which are ascribed to common underlying
structures in other approaches to transformational grammar are
instead accounted for by means of purely semantic relations among
lexical items and/or similarities in output of the interpretive semantic
component.

The practitioners of the lexicalist approach take as their goal the
construction of a theory of an ideal language user's knowledge of his
language. One of the crucial factors in judging the adequacy of the
theory, in addition to its accuracy in representing our linguistic
intuitions, is its predictions about what a child would have to learn
in order to learn the language. As has been pointed out many times

59

before, children learn their language on the basis of exposure to evidence that is highly degenerate relative to the complexity of the grammar that they actually acquire. One can only conclude that the choices among possible grammars are strongly predetermined by the structure of the organism. The aspect of linguistic theory which is of greatest interest, therefore, is the characterization of that part of the speaker's knowledge which does not have to be learned; it is this enterprise which makes linguistics relevant to understanding the mysteries of the human mind.

At such a late date as 1976, it should be unnecessary to repeat this litany, which dates back at least to Chomsky's Aspects of the Theory of Syntax. But I think it is important to emphasize it for two reasons. First, I believe that many linguists doing generative grammar lost sight of the need for a grammar to be learnable, and this led to many of the syntactic and semantic excesses of the last ten years, including most notably the theory of generative semantics and its descendants. Second, it has rarely if ever been pointed out that this conception of the goals of linguistic theory is as germane to semantics as it is to syntax or phonology. A child must manage to associate lexical items and grammatical constructions with meanings which are often extremely abstract and removed from direct experience. For example, it is easy to imagine how a child could learn the word 'dog', but what about the word 'from'? Even the slightest reflection on this semantic ability leads one to the hypothesis that innate mental organization must have a strong influence on how meanings are discovered and how the semantic description of the language must be organized.

The construction of a semantic theory that accounts for the child's ability to learn language has not been the goal of most research in the field of linguistic semantics. Logicians are by and large interested in truth, synonymy, entailment, and so forth, not in the context of characterizing the speaker's knowledge of human language, but in developing a mathematically consistent characterization of a particular class of natural and artificial languages: Lewis (1972) and Montague (1973) exemplify such an approach. Others, such as Katz (1972) and Lakoff (1972) (if I may mention them in one breath) take their goal to be a description of the language-user's knowledge; but at no point do they address themselves to the learnability of the semantic representations they propose. Ironically enough, the one who discusses learnability is Quine (1960), who takes a strongly behaviorist position. As I understand it, his doctrine of the indeterminacy of radical translation amounts to the claim that meanings cannot be learned at all! From the point of view of the linguist, this is a disastrous conclusion, since we must assume we all speak the same language in order to do any research at all. I believe it is the assumption of innate mental structure that enables us to escape Quine's argument.

I will assume that the meaning of a word, sentence, or discourse is an element of general conceptual structure, whose existence is independent of its happening to be expressed in verbal form. This means that a theory of semantic representation is taken to be part of a theory of conceptualization, and that psychological evidence concerning the nature of concepts is highly relevant in constraining semantic theory. Thus the semantic component of a grammar is not simply translating into an arbitrary language 'Semantic Markerese', as Lewis (1972) condescendingly calls it, nor does it carry out the purely mathematical function of the logician's model theory. Rather the choice of semantic representation has strong empirical consequences. Not only must it meet criteria of adequacy in accounting for synonymy, entailment, presupposition, etc. in the language; it must accord with what is known about how humans encode and use any sort of information.

Following Fodor (1975) and Miller and Johnson-Laird (1976), we can think of a concept as a mental procedure, somewhat akin to a computer program, encoded in whatever way the brain encodes procedures so that they are available to be carried out on demand. The 'concept of an X' is a procedure which determines whether a particular given percept (object, event, sensation, memory, another concept, etc.) is or is not an instance of X. For convenience, we will use capitals to designate concepts. Thus for example, the concept DOG is a mental procedure which determines whether a given object is a dog, the concept JOHN HITS THE BALL is a procedure which determines whether a given event is an instance of John hitting the ball, and so forth. It can be seen that a concept associated with a particular sentence is in effect a Tarskian truth-condition for the sentence, where the metalanguage is mental representation; furthermore, the concept associated with a particular word, phrase, or sentence can be taken as its Fregean 'sense' (Sinn) or its Carnapian 'intension'.

We differ from these approaches, however, in claiming that there is no need for a concept to be associated with an utterance; there are plenty of purely visual, aural, and kinesthetic concepts. For example, the perception of a fugue involves forming a concept of its theme; certainly no propositional utterance is necessary.

This psychologically constrained view of semantic representation has a sort of paradoxical advantage, in that it frees the linguist of ultimate responsibility for providing a canonical form for meanings. So many nonlinguistic factors are involved that one could hardly expect language alone to provide enough evidence to decide on the nature of conceptual structure. However, it does become possible for evidence from many other areas of psychological investigation to influence semantic theory, and for evidence from language to bear on psychology. In other words, the problem of semantic representation takes its place as one part of a much larger problem. In my view, this constitutes progress, even if it means for the moment abandoning attempts to completely formalize natural language semantics.

One aspect of linguistic semantics that this approach immediately encourages us to abandon is the attempt to uniformly decompose lexical meanings into conceptual primitives. From the sentence level down to the morpheme level, decomposition is expected, for this is what makes creativity possible in language. Below the morpheme level, it is certainly possible to do great amounts of classification, but complete decomposition appears to be out of the question in principle, not just in practice.

For a simple example, consider the word red. Suppose one were to try to decompose it. An important feature of red is that it is a color. But suppose the semantic feature COLOR is removed from red --what is left to decompose? Redness without color is difficult to imagine. In the early works of Katz, this residue was left in an undecomposed 'distinguisher', which was not supposed to play a role in semantic relations. Bolinger (1965) showed, however, that any aspect of the meaning of a word can be cause for anomaly or entailment, if one is clever enough about creating an appropriate context; thus the role of the distinguisher is questionable. The other side of Bolinger's demonstration is that just about any concept imaginable can play the role which Katz assigns to semantic markers. Since the number of possible concepts is infinite, one can hardly conceive of the decomposition of the lexicon into semantic markers as the proper theoretical goal. A more complete form of this argument against decomposition appears in Fodor, Fodor, and Garrett (1975), and I find their case a very strong one.

Lacking any convincing theory as to how mental information is stored and processed (at present we have mainly arguments as to what it cannot be), we must be content to do lexical analysis in terms of relationships between concepts. Thus, as a substitute for the traditional paradigm 'morpheme x has the semantic marker Y', I will use a paradigm of the form 'utterance x expresses concept Y, which entails concept Z', where Z is the concept that in the earlier analysis would be embodied in a semantic marker. Such a paradigm for analysis enables us to say everything that was said under the old paradigm, without requiring us to make a claim about complete semantic decomposability.

The fundamental relationship of this paradigm is hyponymy: if X is a hyponym of Y, every instance of X is also an instance of Y.

In terms of Miller and Johnson-Laird's procedural semantics, the statement 'X is a hyponym of Y' can be taken to mean that it is impossible to determine whether X truly represents a given percept without doing all the mental computation that would be required to determine whether Y truly represents that percept as well. Hyponymy can thus be thought of as a sort of procedural entailment.

Besides hyponymy, there are many other important relationships among concepts. Two that are very often discussed are part-whole relations (for example, an ear is part of a head) and locative inclusions (for example, a house is contained in a neighborhood). I want to motivate here a much less familiar kind of relationship among concepts, which I will call 'cross-field generalization'. I will show that it plays a major role in the organization of the lexicon, and by inference, in the organization of human concepts.

To discuss cross-field generalization, we need the notion of a 'semantic field'. The idea that meanings can be separated into semantic fields is an old one in the literature, but it is hard to say exactly what counts as a semantic field, or whether it is claimed there is any general procedure for picking them out. Well-known examples of semantic fields are color terms and kinship terms, in which the general concepts 'X is a color' and 'X is related to Y' are elaborated in terms of families of hyponyms. The methodological preliminaries over with, I would like to examine a different sort of semantic field, the class of verbs dealing with spatial position.

The field of verbs of spatial position can be divided into three important subfields, which I will call GO-verbs, BE-verbs, and STAY-verbs. The sentences in (1) exemplify the subclass of GO-verbs.

(1a) The train traveled from Detroit to Cincinnati.
(1b) The hawk flew from its nest to the ground.
(1c) An apple fell from the tree onto Isaac's head.

These sentences all express concepts which pick out types of physical motion. Following Gruber's (1965) terminology, we will refer to the object in motion as the Theme of the sentence, to the Theme's initial position as the Source, and to its final position as the Goal. The semantic similarity between the sentences in (1) is described by saying that they all express hyponyms of a concept GO (X, Y, Z). This concept makes the claim that there has taken place an event consisting of the motion of x from y to z. In other words, the first variable of GO corresponds to the Theme, the second to the Source, and the third to the Goal.

The semantic differences between the sentences are expressed in two distinct ways. First, the different Themes, Sources, and Goals in the three sentences are described by inserting for the variables X,

Y, and Z the interpretations of the various noun phrases in the sentences, according to the way the verb correlates its strict subcategorization feature with its semantic representation. For example, (1a) expresses the concept TRAVEL (THE TRAIN, DETROIT, CINCINNATI), which is a hyponym of the concept GO (THE TRAIN, DETROIT, CINCINNATI), which is in turn a hyponym of GO (X, Y, Z).

The other differences between the sentences are described in terms of different manners of motion which they express. So, for example, the entailments of (1b) might be represented more fully as

$$\begin{bmatrix} \text{GO (THE HAWK, ITS NEST, THE GROUND)} \\ \text{Manner: THROUGH THE AIR} \end{bmatrix}$$

A full explication of fly would of course involve further analysis of the manner marker; what is relevant here, however, is the extraction of the entailment GO (X, Y, Z) from all these verbs of physical motion.

Next consider (2).

(2a) Max is in Africa.
(2b) The cat lay on the couch.
(2c) The statue stands on Cambridge Common.

These describe not a motion, but rather the location of an object relative to some other object. Thus we can claim that the sentences in (2) express hyponyms of a concept BE (X, Y), where X is the Theme (the object being located) and Y is its Location. As in (1), the differences of meaning among the sentences in (2) arise by substituting different expressions for X and Y, and by associating different expressions of manner with the concept BE.

In addition to the verbs of location illustrated in (2), there is a second, smaller class of location verbs with rather different semantic properties:

(3a) The bacteria stayed in his body.
(3b) Stanley remained in Africa.
(3c) Bill kept the book on the shelf.

These differ from (2) in two ways. First, they cannot refer to a point in time, as can (2); this is seen by comparing the sentences in (4). Second, they can serve as a complement to the expression what happened was that, whereas BE-verbs cannot do so; see example (5).

(4a) The bacteria $\begin{Bmatrix} \text{were} \\ \text{*stayed} \end{Bmatrix}$ in his body at 6:00.

(4b) The cat $\begin{Bmatrix} \text{lay} \\ \text{*remained} \end{Bmatrix}$ on the couch at 6:00.

(5) What happened was that $\begin{Bmatrix} \text{Stanley remained in Africa.} \\ \text{Bill kept the book on the shelf.} \\ \text{*Max was in Siberia.} \\ \text{*the statue stood in Harvard Square.} \end{Bmatrix}$

The verbs in (3) thus express hyponyms of a concept we will call
STAY (X, Y), where X is the Theme and Y is its Location.

The evidence from the use of the expression <u>what happened was</u>
indicates a further hyponymy: STAY verbs, like GO verbs, describe
events, that is, they are hyponyms of a concept HAPPEN; BE verbs,
on the other hand, represent states of affairs.

Given these three subfields of verbs of position, let us consider
another semantic field, verbs of possession. These can again be
divided into three subfields, exemplified in (6), (7), and (8).

(6a) Harry gave the book to the library.
(6b) Charlie bought the lamp from Max.
(6c) Will inherited a million dollars.

(7a) The book belonged to the library.
(7b) Max owned an iguana.
(7c) Bill had no money.

(8a) The library kept the book.
(8b) The iguana stayed in Max's possession.
(8c) The leopard retained its spots.

In (6), the thing described by the direct object of the sentence under-
goes a change in whom it belongs to; whereas the sentences in (7)
express states of possession. The sentences of (8) also express a
single unchanging possessor; but <u>at 6:00</u> may be added only to (7),
not to (8), and <u>what happened was</u> may be prefixed only to (8), not to
(7).

Thus there is an important parallel between (6) through (8) and
(1) through (3). Gruber chooses to represent this parallel by claiming that the verbs in (6) are also hyponyms of GO, the verbs in (7)
are hyponyms of BE, and the verbs in (8) are hyponyms of STAY.
The difference between (6) through (8) and (1) through (3) is then expressed by putting a modifier on the concepts GO, BE, and STAY,
which picks out the proper semantic field. For physical motion and
location, the field modifier is 'Positional'; for possession, it is

'Possessional'. Sentence (1a), for example, entails the concept (9a); (6a) entails the concept (9b).

(9a) GO$_{Posit}$ (THE TRAIN, DETROIT, CINCINNATI)
(9b) GO$_{Poss}$ THE BOOK, HARRY, THE LIBRARY)

This now gives us a principle with which we can organize a third very important semantic field, verbs of predication or ascription. These verbs are used to describe what properties things have. The same three-way division into subfields obtains:

(10a) The coach changed from a handsome young man into a pumpkin.
(10b) The metal turned red.
(10c) The ice became mushy.

(11a) The coach was a turkey.
(11b) The metal was vermilion.
(11c) The pumpkin seemed tasty.

(12a) The poor coach stayed a pumpkin.
(12b) The metal stayed red.
(12c) The redness persisted.

The sentences of (10) describe changes of state; (11) describes a state; (12) describes the persistence of a state. Of the two non-motional cases (11) and (12), at 6:00 may be added only to (11), and what happened was may be prefixed only to (12). Thus it is clear that we want the verbs in (10), (11), and (12) to be further hyponyms of GO, BE, and STAY respectively. We will call the field modifier this time 'Identificational'; Locations, Sources, and Goals in this field make claims about what the Theme is, rather than where it is, as in Positional, or whose it is, as in Possessional. Thus for example, (10a) entails the concept (13a). For sentences such as (10b) in which one of the arguments of GO is syntactically absent from the sentences, the argument in the entailed concept contains a free variable, as in (13b).

(13a) GO$_{Ident}$ (THE COACH, A HANDSOME YOUNG MAN, A PUMPKIN)
(13b) GO$_{Ident}$ (THE METAL, Y, RED)

The field modifiers Positional, Possessional, and Identificational on the basic functions GO, BE, and STAY enable us to express important semantic distinctions and generalizations. Combining the

three field modifiers with each of the three functions yields a
description of a particular class of verbs, in such a way that we
account for the similarities and differences among the classes in
a rather natural way. The fact that the three major functions apply
to each of the three semantic fields illustrates what I would like to
call the phenomenon of 'cross-field generalization'. A basic concept
of what 'location' is differs from one field to another: in the Positional field a 'location' is a spatial position; in the Possessional field
it is a possessor; in the Identificational field it is a property. From
any of these given concepts of 'location' an entire field of verbs is
elaborated, using the three basic functions GO, BE, and STAY to
describe states and event involving that field.

As evidence that cross-field generalization is of genuine linguistic significance, observe that it is common for particular verbs
to be involved in more than one semantic field, while still preserv-
ing their classification as GO, BE, or STAY verbs. Consider the
following examples:

(14a) The coach turned into a driveway.   (Positional)
       The coach turned into a pumpkin.   (Identificational)
(14b) The train went to Texas.   (Positional)
       The inheritance went to Philip.   (Possessional)
(14c) Max is in Africa.   (Positional)
       Max is a doctor.   (Identificational)
(14d) Bill kept the book on the shelf.   (Positional)
       Bill kept the book.   (Possessional)
(14e) The coach remained in the driveway.   (Positional)
       The coach remained a pumpkin.   (Identificational)

In each pair, the same verb is used in two different semantic fields.
Since these uses are not a priori related, it is a significant generalization that a sizable number of verbs exhibit such behavior. The
theory I am proposing claims that the relationship between these uses
is simple and nonaccidental: the verb stays fundamentally the same,
changing only its semantic field via a cross-field generalization. One
of the ways in which words are expected to extend their meanings,
then, is by keeping all semantic structure intact except that which
picks out the semantic field.

This theory claims that sentences represent concepts of fundamentally a simple form, namely giving the 'location' or 'locations'
of something at a particular time or during a particular interval;
the richness of expression available to natural language comes in
part from extending the concept of location to other than physical
position.

In addition to the three semantic functions discussed so far, there are two which describe different kinds of causation. Compare (15), (16), and (17)

(15a) The rock fell from the roof to the ground.
(15b) Noga stayed sick.
(15c) Dick received the money.
(15d) The air went out of the balloon.

(16a) Linda lowered the rock from the roof to the ground.
(16b) David kept Noga sick.
(16c) Dick acquired the money.
(16d) Laura sucked the air out of the balloon.

(17a) Linda dropped the rock from the roof to the ground.
(17b) David left Noga sick.
(17c) Dick accepted the money.
(17d) Laura released the air from the balloon.

The events in example (15) are also described in (16) and (17), but the latter two also claim that the events are due to the agency of the subject. In turn, (16) and (17) differ in the kind of action performed by the Agent: the Agent in (16) is bringing the event about, or causing it; in (17) the Agent is ceasing to prevent the event, or letting it happen. We can symbolize these two kinds of agency as CAUSE (X, E) and LET (X, E) respectively, where X is the Agent and E is the Event. Then if (15a, b), for example, are represented as (18a, b) respectively, we can represent (16a, b) as (19a, b) and (17a, b) as (20a, b).

(18a) GO_{Posit}(THE ROCK, THE ROOF, THE GROUND)
(18b) $STAY_{Ident}$(NOGA, SICK)

(19a) CAUSE (LINDA, GO_{Posit}(THE ROCK, THE ROOF, THE GROUND))
(19b) CAUSE (DAVID: $STAY_{Ident}$(NOGA, SICK))

(20a) LET (LINDA, GO_{Posit}(THE ROCK, THE ROOF, THE GROUND))
(20b) LET (DAVID, $STAY_{Ident}$(NOGA, SICK))

CAUSE is quite familiar from the literature, LET less so. There are two interesting distinctions between them. First, CAUSE allows an expression of instrument, but LET appears not to do so. In (21), for example, the with-phrases can be interpreted only as accompaniment, not as instrument.

(21a) Linda dropped the rock with a cable.
(21b) Dick accepted the book with a $5 bill.
(21c) ?David left the air in the balloon with a knot.

The second difference is that the second argument of LET may be either an event or a state of affairs, as can be seen from the contrast in (22). Example (22a) must be interpreted as David permitting Laura to go out of the room; on the other hand, (22b) does not say anything about Laura's movement, but only where she is allowed to be.

(22a) David let Laura out of the room.
(22b) David allowed Laura out of the room.

In other words, the verb allow can govern a state of affairs. By contrast, CAUSE requires its second argument to be a real event. All the causative locational verbs such as hold, keep, and retain are hyponyms of 'cause to stay' rather than 'cause to be'. The verb cause itself might appear to be a counterexample, since it does occur in sentences like Dollie caused Martin to be happy, where be happy appears just to be a state of affairs. I will show shortly, though, that the verb cause has a more complicated analysis than just the concept I have symbolized as CAUSE. In any event, one should be immediately suspicious of calling this example a case of CAUSE $(X, BE(Y, Z))$, since it means about the same as Dollie caused Martin to become happy, which is a hyponym of 'cause to go'.

The examples in (16) and (17) show that the concepts CAUSE and LET occur in all three semantic fields we have investigated, simply by taking as their second argument a GO, BE, or STAY whose location is in the appropriate field. Thus CAUSE and LET can be thought of as predicative concepts that can elaborate the semantic possibilities of any field.

Next I would like to use the notion of cross-field generalization to motivate a semantic field whose existence is less obvious than the three fields we have considered so far. This field is nonobvious enough that it appears to have up to now escaped attention, but I will try to show that it is a genuine semantic field with internal structure parallel to the other three.

To start, consider the interpretations of (23a, b).

(23a) Laura kept David in the room.
(23b) Laura kept David working. (in underlying structure,
       Laura kept David [$_S$David working])

The interpretation of (23a) is a hyponym of the concept (24).

(24) CAUSE (LAURA, STAY$_{Posit}$(DAVID, THE ROOM))

If the verb <u>keep</u> is to be essentially the same in (23b), we must provide (23b) with a similarly structured interpretation. But clearly
none of the previous semantic fields will do. So we introduce a field
call 'Circumstantial': if an individual is in a Circumstantial Location,
where the location is an event or state of affairs, this is taken to
mean that the individual is involved as a protagonist in that event or
state of affairs. Then (23b) will entail the concept (25).

(25) CAUSE (LAURA, STAY$_{Circ}$(DAVID, DAVID WORK))

(25) claims that Laura caused David to stay in the situation of working, precisely the desired interpretation. Furthermore, this interpretation is of precisely parallel form to its Positional counterpart
(24). Some other examples of verbs of Circumstance, given with
their Positional uses where such exist, are given in (26)-(34).

(26a) Linda kept Laura (away) from the cookies.
       CAUSE (LINDA, STAY$_{Posit}$(LAURA, NOT THE COOKIES))
(26b) Linda kept Laura from screaming.
       CAUSE (LINDA, STAY$_{Circ}$(LAURA, NOT (LAURA SCREAM)))

(27)   The car began sputtering.
       GO$_{Circ}$(THE CAR, Y, THE CAR SPUTTER)

(28a) John avoided the beach.
       STAY$_{Posit}$(JOHN, NOT THE BEACH)   (or causative)
(28b) John avoided playing checkers.
       STAY$_{Circ}$(JOHN, NOT(JOHN PLAY CHECKERS))(or causative)

(29a) Dick forced the ball into the hole.
       CAUSE (DICK, GO$_{Posit}$ (THE BALL, Y, THE HOLE))
(29b) Dick forced David to shut up.
       CAUSE (DICK, GO$_{Circ}$(DAVID, Y, DAVID SHUT UP))

(30)   Max caused Seymour to die.
       CAUSE (MAX, GO$_{Circ}$(SEYMOUR, SEYMOUR DIE))

(31)   Sheila stopped laughing.
       GO$_{Circ}$(SHEILA, Y, NOT(SHEILA LAUGH))

(32a) Manny released the air from the balloon.
       LET (MANNY, GO$_{Posit}$(THE AIR, THE BALLOON, Z))

(32b) Manny released Moe from washing the car.
LET (MANNY, GO_{Circ}(MOE, MOE WASH THE CAR, Z))

(33a) David allowed Laura in the room.
LET (DAVID, BE_{Posit}(LAURA, THE ROOM))
(33b) David allowed Laura to wash the car.
LET (DAVID, BE_{Circ}(LAURA, LAURA WASH THE CAR))

(34) Moe exempted Jack from fighting.
LET (MOE, BE_{Circ}(JACK, NOT (JACK FIGHT)))

It can be seen that quite a number of popular verbs are members of the semantic field of Circumstantial verbs, and that the same concepts of GOing, BEing, STAYing, CAUSing, and LETting appear in the Circumstantial field as in the Positional field.

There are two points to observe about these representations. First, where a verb that takes a sentential complement also has a Positional use, the two variants of the verb express concepts which, other than the semantic field, are identical. In the present theory it is no accident that the verb occurs in these two seemingly disparate syntactic and semantic contexts: the contexts are in fact closely related by cross-field generalization.

A second point to note is that complement type is related to some extent to semantic representation. Gerundives typically correspond to Locations or Goals; from-ing complements are negated Locations or negated Goals; to-infinitive complements are Goals of various sorts (including Goals of intentions, which we have not discussed here); and that-complements are typically Themes (again we have no examples here). The correspondence is hardly exact though, in part because there are far more semantic roles for clauses than there are complement types. But the distribution is hardly random either.

One might with some justification wonder if the representations given in (26) through (34) are rather baroque; it is entirely plausible to suggest that the mysterious Circumstantial GO is superfluous in the representation of force, and certainly in that of the arch-causative verb cause. I have claimed that a representation such as (35b) is correct for sentence (35a), yet (35c) appears intuitively correct and is one function simpler.

(35a) John $\begin{Bmatrix} \text{forced} \\ \text{caused} \end{Bmatrix}$ Bill to scream.

(35b) CAUSE (JOHN, GO_{Circ}(BILL, Y, BILL SCREAM))
(35c) CAUSE (JOHN, BILL SCREAM)

There are at least three arguments against (35c). First, without a Circumstantial function, <u>cause</u> and <u>keep</u> cannot be differentiated: both of them would have to be represented as (35c). (35b) represents the difference, since <u>keep</u> substitutes STAY$_{Circ}$ for the GO$_{Circ}$ in (35b). Second, (35b) but not (35c) can explain why (36a) represents a change of state, even though the complement represents a state of affairs.

(36a) Dollie caused Martin to be happy.

(36b) CAUSE (DOLLIE, GO$_{Circ}$(MARTIN, Y, BE$_{Ident}$(MARTIN, HAPPY)))

(36c) CAUSE (DOLLIE, BE$_{Ident}$(MARTIN, HAPPY))

A representation of (36a) parallel to (35c) is (36c), which we can reject on two grounds: first, it violates the otherwise motivated constraint that the final argument of CAUSE must be an event; and second, it does not represent the change of state which the sentence entails. But a representation like (36b), parallel to (35b), overcomes both objections at once. The second argument of CAUSE is an event, namely Circumstantial GO, and this GO represents a change of state.

The third argument for the representation (35b) is that it provides an account of the semantic difference which was used by Rosenbaum (1967) to argue for the presence of an underlying direct object with these verbs. Rosenbaum's examples were of the form illustrated in (37).

(37a) John forced the doctor to examine Bill.

(37b) John forced Bill to be examined by the doctor.

From the difference in meaning between (37a) and (37b), among other things, Rosenbaum argued that they have the underlying syntactic structures (38a) and (38b) respectively.

(38a) John forced the doctor [$_S$the doctor examine Bill]

(38b) John forced Bill [$_S$the doctor examine Bill]

Since the underlying structure of the complement sentence in (38) is <u>the doctor examine Bill</u> in both cases, a representation like (35c) cannot differentiate the readings of the two sentences. But if Circumstantial GO is included, the difference in meaning can be represented quite plausibly as (39a) vs. (39b).

(39a) CAUSE (JOHN, GO$_{Circ}$(THE DOCTOR, Y, THE DOCTOR EXAMINE BILL))

(39b) CAUSE (JOHN, GO$_{Circ}$(BILL, Y, THE DOCTOR EXAMINE
       BILL))

In other words, the use of Circumstantial GO enables the system to
express certain important semantic differences which have crucial
effects on syntactic structure. The direct object of <u>force</u> is given a
real semantic function. Hence the syntax of <u>force</u> is directly related
to and explained by its semantics: there is a one-to-one correspondence between syntactic and semantic arguments, as there should
be.

We see therefore that the concept of Circumstantial location, although intuitively somewhat murky and philosophically rather suspect,
leads to a much more adequate formal system than could be attained
without it.

Now, in case the generalization from Positional to Circumstantial
should still seem marginal and unmotivated, we should observe that
it is in fact quite pervasive in the language. A few random examples
from Jespersen, in which the generalization is immediately evident,
are these:

(40) He <u>came</u> to be called Batman.
      They <u>led</u> me to believe something ridiculous.
      We couldn't <u>drive</u> him to confess.
      Will you ever <u>bring</u> yourself to acknowledge that?
      I hereby <u>direct</u> you to shred the documents.
      The <u>way</u> to find out is still unknown.

Such examples are not metaphors in the usual sense--they are not
used for artistic effect, and there is no sense of clashing semantic
markers that is characteristic of true metaphor. Rather, they are
generalizations of the meanings of verbs along what I would claim
are innately determined lines.

As a more subtle example, consider the meaning of the verb
<u>force</u>, which we have so far analyzed only up to synonymy with the
verb <u>cause</u>. <u>John forced the ball into the hole</u> can be paraphrased
more accurately by 'cause to go' plus a manner phrase, something
like 'John caused the ball to go into the hole by applying pressure
against its resistance'. Surprisingly, exactly the same manner
phrase is right for the circumstantial reading: <u>John forced Sue to
speak up</u> can be paraphrased as 'John caused Sue to speak up by
applying pressure against her resistance'. In other words, the concepts of 'pressure', 'applying pressure', and 'resistance' generalize
from their physical sense to this abstract sense, all in precisely the
right way that they can be combined identically in both semantic
fields to paraphrase the sense of the verb <u>force</u>. Surely this is no

coincidence; to me it argues that the choice of extensions from the
Positional field to the Circumstantial is highly predetermined in
human cognition, and that the generalization of a verb's meaning
follows certain innate lines of analogy. In the semantic theory I
have been proposing, these generalizations fall out immediately from
the choice of semantic fields and from the theory of their organization.

As a final example of cross-field generalization in grammar, I
would like to bring up a case which I am just beginning to investigate,
for which the results are somewhat more speculative but very promising. One important subfield of the class of spatial location verbs has
not yet been mentioned, one which deals with spatial extent. This
class raises a number of apparent difficulties in the analysis I have
given so far. Consider example (41).

(41) The road $\begin{Bmatrix} \text{extended} \\ \text{reached} \end{Bmatrix}$ from Johnstown to Altoona.

The from and to in this example strongly suggest that the semantic
representation of (41) should be a hyponym of GO. To strengthen
this conjecture, we observe that the verb goes itself can be substi-
tuted for the verbs in (41), and that both extend and reach can
describe physical motion, as in (42).

(42) John extended his arm over the table.
      John reached Altoona.

Yet (41) does not express change of any sort, and it fails the what
happened was test for eventhood, which picks out verbs of motion:

(43) *What happened was that the road $\begin{Bmatrix} \text{extended} \\ \text{reached} \end{Bmatrix}$ from New
      York to Los Angeles.

An example with similar problems, but in the Identificational field,
is (44).

(44) This theory ranges from the sublime to the ridiculous.

Sentences (41) and (44) differ from all the previous examples of
motional verbs in one crucial way: they do not make essential
reference to the passage of time, and because of this they describe
not events but states of affairs. Since the use of happen implies
passage of time, (43) is anomalous. Thus the difficulties with (41)
and (44) follow from the fact that they are not in fact hyponyms of
Positional GO and Identificational GO.

In dealing with these examples, we cannot follow our earlier procedure of inventing a new kind of 'location', since the Sources and Goals are a kind of 'location' with which we are already familiar. Rather we seem to need to extend the concept GO itself, so that it subdivides into two fundamental concepts, which I will call 'Transition' and 'Extension'. All previous examples of GO have been Transitional GO, expressing the locations of the Theme over time. Sentences (41) and (44), though, are Extensional GO, expressing what locations the Theme occupies without reference to time. We can represent them as hyponyms of the concepts (45a, b) respectively.

(45a) $\text{GO}_{\text{Ext, Posit}}$(THE ROAD, ALTOONA, JOHNSTOWN)
(45b) $\text{GO}_{\text{Ext, Ident}}$(THIS THEORY, THE SUBLIME, THE RIDICULOUS)

Transitional GO claims that the Theme is first at the Source and then at the Goal; extensional GO claims that one end of the Theme is at the Source and simultaneously the other end is at the Goal.

Now we must ask whether the other basic concepts can also be used in this extensional sense. Since BE never refers to passage of time in any case, we would expect no distinction between Transitional BE and Extensional BE. A possible candidate for an expression of Extensional STAY is the verb contain. Transitional STAY, which we have been using exclusively up to now, claims that there is no time during a given interval when the Theme is not at the Location. Contain claims that there is no part of the Theme which is not at the Location; this seems to bear the same relationship to Transitional STAY as Extensional GO bears to Transitional GO. (46) gives the representation I am proposing.

(46) The circle contains the square.
$\text{STAY}_{\text{Ext, Posit}}$(THE SQUARE, THE CIRCLE)

Extensional STAY might be taken to mean approximately 'stay within the boundaries of'; the verb of this paraphrase is of course significant.

What sorts of notions could instantiate a nontemporal, that is, Extensional, causality? One attractive possibility is that verbs expressing logical connections are of this sort. 'P implies Q', for example, could be represented as a causation, as in (47a). There is no standard logical connective expressing 'P lets Q', but this sense seems to be conveyed by 'Q is consistent with P', as in (47b). By filling in the Agent of CAUSE or LET with a specified argument which represents the body of knowledge known as logic, we can represent 'P is logically possible' with some such expression as (47c). The parallel expression (47d) is then of course 'P is logically necessary'.

(47a) P implies Q
       $CAUSE_{Ext}(P, Q)$
(47b) Q is consistent with P
       $LET_{Ext}(P, Q)$
(47c) P is logically possible.
       $LET_{Ext}(LOGIC, P)$
(47d) P is logically necessary.
       $CAUSE_{Ext}(LOGIC, P)$

Other kinds of necessity and possibility can be expressed by substituting other kinds of general systems, such as MORALITY, AUTHORITY, THE PRESENT SITUATION, and so forth, for LOGIC in these formulas. This gives us essentially the range of readings of the modals <u>must</u> and <u>may</u>, which are thus Extensional CAUSE and Extensional LET respectively:

(48) John must leave.
$$CAUSE_{Ext}(\begin{Bmatrix} \text{MORALITY} \\ \text{AUTHORITY} \\ \text{THE PRESENT SITUATION} \end{Bmatrix}, \text{ JOHN LEAVE})$$

John may leave
$$LET_{Ext}(\begin{Bmatrix} \text{MORALITY} \\ \text{AUTHORITY} \\ \text{THE PRESENT SITUATION} \end{Bmatrix}, \text{ JOHN LEAVE})$$

So, if this last speculation is correct, the present theory can express the troublesome ambiguities of these modals in quite a simple way. Furthermore, the theory has as a natural consequence the semantic parallelisms which Lakoff (1972, Section VIII) points out between the pairs <u>require/permit</u>, <u>necessary/possible</u>, and <u>must/may</u>. He conjectures that they share part of their conceptual structure, and in our representation the shared part is extremely simple and general.

(49) CAUSE   LET
      require   permit
      necessary   possible
      must   may

We see then that a number of further semantic fields of verbs are conceivably amenable to the same analysis we proposed in the original three cases. There is no a priori reason why Transitional and Extensional verbs should have anything at all in common, yet the fact that the same lexical items appear systematically in both fields argues strongly that there is a cross-field generalization that the theory must capture. The theory I have been proposing can express the generalization by abstracting the fundamental concepts GO, BE, STAY, CAUSE, and LET away from the particular field which they organize. We see then that these five concepts are very powerful unifying concepts in the lexicon. In turn, since I have argued that meanings are psychologically real, this amounts to the claim that cross-field generalization is an extremely important element of conceptualization. Is there other evidence for such a claim?

First consider a type of evidence drawn from within the language: the process of metaphor. In a metaphor, the structure of one semantic field is grafted onto another semantic field; the aesthetic effect arises at least in part from the perceiver's restructuring of a familiar field in some novel way. The fact that we can interpret metaphors at all argues that we are capable of performing new cross-field generalizations on demand.

The cross-field generalizations I have been discussing up until now, namely those which are involved in grammar, do not seem artistic in the way that metaphors are; and it is reasonable to ask why they are not so. There are two possible theories. The weaker one is simply that we are so used to the generalizations of GO, BE, etc. that they are aesthetically worn out; there is nothing novel about them any more. A stronger hypothesis is that the cross-field generalizations of concepts like 'location', 'event', 'state', and so forth are innately determined; GO, BE, etc. are fundamental conceptual building blocks out of which fields are elaborated. Thus their generalization across semantic fields is conceptually 'natural' in some sense. In metaphor, on the other hand, a cross-field generalization is invoked which is not innate in the same sense; there is thus an element of unnaturalness, an organization of a field which is not native to the organism but which nevertheless can be entered into and played with.

Turning to less linguistic matters, here is a different sort of example of our ability to perform cross-field generalizations, in this case in real time. Consider the ability of a musician to follow a conductor's physical gestures--not only to follow his rhythm, but to be able to translate the force, direction, and shape of the conductor's gestures into tone, attack, and phrasing without explicit coaching as to what the gestures signify. Similarly, consider the ability of a dancer to create appropriate dances for given music--again, not just rhythmically correct dances, but dances which correspond to the expression of the music in many complex and subtle ways. Again, there is no a priori reason why human beings should have the ability to translate from physical gesture into sound and back again in such a way that there is substantial interpersonal agreement on how appropriate the translation is. The fact that humans do have this ability argues that there must be certain generalizations about how physical gestures and musical gestures are represented conceptually, and that these generalizations are determined at least in part along lines laid down by the nature of the organism. This is precisely the sort of cross-field generalization I have been proposing as part of semantic theory; the fact that it shows up in other aspects of our mental activity gives independent support to the claim that these semantic representations have psychological reality.

How does this theory bear on the learnability of the language--a factor which I have claimed is crucial in judging the adequacy of semantic theories? It seems to me to accord very well with the work of Piaget, who has been concerned with how children develop extra-linguistic principles involved in understanding the behavior of the physical world: the conservation of objects, their existence independent of perception, their combinatorial properties, and so forth. He emphasizes the nonlinguistic nature of these notions, showing how the child's ability to reason about and describe situations involving these notions develops later than his ability to put the notions to practical use.

Piaget inquires about the nature of logical reasoning, arguing that logic, in the logician's sense, is not the basis of thought, but rather is only the final step in a long sequence of developmental stages of reasoning. The beginning of the sequence is the application of principles of conservation and identity to the perception and manipulation of the physical world. By gradual stages of abstraction, a child develops the ability to understand situations which he does not perceive completely and in which he is not directly involved. The child finally learns to comprehend situations completely independent of the point of view of the observer and to generalize to abstract situations totally beyond experience, for example, logical truths.

According to the semantic theory I have been proposing, one crucial step in moving to abstract reasoning is recognizing a particular phenomenon as an instance of generalized Location. For example, understanding the full generality of complement verbs requires learning the concept of Circumstantial location, and realizing that the same principles of organization apply in the new domain as in more familiar domains. Once this realization is reached, the field of Circumstance is largely determined, and it remains to the child only to figure out which complement verbs fit which of the concepts available in the field. This is surely easier than figuring out every complement verb from scratch. Such use of cross-field generalization is like the kind of learning process that Piaget envisions in connection with other extensions of physical comprehension. In fact, the analysis of language may provide insight into where we ought to look for cognitive extensions of physical principles. Since the linguistic extensions are physically unmotivated, any account of why these and not other generalizations occur may bear on a theory of the structure of cognition.

The linguistic evidence I have presented here therefore appears to be complemented by observations of a nonlinguistic nature about conceptualization and human learning. It seems to me that a clear message for semantic theory emerges: contrary to current fashion, the semantics of natural language should not be approached by developing alternative versions of formal logic. Rather, we should look for insight by studying the innate conception of the physical world and how conceptual structures generalize to wider, more abstract domains. Such an approach seems to me an exciting and promising way of learning about the relationship of language and thought.

REFERENCES

Bolinger, Dwight. 1965. The atomization of meaning. Lg. 41.555-573.

Bresnan, Joan W. 1972. Theory of complementation in English syntax. Ph.D. dissertation, Massachusetts Institute of Technology.

_____. 1973. Syntax of the comparative clause construction in English. Linguistic Inquiry 4:3.275-344.

Chomsky, Noam. 1965. Aspects of the theory of syntax. Cambridge, MIT Press.

_____. 1972. Studies on semantics in generative grammar. The Hague, Mouton.

Davidson, D. and G. Harman (eds.). 1972. Semantics of natural language. Dordrecht, Reidel.

Emonds, Joseph. 1970. Root and structure-preserving transformations. Bloomington, Indiana University Linguistics Club.

Fodor, Jerry. 1975. The language of thought. New York, Crowell.

_____, Janet Fodor, and Merrill Garrett. 1975. The psychological unreality of semantic representations. Linguistic Inquiry 6:4.515-532.

Gruber, Jeffrey. 1965. Studies in lexical relations. Bloomington, Indiana University Linguistics Club.

Jackendoff, Ray. 1972. Semantic interpretation in generative grammar. Cambridge, MIT Press.

_____. 1976. Toward an explanatory semantic representation. Linguistic Inquiry 7:1.89-150.

_____. Forthcoming. Lexicalist syntax: A study of phrase structure. Linguistic Inquiry Monograph Series #2. Cambridge, MIT Press.

Katz, Jerrold. 1972. Semantic theory. New York, Harper and Row.

Lakoff, George. 1972. Linguistics and natural logic. In: Davidson and Harman (1972:545-665).

Lewis, David. 1972. General semantics. In: Davidson and Harman (1972:169-218).

Montague, Richard. 1973. The proper treatment of quantification in ordinary English. In: Approaches to natural language. Edited by Hintikka, Moravcsik, and Suppes. Dordrecht, Reidel. 221-242.

Miller, George and Philip Johnson-Laird. 1976. Language and perception. Cambridge, Harvard University Press.

Piaget, Jean. 1972. Psychology of intelligence. Totowa, New Jersey, Littlefield, Adams, & Co.

Quine, Willard v. O. 1960. Word and object. Cambridge, MIT Press.

Rosenbaum, Peter. 1967. The grammar of English predicate complement constructions. Cambridge, MIT Press.

METALANGUAGE, PRAGMATICS, AND PERFORMATIVES

GEOFFREY LEECH

University of Lancaster

Abstract. The paper explores the validity of an alternative to the abstract performative hypothesis, whereby performative sentences are regarded as metalinguistic statements, and are shown to be pragmatically rather than semantically related to equivalent non-performative sentences.

1. The performative hypothesis and the pragmatic analysis

In his article 'On Declarative Sentences' (1970), Ross, after putting forward his 'performative hypothesis' (or 'abstract performative hypothesis'), considered an alternative to that hypothesis, which he thought might well prove to be superior to it. This alternative hypothesis, 'the pragmatic hypothesis', differed from the performative analysis only in the following respect: according to the performative hypothesis elements referring to the speaker, speech act, and hearer of a sentence are present in the highest, performative clause of its deep or semantic structure; whereas according to the pragmatic hypothesis, these elements would not be in the semantic structure, but would be, to use Ross's phrase, 'in the air'. Ross saw the pragmatic hypothesis as roughly isomorphic to the performative hypothesis, at least to the extent that all the advantages of the performative hypothesis would also be claimed for the pragmatic hypothesis. But he saw no way of giving a local habitation and a name to the airy nothings which the pragmatic hypothesis postulated: the pragmatic hypothesis could not be formulated.

In the years since Ross wrote his paper, work in pragmatics has made pragmatic entities such as 'speaker', 'speech act', and 'hearer'

seem less mysterious than they seemed to Ross. Searle's theory of
speech acts and Grice's theory of conversation, if we allow them the
name of 'theory', could not exist without them. In an unpublished
paper 'Speech Acts and Recent Linguistics', Searle has in fact argued
that the pragmatic hypothesis is more soundly based than the performative hypothesis; and that 'the speaker, the hearer, and the speech act
are not in the air; they are very much on the ground' (p. 10). In fact
'pragmatic hypothesis' may be regarded as something of a misnomer,
since if the alternative to the performative hypothesis is to postulate
that entities such as 'speaker' and 'hearer' exist in the situation in
which an utterance occurs, this is merely to state a commonplace
about language, which none but the purest of formal grammarians
could ignore. Let us therefore speak of a 'pragmatic analysis',
rather than a 'pragmatic hypothesis'.

I am going to try to give fuller support to Searle's position, by
attempting a reasonably precise formulation of the pragmatic analysis, and arguing that the advantages of the performative hypothesis
can equally well be advantages of the pragmatic analysis, which,
moreover, has certain additional advantages. To do this, however,
I shall depart from Searle's views on performatives, by taking full
account of the metalinguistic character of performative sentences.

2. Indirect speech and modes of mention

An obvious but strangely neglected fact about most performative
sentences is that they are, syntactically and semantically, a class
of indirect speech (oratio obliqua) statements; that is, (1) and (2) are
basically the same type of utterance, the difference being that whereas
(1) reports a speech act by Gerald, (2) reports a speech act by its own
speaker, viz. the speech act which he is currently engaged in performing:

(1) Gerald declares that no one was to blame.
(2) I (hereby) declare that no one was to blame.

For this reason, as Davidson (1969:172) puts it, 'performatives tend
to be self-fulfilling. Perhaps it is this feature of performatives that
has misled some philosophers into thinking that performatives, or
their utterances, are neither true nor false'.

In order to characterise the semantics of performatives, we need,
therefore, some account of the conditions under which an indirect
speech utterance can be a true report of another utterance, and in
particular, an account of the difference in this respect, between
direct and indirect speech reporting. What, for example, is the
semantic difference between (3) and (4)?

(3) Gerald said that no one was to blame.
(4) Gerald said 'No one is to blame'.

It is clear that (3) can be a true report of a wider range of utterances
(see Zwicky 1971) than (4). Sentence (3), for example, could truly
report (5) through (8), whereas (4) could truly report only (5):

    (5) 'No one is to blame.'
    (6) 'There's nobody to blame.'
    (7) 'I don't think you can blame anybody for this.'
    (8) 'It's no one's fault.'

I have suggested in another paper (Leech 1976) that the semantic
difference between (3) and (4) can be handled by a general theory of
the metalinguistic use of natural language, and in particular by a
distinction between MODES OF MENTION:

    (9) Gerald said: /aɪ'wəʊmpbɪ rɪ'spɒnsɪbl/
        (PHONIC MODE OF MENTION)
  (10) Gerald wrote: 'I Won't Be Risponsable'
        (GRAPHIC MODE OF MENTION)
  (11) Gerald said 'I won't be responsible'.
        (FORMAL MODE OF MENTION, = DIRECT SPEECH REPORT)
  (12) Gerald said that he wouldn't be responsible.
        (CONTENT MODE OF MENTION, = INDIRECT SPEECH
        REPORT)

The distinction between modes of mention can be informally drawn
by noting the varying truth conditions of (9) through (12). The phonic
mode of mention commits the reporter to reporting the actual pronunciation Gerald used; (9) would thus be a false report if Gerald had
been speaking in an American accent. The graphic mode commits the
reporter to the actual written form of the message, including, for
example, spelling errors. The formal mode commits him to the
actual lexico-syntactic form of the utterance, that is, verbatim reporting. The content mode commits him not to the actual words
spoken, but to the sense or purport of the utterance. I have used the
nontechnical terms 'phonic', 'formal', 'content', etc. because these
categories are categories of natural language semantics, not necessarily synonymous with technical terms such as 'phonological',
'syntactic', 'semantic' in a particular linguistic theory. The content
mode is a particularly broad category, since an indirect report need
not give the semantic form of the reported utterance in any strict
logical form: it is sufficient, in general, that the report gives the
pragmatic force of the original. Consider the following exchange:

(13) GERALD: Where's the bathroom?
      BILL: I haven't the slightest idea.

Bill's utterance here would be truly reported by (14) or (15) as well
as by (16):

(14) Bill said he didn't know where the bathroom was.
(15) Bill said he didn't have a clue.
(16) Bill told Gerald that he didn't have the slightest idea.

A formal account of modes of mention runs briefly as follows. The
naming of linguistic entities in natural language is accomplished by presenting the linguistic referent as part of the semantic representation
of the reporting utterance;[1] or, more strictly, in the case of quotation, by presenting a TOKEN of a TYPE of which the referent itself
is a TOKEN. Different modes of mention arise from the fact that
the concept of a type-token relationship is ambiguous. To establish
two linguistic occurrences as co-tokens of the same type, we need to
establish their equivalence at some level of linguistic description or
other, but the type-token relation varies according to what level is
selected. For example, The and the are co-tokens of the same type
at the formal level, but not at the graphic level; nobody and no one
are co-tokens at the content level, but not at the formal level. Thus
a mode of mention of category m is a mode of referring to a linguistic
referent by presenting a co-token of it at level m. At the content
level, the co-token incorporated into the semantic representation reporting utterance is itself in the form of a semantic representation,
and can therefore be integrated into the reporting utterance as far as
syntactic processes are concerned. Hence there is a characteristic
shift of tense and pronouns in past-tense indirect speech reporting,
in accord with anaphoric relations with the rest of the reporting sentence.

3. A sketch of the pragmatic analysis

As a preliminary to the formulation of the pragmatic analysis, I
shall define a speech act ('A') in relation to four terms, 's' (= 'speaker'),
'h' (= 'hearer'), 't' (= time of utterance), 'u' (= 'utterance'). Thus the
information contained in Ross's deep-structure representation of a
sentence:

(17) (I) (($\begin{bmatrix} +V \\ +\text{performative} \\ \ldots\ldots \end{bmatrix}$) (you) (It was written by Ann and myself))

can also be specified in a pragmatic representation of an utterance as part of a speech situation:

(18) Direct speech

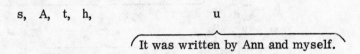

s, A, t, h,   u

It was written by Ann and myself.

In indirect speech sentences, there is both a PRIMARY SPEECH SITUATION, that of the reporting utterance, and a SECONDARY SPEECH SITUATION, that of the reported utterance:

(19) Indirect speech

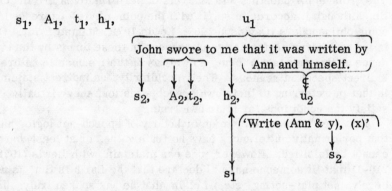

s_1, A_1, t_1, h_1, u_1

John swore to me that it was written by Ann and himself.

s_2, A_2, t_2, h_2, u_2

'Write (Ann & y), (x)'

s_2

s_1

(SYMBOLS: $\rightarrow$ = 'refers to'; $\leftarrow\!\!\!\!\!\!\!\!\rightarrow$ = 'refers to in the content mode'; $\leftrightarrow$ = 'is identical to'; s_1 = 'primary speaker'; s_2 = 'secondary speaker'; etc.)

Performative sentences, in this account, constitute the subclass of indirect speech sentences such that $s_1 = s_2$, $A_1 = A_2$, $t_1 = t_2$, $h_1 = h_2$, and $u_1 = u_2$. In other words, performative sentences are sentences which report their own speech situation:

(20) Performative sentence

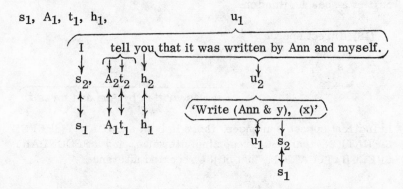

The grounds for adopting this analysis of performatives are linguistic, although it accords in spirit with the point of view expressed by some philosophers (Davidson 1969, Lewis 1972, Stampe 1975). One is led to analyse performative utterances in these terms by the evidence of their syntactic form, as well as of their semantic nature as indirect speech utterances. Their peculiarity, as indirect statements, is that by referring to their own speech situation, they virtually satisfy the conditions for their own truth.

This view runs counter to an orthodoxy of speech-act logic, namely that performative utterances have no truth value, or at least that they cannot be falsified. However, one can maintain, with Lewis (1972: 210-1) that 'If someone says "I declare that the Earth is flat" (sincerely, not play-acting, etc.) I claim that he has spoken truly: he does so declare'. Similarly, if someone says 'I pronounce you to be man and wife', and one happens to know he considers himself to have no authority to solemnize a marriage, one can deny his pronouncement with 'No you don't!'. The reason that performative sentences appear unfalsifiable is that a condition under which they can be plausibly denied rarely arises.

To justify (20) as a reasonable analysis of a performative sentence, I need to show that it follows, from a normal semantic reading of a sentence with overt performative characteristics, that it can refer to its own speech situation. This, in turn, means justify all five equations in (20):

(a) $s_1 = s_2$

(b) $h_1 = h_2$

(c) $t_1 = t_2$

(d) $A_1 = A_2$

(e) $u_1 = u_2$

The first two equations (a) and (b) are established by the normal rules for interpreting first and second person pronouns. Equation (3) is based on the semantics of tense in English. The simple present tense has two possible uses when attached to a non-stative (or 'event') verb such as tell: (i) it is used to refer to a time period, such that the present moment (t_1) is included in that time period, and such that the reported event habitually or repeatedly takes place in that time period; (ii) it is used to refer to a single present moment of time, at which a single occurrence of the event reported takes place. This same habitual/non-habitual ambiguity is found with all tenses and aspects of the verb; see, for example, Leech (1971:2-10). The latter sense, which may be called the 'instantaneous present', is only an acceptable interpretation if the described event is actually simultaneous with the moment of speech. [2] Hence, it occurs in only a few contexts, such as sports commentaries (Johnson scores!), cookery demonstrations (I pour the mixture into the saucepan), and, above all, with performatives. A performative sentence provides the ideal condition for the instantaneous use of the present, since in the case of an utterance reporting its own speech act, the coincidence of speech act with the present moment of time is absolutely assured.

Sentence (20), like all sentences containing the simple present tense, is theoretically ambiguous between habitual and instantaneous interpretations: in the habitual sense, for example, it could be an answer to the question

(21) What do you generally do when I accuse you of plagiarism?

But the instantaneous interpretation is the one which is relevant to performatives; that is, it is given, for the purpose of the pragmatic analysis of performatives, that $t_1 = t_2$.

The fourth equation ($A_1 = A_2$) must be accepted for lack of any realistic alternative. What other speech act can u_1 be referring to in (20), if not to its own speech act? Nothing, unless there can be two distinct speech acts, such that they take place between the same speaker and the same hearer at the same moment of time. Perhaps in theory, this is possible: the speaker could be writing one message at the same time as speaking another message, and could be using the spoken message to report the written message (Lewis 1972:210). But such a feat of verbal dexterity is so improbable as to be dismissed as a realistic interpretation of (20). Thus by an argument of elimination, we conclude that if, in an indirect-speech report, $s_1 = s_2$, $h_1 = h_2$, and $t_1 = t_2$, then A_1 must $= A_2$.

To complete the overall equation between reporting and reported speech situations, it must also be shown that $u_1 = u_2$. On the face of it, this looks contradictory, since u_1 contains the performative prefix

'I tell you that . . .', whereas u_2, as I have represented it, does not.
But since a performative sentence is an indirect speech report, it
reports an utterance in the content mode. Therefore, all that is
claimed by the equation $u_1 = u_2$ is that the communicative import of
the reported utterance is the same, in the broad pragmatic sense,
as that of the reporting utterance. In fact, the effect of the performative utterance is to assert that the pragmatic force of u_2 is that spelled
out in u_1. Once the equation is seen to be non-contradictory, it
follows, by the argument of elimination used for equation (d), that
$u_1 = u_2$. This equation, which completes the case for regarding performative utterances as referring to their own speech situations, in
fact holds the key to the nature of performatives, which is that they
report themselves as having a particular communicative import.

Three incidental facts about performatives reinforce this analysis.
(I) The class of performative verbs is coextensive, so far as I can see,
with a class of locutive verbs which we may call 'content descriptive'.
Apart from the general verb say, most locutive verbs seem to fall
into two major categories which we may call 'phonically-descriptive'
(gasp, murmur, giggle, shout, whine, etc.) and 'content-descriptive'
(state, request, order, advise, promise).[3] A formal distinguishing
feature of these categories is that phonically-descriptive verbs appear
to be more acceptable in direct speech reports than in indirect speech
reports,

  (22) 'Prices have slumped', murmured/gasped/giggled Fred.
  (23) ?Fred murmured/gasped/giggled that prices had slumped.

whereas content-descriptive verbs are more acceptable in indirect
speech reports than in direct speech reports:

  (24) ?'Prices have slumped', stated/claimed/suggested Fred.
  (25) Fred stated/ claimed/suggested that prices had slumped.

As far as I can tell, every content-descriptive verb can act in a performative function, while no phonically-descriptive verb can do so:

  (26) I (hereby) claim/announce/suggest that prices have slumped.
  (27) *I (hereby) gasp/murmur/giggle that prices have slumped.

If this is an accurate generalisation, then the class of 'performative
verbs' is independently defined, in a way which accords with the
semantic function of performative utterances. It does not have to be
specially marked (as in Ross's analysis) for that function.

(II) Performative verbs cannot be followed by a direct quotation:

(28) *I order you 'Go to bed'.

This again is predictable from the analysis: since the equation $u_1 = u_2$ would be contradictory in the formal mode, one cannot make an utterance refer to itself by direct speech reporting. A determined attempt to do so would actually produce an infinitely long sentence:

(29) *I order you "I order you 'I order you . . .

(III) The optional adverb <u>hereby</u> accompanying performatives has its own story to tell. Analogy with similar adverbs <u>hereto,</u> <u>herewith</u>, etc. argues for a semantic analysis of this adverb as meaning 'by this', or more explicitly 'by means/virtue of this utterance'. Such an interpretation makes the adverb an overt marker of the fact that a performative utterance describes itself as being used as the means of conveying a particular communicative force and content.

Hence a performative utterance is one which reports its own speech situation and therein refers to itself in the content mode.

I have already argued the pragmatic equivalence of u_1 and u_2 in (20), and since u_2 in (20) and u_1 in (18) are equivalent (i. e. co-tokens) in the content mode, this also means that u_1 in (20) can be pragmatically equivalent to u_1 in (18). That is, the following can be pragmatically equivalent:

(30) It was written by Ann and myself.
(31) I tell you that it was written by Ann and myself.

A similar argument can be made for any pair consisting of a performative sentence and its non-performative equivalent (i. e. the performative sentence minus its performative clause prefix). Therefore, the principle can be stated that: a performative utterance can be pragmatically equivalent to a corresponding non-performative sentence, but differs from it in making explicit its own speech act force.

4. Comparison of the performative hypothesis and the pragmatic analysis

It is now time to return to the performative hypothesis, and to see how the pragmatic hypothesis measures up against it. The two main attractions of the performative hypothesis are (a) that it accounts, by means of the performative deletion transformation, for the semantic equivalence, or quasi-equivalence, between performative sentences and equivalent non-performative sentences (or, in Ross's terms, between overt and covert performative sentences); and (b) that it enables us to simplify our grammar, by accounting for both a set of constraints on main clauses and an apparently different set of constraints on subordinate clauses by means of the same set of rules.

With regard to (a), we have seen, from discussion so far, that the pragmatic analysis provides its own account of the quasi-equivalence of performatives and non-performatives. Moreover, it could be claimed that the pragmatic analysis is more successful in this respect. The principle given at the end of section 3 helps to explain what seems to be a general fact about performative sentences: viz., that they are rare in comparison with non-performative sentences, and that they are only used when the speaker wants to lay particular stress on the illocutionary force of the utterance. Thus there is a clear difference in force between overt and covert imperatives such as:

(32) I (hereby) order you to be quiet.
(33) Be quiet.

If, for example, the speaker (32) is an officer speaking to an N.C.O., he makes it clear, by formally expressing the illocutionary force of his utterance, that he is speaking in his authority as an officer, and therefore, no doubt, that certain disciplinary consequences may ensue if his command is not obeyed. Whereas (33) could implicitly have this force, (32) makes the hearer understand that this force, and no other, is intended. Pragmatically, it seems, a performative sentence should be defined positively, as one which lays special emphasis on its speech-act role, whereas the performative hypothesis defines it negatively, as a sentence which happens not to have had its performative prelude deleted. With regard to (b), Ross presents fourteen arguments which purport to show that the grammar would be simpler if the performative hypothesis were accepted. Since his article, many other arguments have been put forward both for and against the hypothesis, [4] but I shall confine myself in the main to Ross's arguments.

These arguments, and in fact, almost all arguments for the performative hypothesis, group, broadly, into four categories. [5]

The first type of argument is the one that is most directly answerable in terms of the pragmatic analysis:

(34) According to $\left\{ \begin{array}{l} \text{The Times} \\ \text{you} \\ \text{*me} \end{array} \right\}$, food prices will skyrocket.

(35) Fred_i claims that according to $\left\{ \begin{array}{l} \text{the Times} \\ \text{you} \\ \text{me} \\ \text{*him}_i \end{array} \right\}$, food prices will skyrocket.

The essence of this argument is that there is a particular restriction on the 'according to x' construction in main clauses, viz. that x cannot be a first person pronoun; and that there is a different restriction on this construction in a subordinate clause, viz. that x cannot be a third person pronoun coreferential to the subject of the higher clause. These appear to be independent restrictions, but by virtue of the performative analysis, the former becomes a special case of the latter; i.e., in (34), me is coreferential to the subject of the higher performative clause. Thus the performative hypothesis enables us to state one rule which covers two superficially independent sets of data. The higher clauses in examples such as (35) illustrating the rule are always clauses introducing indirect quotation. [6]

For example, Ross's generalisation, as he points out, does not cover cases like:

(36) Satchel Page$_i$ drives a truck that gets, according to him$_i$, 37.8 miles per gallon.

In terms of the pragmatic analysis, therefore, the generalisation may be simply and adequately recast in the following form:

(37) In a statement modified by a phrase 'according to x', 'x' cannot refer to the speaker of the statement.

This principle covers both direct speech cases like (34) and indirect speech cases like (35), assuming pragmatic representations such as (18) and (19). Thus for data like this, as in other, similar arguments employed by Ross, the pragmatic analysis does the same work as the performative hypothesis. Moreover, the pragmatic analysis allows a rational explanation for this restriction. Semantically, the function of the 'according to x' construction is to point out that the speaker is reporting what x has claimed, without associating himself with x's commitment to its validity; thus 'according to x', where x is the speaker of the associated statement, is odd for the reason that it is odd for a person to simultaneously commit himself and not commit himself to the validity of a statement.

A second set of arguments used by Ross involves, like the argument above, coreferential relations obtaining between elements in a subordinate clause and elements in a main clause, and in particular, restrictions on the use of pseudo-reflexive pronouns:

(38) The paper was written by Ann and $\left\{\begin{array}{l} \text{*himself} \\ \text{*themselves} \\ \text{myself} \end{array}\right\}$.

(39) Tom $\begin{Bmatrix} \text{claims} \\ \text{believes} \\ \text{realises} \end{Bmatrix}$ that the paper was written by Ann and

$\begin{Bmatrix} \text{himself.} \\ \text{*themselves.} \\ \text{myself.} \end{Bmatrix}$

Here again, it appears that a different set of restrictions operating main clauses and subordinate clauses can be explained by a single rule, assuming the performative hypothesis. The rule is that a pseudo-reflexive can occur in coordination with another NP only if the pronoun is coreferential to an NP which commands it. If (38) and (39), in deep structure, have a highest performative clause, this rule will account for the acceptability of myself in (38) and (39), as well as of himself in (39). The same sort of rule can be formulated for other contexts in which pseudo-reflexive pronouns occur: as for x-self; like x-self; etc.

The difficulty with Ross's rules of this type is that when one considers a sequence of sentences, rather than a single sentence, the sentences which the rules exclude as ungrammatical no longer seem so:

(40) Klinkhorn left Miami in 1953. For some time there had been an estrangement between his wife and himself.

(41) Guerrero's friends made their peace with the junta. As for himself, there was little he could do but await arrest and the inevitable firing-squad.

(42) No composer has enjoyed a better family background than Mozart. His father and sister, like himself, were remarkable musicians.

We see from these examples that the conditions governing the use of pseudo-reflexives, like those governing the use of third person pronouns, stretch beyond the sentence, and that Ross's rules are inadequate. As a first approximation, it seems that referent of x-self must be contextually recoverable (whether from the same sentence, or a preceding sentence, or from the extralinguistic speech situation), and that there must be another, subsequently mentioned referent, or set of referents, with which the referent of x-self is in contrast. The contrasting referents are those of his wife in (40), Guerrero's friends in (41), and his father and sister in (42). The speaker, being contextually recoverable, is always a candidate for being referent of x-self. Whatever the precise formulation of rules for pseudo-reflexives may be, it is difficult to see how the performative hypothesis can play a role in it. Therefore this type of argument may be disregarded.

A third type of argument for the performative hypothesis rests on the observation of certain phenomena which seem to presuppose for their proper explanation, the existence of a higher performative clause, of which vestiges remain in surface structure.

The distribution and meaning of speech-act adverbials, whether single adverbs or clauses, can be most simply accounted for by this means:

(43) I don't believe a word of it, <u>bluntly</u>/<u>frankly</u>.
(44) <u>I tell you bluntly</u>/<u>frankly</u> that I don't believe a word of it.

(45) What's the capital of Outer Mongolia, <u>since you're so clever</u>?
(46) <u>I ask you</u> what the capital of Outer Mongolia is, <u>since</u> you're so clever.

The first thing to notice about this type of argument is that it does not necessarily support the view that all overt non-performatives have an underlying performative clause: it can be reconciled with the pragmatic analysis if we merely accept the hypothesis of an underlying performative utterance in cases where there are overt signals to that effect. This would mean placing speech adverbs like <u>bluntly</u> alongside other parenthetical adverbial constructions which, to a greater or lesser extent, reflect a performative origin: for example, <u>I say</u>, <u>putting it bluntly</u>, <u>to put it mildly</u>, <u>frankly speaking</u>, etc.

It is true that examples like (43) through (46) can be taken to justify the existence of a performative deletion transformation, and thereby to strengthen the performative analysis in general. But they also suggest that such deletion of performatives is selective, and lexically constrained. For example, the roughly synonymous <u>openly</u> and <u>because</u> cannot easily replace <u>frankly</u> and <u>since</u> in (43) and (45). Thus the performative deletion solution is not so simple and economical as it might seem. In addition, there are other, non-speech-act classes of adverbial which seem to be surface-syntactic reductions of higher predications:

(47) <u>Strangely</u>, no one has mentioned it.
       (= 'it is strange that . . .')
(48) The unions are determined to continue their strike.
       <u>Equally</u>, the employers have no intention of increasing their offer.
       (= 'It is equally $\begin{Bmatrix} \text{true} \\ \text{the case} \end{Bmatrix}$ that . . .')

The argument for performative clause deletion in the case of <u>bluntly</u>
etc. would also argue for an 'It is true that' clause deletion transformation in the case of (48). However, in view of the restriction of
such evidence to individual adverbial forms, there is reason to prefer,
both for speech-act adverbs and other cases, a solution in terms of
lexical specifications and lexical rules, [7] rather than by syntactic
transformations.

Yet a further type of counterargument to the pragmatic analysis
is based on a wider kind of syntactic evidence. An example is
Sadock's argument (1974:32-4) in claiming, as a point in favour of
the performative hypothesis, that it explains why imperatives have
no overt subject. He points out that there is a requirement with verbs
like <u>order</u> and <u>request</u> that the subjects of their complement clauses
have to be coreferential with their indirect objects, and moreover that
these subjects have to be transformationally deleted. This analysis
accounts for the non-occurrence of structures like (50) on the
semantic level, and of structures like (51) on the syntactic level:

(49) I order you [you open the door].
(50) *I order you [Sheila open the door].

(51) *I order you that you open the door.
(52) I order you to open the door.

Sadock's point is that given the performative analysis, all imperatives
will be derived from a semantic structure like (49), and deletion of the
subordinate clause subject as in (52), together with the deletion of the
performative clause, will ensure that an imperative sentence like
<u>Open the door</u> ends up without a subject.

The argument, however, rests on doubtful assumptions. First, not
all imperatives have no subject.

(53) You open the door! [8]

Second, it is not clear why the deleted 'you' in (52) should be regarded
as the second 'you' rather than the first 'you' of (49). It seems
generally true of sentences with locutive verbs that the NP referring
to the hearer (= indirect object) is optional, and this is supported, in
the case of verbs like <u>order</u>, by the occurrence of:

(54) The colonel ordered that the bridge should be destroyed.

and even of:

(55) I order that all N. C. O. s report here immediately.

Third, the assumption that it is the indirect object, not the subject of the subordinate clause, that is missing from the surface syntax makes the syntactic form of (53) explicable in terms of the subject-raising transformation, which applies to many other locutive verbs.

One substantive difference between the performative and pragmatic analyses is that the former treats the speech act as an aspect of sentencehood, while the latter treats it as an aspect of a speech situation, which may remain constant for a series of sentences forming a discourse or text. For an encyclopaedia article consisting of 100 sentences, the performative analysis has to maintain that the same performative clause, presumably something like 'I state to you that . . .' is repeated redundantly in the semantic structure of every sentence. This is particularly implausible in that encyclopaedia articles by stylistic convention avoid first and second person reference.

Moreover, as I have indicated, the facts about anaphora and co-reference which Ross attempts to deal with in a sentential context require handling within a discourse framework.

5. Conclusion

I have tried to show that the generalisations expressed in terms of the performative hypothesis either are incorrect, or are accounted for equally well, or better, in terms of the pragmatic analysis.

Since not all arguments in favour of the performative hypothesis have been discussed, I cannot claim to have made more than a prima facie case for the pragmatic analysis. In particular, mention must be made of one argument which in my view tends to support the performative hypothesis, but not the pragmatic analysis. This is the argument about pronouns presented by Harada (1971), and developed by Sadock (1974:28-9). The performative hypothesis, it is claimed, makes the independent feature-specification of pronouns redundant, since 1st person, 2nd person, and 3rd person pronouns are predictable from a syntactic deep structure containing a performative clause and referential indices. Thus three transformations, operating disjunctively and in order, can progressively replace (a) NPs coreferential to the highest subject by 1st person pronouns; (b) NPs coreferential to the highest indirect object by 2nd person pronouns; and (c) all other anaphoric NPs by third person pronouns. Although similar rules, referring to s_1 and h_1, can be formulated in the pragmatic analysis, it is not clear that any pragmatic rules, apart from these, would need to be ordered. Hence the fact that pronoun assignment rules need, for simplicity, to be ordered, is an argument in favour of their being syntactic transformations.

Perhaps further work in pragmatics will invalidate this argument. For instance, it seems that the rules for assigning 'proximal' and 'distal' markers to deictic items (<u>this</u>/<u>that</u>, <u>here</u>/<u>there</u>, <u>come</u>/<u>go</u>, etc.) would in part be based on an ordering of rules similar to that of pronouns; viz. (a) 'Mark as proximal those items which have reference to aspects of the speech situation'; (b) 'Mark all other deictic items as distal'. In this way, an account would be given of the 'unmarked' use of distal items, as in <u>He went to London,</u> where the only implication in the use of <u>go</u> as opposed to <u>come</u> is that London is not 'here'. Thus ordering may be a general principle of pragmatic rules, as of syntactic and phonological rules.

This case, however, reminds us that there is a residue of truth in Ross' original contention that the pragmatic hypothesis was too vague to be formulated. To the extent that the formalisms of pragmatics are less developed than those of syntax, the details of the pragmatic analysis must be taken on trust. But at face value, the evidence is strongly in favour of the pragmatic analysis.

NOTES

In writing this paper, I have enjoyed the benefits of comments by Robert L. V. Hale, and of discussion with members of the Department of Linguistics and Modern English Language, University of Lancaster.

1. Cf. the philosophical distinction between 'use' and 'mention', as discussed, for example, by Searle (1969:73-6). Searle appears to deny that 'presenting' is a means of 'referring': '. . . if we wish to speak of a word we don't need to name it or otherwise refer to it' (p. 75). But surely the virtual equivalence of the statements (a) and (b) requires that we treat <u>Les</u> as a referring expression:

(a) <u>Les</u> is easy to pronounce.
(b) The French plural definite article is easy to pronounce.

2. In natural language we cannot, for obvious practical reasons, treat lack of duration and simultaneity as implied by the 'instantaneous present' in a strictly literal sense. The fuzziness of time categories in a language like English can be illustrated by the sentence <u>Everything in the world is younger than it is,</u> which would be a tautology, rather than a contradiction, if we took the lapse of time between the first and second occurrences of <u>is</u> seriously. That in practice a certain latitude enters into the interpretation of time categories is notoriously evident in the procrastinatory use of expressions such as <u>this moment, in a minute, in a second,</u> etc.

3. I assume a distinction between illocutionary and perlocutionary verbs. Thus <u>persuade, convince, remind,</u> etc. are perlocutionary, in that they indicate that the speech act has a particular result. These verbs cannot be used performatively, since to do so would be to assume

in advance that the result is achieved. Another class of locutive verbs, including hint, imply, and insinuate, cannot be performative because they specify an indirect mode of communication incompatible with performativity.

4. See especially Matthews' (1972) criticisms of Ross, and Sadock's arguments both for and against the hypothesis (in Sadock 1974, Chs. 2 and 3). Sadock arrives at a revision of the performative hypothesis which does not, however, affect the issues discussed in this paper.

5. Some other arguments, outside these categories, presented by Sadock will be discussed later in this section.

6. According to Leech (1976), indirect quotation is introduced not only by speech-act verbs, but also propositional attitude verbs such as believe, want, wonder, imagine. This extension of the indirect speech analysis to 'thought quotation' is argued on the grounds that it enables generalisations to be made about reporting sentences regarding semantic ill-formedness, referential opacity, and presuppositions. Such an analysis explains why there is a common pattern of acceptability covering cases like:

$$\text{Tom}_i \left\{ \begin{array}{l} \text{said} \\ \text{believed} \end{array} \right\} \text{that} \left\{ \begin{array}{l} \text{someone} \\ ?{*}\text{he}_i \end{array} \right\} \text{was lurking nearby.}$$

which Ross sees as supporting the performative hypothesis, on the grounds that lurk cannot occur with a subject coreferential to a subject of the next higher clause: hence the oddity of ?*I am lurking nearby. As Ross states it, the restriction is clearly inaccurate, since there is nothing wrong with examples like:

Tom happened to be lurking in the shrubbery.

The pragmatic analysis, combined with the extended analysis of indirect quotation, would allow us to state the restriction simply as follows: 'It is odd for a person to predicate lurk of himself (whether in speech or in thought)'. This phenomenon has nothing to do with grammatical restrictions, but seems to be a consequence of the strangeness of a speaker's attributing to himself unfavourable associations such as furtiveness, cowardliness, etc., which lurk has in common with semantically related verbs like skulk, sneak, slink. On the relation between belief sentences and indirect-speech sentences, see also Jackendoff (1975).

7. In Leech (1974), lexical rules of limited productivity are discussed in detail (Ch. 10) and are applied to speech-act adverbials (pp. 356-360).

8. The view that the you in You behave yourself, etc. is a subject, rather than a vocative, is supported by imperatives like Mary, you

behave yourself, where the vocative is obviously Mary, not you.
Also, vocatives, unlike you in the above construction, are marked
off intonationally from the rest of the sentence.

REFERENCES

Davidson, D. 1969. On saying that. In: Words and objections:
  Essays on the work of W. V. Quine. Edited by D. Davidson and
  J. Hintikka. Dordrecht, Reidel.
Harada, S. I. 1971. Where do vocatives come from? English
  Linguistics 5. 2-44.
Jackendoff, R. 1975. On belief contexts. Linguistic Inquiry 6:1. 53-
  94.
Lakoff, G. 1974. Pragmatics in natural logic. Linguistic Agency
  University at Trier.
Leech, G. N. 1971. Meaning and the English verb. London, Longman.
_____. 1974. Semantics. Harmondsworth, Penguin.
_____. 1976. Natural language as metalanguage: An approach to some
  problems in the semantic description of English. To appear in
  Transactions of the Philological Society, 1976.
Lewis, D. 1972. General semantics. In: Semantics of natural
  language. Edited by D. Davidson and G. Harman. Dordrecht,
  Reidel.
Matthews, P. H. 1972. Review of: Readings in English transfor-
  mational grammar. Edited by R. A. Jacobs and P. S. Rosenbaum.
  In: JL 8:1. 125-35.
Ross, J. R. 1970. On declarative sentences. In: Readings in
  English transformational grammar. Edited by R. A. Jacobs and
  P. S. Rosenbaum. Waltham, Massachusetts, Ginn. 222-272.
Sadock, J. M. 1974. Towards a linguistic theory of speech acts.
  New York, Academic Press.
Searle, J. R. 1969. Speech acts: An essay in the philosophy of
  language. London, Cambridge University Press.
Searle, J. R. Undated. Speech acts and recent linguistics. Mimeo.
Stampe, D. W. 1975. Meaning and truth in the theory of speech
  acts. In: Syntax and semantics, Volume 3: Speech acts. Edited
  by P. Cole and J. L. Morgan. New York, Academic Press. 1-39.
Zwicky, A. M. 1971. On reported speech. In: Studies in linguistics
  semantics. Edited by C. J. Fillmore and D. T. Langendoen.
  New York, Holt, Rinehart and Winston. 73-8.

SEMANTICS AND SYNTAX:
THE SEARCH FOR CONSTRAINTS

BARBARA HALL PARTEE

University of Massachusetts, Amherst

Abstract. I am concerned with the goal of developing a theory of
semantics for natural language which has as much rigor and explicitness as linguists have attempted to provide for the theory of syntax.
I am equally concerned with the connections between rules of syntax
and rules of semantics; I believe that in the search for constraints on
the theory of language, one possibly fruitful approach is to try to constrain as tightly as possible the connections between these two sets of
rules, in conjunction, of course, with constraints on the form of syntactic and semantic rules separately.

Montague's theory of grammar, which I do not try to describe here
in any detail, has two important benefits which merit serious attention
from linguists. The first is that it does provide an explicit and rigorous semantics; and the second is that it requires a semantic interpretation rule corresponding to each syntactic formation rule. Recent
work has shown that transformational syntax and Montague's theory
are not so incompatible as they might seem at first, and the possibility of a combined theory with a largely nonabstract transformational
syntax coupled with Montague's semantics and Montague's constraint
on the link between them offers a first step toward the combined goals
of greater adequacy and tighter constraints.

I am going to illustrate the way in which a tight constraint between
semantic and syntactic rules can have the effect of constraining the
syntax itself with some discussion of relative clause formation and
Tough-movement vs. Tough-deletion.

1. Goals. The research I am reporting on here is a part of the ongoing effort to develop a theory of syntax and semantics which is explicit and which approaches the goal of descriptive adequacy with as tight constraints as possible on the form of grammars. In syntax such research has a relatively long history; only recently have theories of semantics begun to acquire the rigor and explicitness that is a prerequisite to any serious discussion of adequacy and constraints.

The introduction of explicit semantics in grammatical theory can have a number of effects on linguistic argumentation. In particular, the burden of treating such matters as anomaly and synonymy may be shared in various ways by the syntactic and semantic components. The net result of such effects is that the comparison of theories makes sense only when the syntax and semantics are equally explicit, and are taken into account together.

2. Constraints

2.1 Adequacy vs. constraints. There is constant conflict between the goal of descriptive adequacy and the goal of maximizing constraints. We need a certain amount of descriptive power to achieve adequacy, but we want to limit descriptive power as much as possible. Much of the theoretical debate of the last ten years can be viewed as a debate over where to put the needed power and where to put constraints. The constraint that transformations must preserve meaning, which was shared by the Katz-Postal-Aspects theory (Katz and Postal 1964; Chomsky 1965) and the theory of generative semantics, was one very tight constraint on the relation between syntax and semantics. That constraint required semantic interpretations to apply to deep structures only; but a controversial amount of power was provided in the syntax and in the use of such devices as global derivational conditions. Interpretive semanticists have tended to prefer stronger constraints on the form of the syntax, while allowing considerable power in the variety of syntactic levels where semantic rules can operate. [1]

Montague's theory of grammar has a somewhat different organization than any of the current transformational models. I want to sketch his theory very briefly--just enough to show how it includes two very strong constraints and where its excess of power lies. Then I suggest further constraints that can be imposed by incorporating some aspects of transformational grammar, and offer the resulting, combined theory as a step toward the joint goals of greater adequacy and tighter constraints.

In Montague grammar, sentences are derived 'bottom-up', so to speak, by rules which combine phrases to produce larger phrases. The form of the syntactic rules is given in (1), where α, β, and γ are strings of terminal symbols, A, B, and C are syntactic categories, [2]

(1) Montague grammar

Syntactic rule n: If $\alpha \, \epsilon \, A$ and $\beta \, \epsilon \, B$, then $\gamma \, \epsilon \, C$, where
$\gamma = F_i(\alpha, \beta)$

Semantic rule n: If α is interpreted as α', and β is
interpreted as β', then γ is inter-
preted as γ', where $\gamma' =$
$G_k(\alpha', \beta')$

and F_i is some syntactic operation that operates on the input expressions to give the resulting phrase. I will return to a discussion of
these syntactic operations F_i shortly. The derivation tree given in (2)

(2) Example of derivation tree

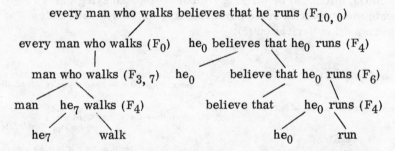

illustrates the operation of such rules in building up the sentence that
appears at the top of the tree. The tree is to be read bottom-up; the
parenthesized F_i to the right of any expression tells what operation
was used to form that expression from the phrase(s) just below it in
the tree. I will not try to describe this particular derivation in any
detail; it conforms to the grammar of Montague's paper 'The Proper
Treatment of Quantification in Ordinary English'.[3] Cooper and Parsons (1976) have shown how Montague's grammar can be converted
into a transformational grammar, so I have included in (3) the Cooper-
deep-structure corresponding to the derivation in (2). By comparing
the two, one can more readily see how Montague's syntactic operations F_i include not only concatenation but also some operations that
would be done by transformations in a transformational grammar.

Within Montague's theory, the input to semantic interpretation is
the syntactic derivation tree. The semantic rules also apply bottom-
up and their form is given in (1), where α, β, and γ are strings as
before, α', β', and γ' are semantic interpretations, and G_k is
some semantic operation that acts on the input interpretations to give
the interpretation of the resulting phrase. The semantic interpretation

(3) Corresponding 'abstract deep structure' (Cooper and Parsons)

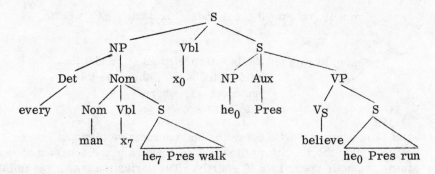

of the derivation tree in (2) is shown in (4); the expressions at each node of (4) are the interpretations of the phrases at the corresponding nodes in (2), produced by working bottom-to-top, applying the semantic interpretation rules corresponding to the syntactic rules that were used in derivation (2).

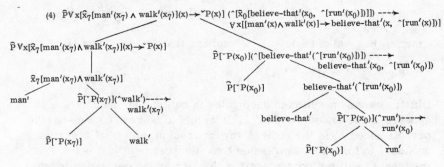

Semantic interpretation of derivation tree 3, translation stage. (Model-theoretic semantics is used to interpret the formulas of intensional logic.)

At each step, the result is an expression of an interpreted intensional logic whose model-theoretic semantics is also given explicitly by Montague. The expressions in (4) are probably completely unintelligible without familiarity with Montague's technical notation; my reason for including (4) here is just to make vivid what one form of a completely explicit semantics looks like. If we ignore all dotted arrows and what follows them, the expressions at each node are the expressions directly produced by applying the interpretation rules to the constituent expressions next lower on the tree; what follows a dotted arrow is a reduction of the given expression to a logically equivalent simpler form.

There are two major constraints imposed by Montague's theory. One is the constraint on the connection between semantics and syntax given in (5):

(5) Basic syntax-semantics constraint. There is one semantic interpretation rule for each syntactic formation rule. The interpretation of constituents must be preserved as part of the interpretation of the whole. All phrases of a given syntactic category receive interpretations of the same 'logical type'.

This constraint bears some resemblance to the Katz-Postal theory of projection rules, but the rules apply to derivation trees rather than to deep structures. The second major constraint is what I call the 'local grammaticality' constraint: no ill-formed intermediate stages are allowed. This constraint says in effect that well-formed surface expressions must be generated directly; Montague does not generate structures which must undergo later obligatory rules.

But Montague's theory does have two points at which the available power appears to be excessive. [4] These are the form of the syntactic operations F_i and that of the semantic operations G_k; Montague places no restrictions on these other than that they be functions. Not only can Montague's syntactic operations F_i include concatenation and such transformation-like operations as substitution and deletion, but they can in principle perform any describable operation on α and β, such as substituting the mirror image of β for every word in α that begins with 'q'.

2.2 Adding constraints to Montague grammar. In earlier work, I emphasized the strength of the two basic constraints already in Montague's system, and indicated how certain sorts of linguistic analyses are thereby ruled out. In that work I was implicitly assuming that only 'reasonable rules' would be allowed, but without some actual constraints on the syntactic and semantic operations F_i and G_k, the overall theory is still much too powerful. What I want to propose here are ways to constrain the syntactic and semantic operations.

The constraints I propose to add to the syntactic operations F_i are outlined in (6). Paradoxically, I think it is easier to constrain the syntax by first enriching it: in particular, I first propose to generate labelled, bracketed strings, that is, P-markers, where Montague simply generates strings. Thus, the derivation tree given in (2) would be replaced by one in which each node is occupied by a labelled bracketed string or P-marker indicating the derived constituent structure of each generated phrase or sentence. With that done, we can then require that each syntactic operation F_i be a composition of certain elementary operations, defined over proper analyses of the

(6) Constraints on syntactic operations F_i:

    (a) Domain: labelled bracketed strings
    (b) Operations: (i) concatenation
                   (ii) elementary transformational operations
    composition of (iii) substitution of a specified constituent
                             for all occurrences of a given indexed
                             element (e. g. he_n)

input P-markers, where the elementary operations include the following: (i) concatenation;[5] (ii) certain elementary transformational operations such as deletion, substitution, and feature-changing,[6] the exact best choices of course being a matter for continued research as they are in transformational syntax; and (iii) an operation familiar to logicians and employed by Montague, substitution of a specified constituent for all occurrences of a given indexed element such as the free variable he_i that occurs in (2).[7] This last operation will be a controversial addition; I would suggest that it either be added as a primitive operation or disallowed altogether; in either case the other elementaries should be kept sufficiently restricted so that operations like this third one will not be definable in terms of the others. I would claim at the very least that something like (iii) will be needed in the interpretive rules if it is not included in the syntactic rules, so that such rules are part of our linguistic competence in one form or another.

The constraints proposed here on the syntactic operations would make Montague's rules equivalent to a kind of combination of phrase-structure rules and transformational rules. Viewed in this light, Montague grammar can be taken as suggesting a reorganization of transformational grammar in which phrase-structure rules are applied bottom-to-top, transformations are applied as soon as their domains have been built up, that is, interspersed among applications of phrase structure rules, and semantic interpretation rules apply to the derivational history, or T-marker, rather than to any level of constituent structure.

Turning to the semantics and how to constrain it, we observe that in the grammar illustrated in (2) and (4), the first stage of interpretation consists of translation into an interpreted, unambiguous formalized language of intensional logic. Montague's specification of the logic provides one kind of way to constrain the semantic operations, by hypothesizing that the logic gives in effect a universal inventory of primitive semantic operations analogous to the elementary syntactic operations. We can require that each semantic operation G_k be definable as a composition of those primitive operations; further research on semantic constraints would include centrally the question

of whether Montague's list as given in (7) can be further narrowed
down. [8]

(7) Constraints on semantic operations G_k

composition of   (i)   propositional connectives: and, or, not
     (ii) quantification
    (iii) λ-abstraction ('function-formation')
    (iv) function-argument application
    (v) 'intension', 'extension' operators
    (vi) introduction of logical constants, e.g.
      = , necessity, etc.

3. Illustrations

Finally, I want to illustrate some of the implications of the constraints sketched above. First, suppose we limit our attention to a
subset of syntactic rules involving only concatenation, so that a
derivation tree can be viewed as directly equivalent to a constituent-
structure tree. Then in a tree such as that in (8), one immediate
effect of Montague's basic constraint (5) is that the semantic interpretation of the D-plus-E construction cannot depend on B or A. A concrete example of this sort, which I will mention only briefly because
I have discussed it in print elsewhere (Partee 1973), concerns

(8)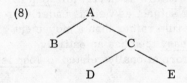

Semantic interpretation of
D E construction cannot
depend on B or A

restrictive relative clauses. I have argued that the NP-S analysis
given on the left in (9) is ruled out in Montague's theory since there
is no way to give an appropriate interpretation to the smaller NP
the boy without reference to the fact that that NP is part of a larger
NP containing a relative clause. The structure on the right can be
interpreted straightforwardly, and is in fact illustrated in the derivation tree given in (2) and interpreted in (4).

Finally I want to examine the implications of some recent work on
the easy-to-please construction. Assuming a VP-complementation
source and ignoring certain details, we can say that the classic analysis of Tough-movement posited a deep structure as in (10) for the
sentence John is easy to please. Lasnik and Fiengo (1974) noted a
number of problems with the classic treatment; to take one example,
they observed that Tough-movement, supposedly an optional rule,

(9) Restrictive relative clauses

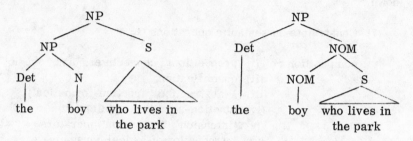

(10) Tough-movement--'classic' deep structure

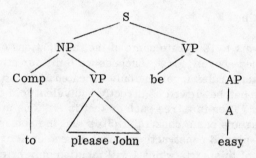

must derive (11a) from the ungrammatical source (11b). For this and other reasons, they proposed a deep structure as in (12) for John is easy to please, with John as underlying subject as well as underlying object of please, and a Tough-Deletion rule rather than a movement rule. The sentence To please John is easy then has an entirely separate source and is no longer transformationally related to John is easy to please.

(11) (Lasnik and Fiengo)
   (a) John was intentionally hard to please
   (b) *To please John was intentionally hard

(12) Lasnik and Fiengo Tough-deletion deep structure

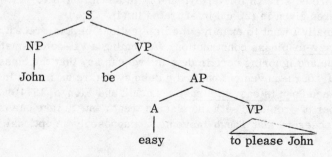

Jackendoff (1975) has argued that Lasnik and Fiengo's proposed deep structure does not in fact permit the correct statement of constraints such as those illustrated in (11a-b). He argues that it is the end-of-cycle structure that is relevant if traces are not used, and can actually be the surface structure if traces are used. The tree in (13) illustrates the surface structure that would result equally from movement or deletion; if Jackendoff is right, it is this structure that determines both the semantic interpretation and the restrictions on adverbs like 'intentionally', etc. The trace is interpreted as a variable bound by John.

(13) Jackendoff surface structure (for either deletion
      or movement)

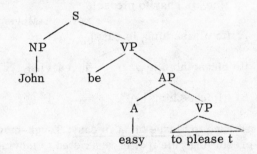

At this point we might pause and ask why, within the current interpretivist framework, there is an Aspects-type deep structure at all. Are there now any reasons other than historical ones for generating a whole deep structure top-down and then applying transformations cyclically bottom-up, as opposed to building everything up from bottom to top, applying transformations as we go? Strict subcategorization, being local, can still work in essentially the same way. Selectional restrictions have generally been transferred to the semantics and in cases like (11a-b) appear to be better statable at certain levels of derived structure than at deep structure anyway. One major motivation for generalized phrase-marker deep structures that was discussed by Chomsky in 1965 but is no longer applicable was the principle of deep structure semantic interpretation. If semantic interpretation is now viewed as cyclic or surface only, there appear to be no remaining arguments for starting derivations by generating a whole deep structure and then transforming it, as opposed to a Montague-style bottom-up derivation. And the bottom-up derivation allows the reintroduction of a strong constraint on the relation between syntactic and semantic rules, while maintaining constraints on the form of syntactic rules as strong as those in the interpretivist syntax. There is in addition the stronger constraint of local grammaticality, forbidding later transformations to fix up ill-formed structures, so that structures such as Lasnik and Fiengo's (13) would be ruled out. Note also that the principle of cyclic application of rules follows from the proposed bottom-to-top generation.

The derivation tree in (14) shows how <u>John is easy to please</u> would be generated in such a theory. Phrase-structure-like rules would

(14) MG-TG derivation tree

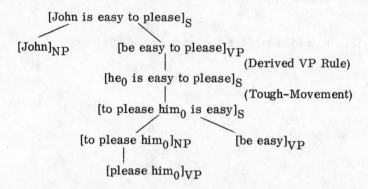

build up the open sentence <u>to please him_0 is easy</u>; Tough-movement can be a meaning-preserving rule if it is restricted to moving free variables, producing <u>he_0 is easy to please</u> as the next stage. The Derived Verb Phrase rule which I have discussed elsewhere (Partee 1975a) deletes a free variable subject and interprets the result by λ-abstraction. The derived verb phrase is the level at which the verb-phrase adverb 'intentionally' can be applied, [9] whereas such an adverb could not apply to the underlying verb phrase 'be easy'. The last step in the derivation is just a phrase structure rule, combining the subject and the verb phrase.

4. Summary

4.1 The final tree above could be converted into a generative semantics style deep structure, along the lines of (3) above, with various abstract 'triggers' as part of the constituent structure. The deep structure then becomes a mixture of real grammatical relations and triggers for syntactic and semantic operations. But if semantic interpretation operates on syntactic structure, it seems preferable not to have to include purely semantic elements or triggers as part of syntactic structure.

4.2 The Extended Standard Theory with traces can probably be made strongly equivalent to the derivation outlined in (14). But I have argued that there is no longer a clear motivation for a level of deep structure within EST, and the 'concreteness' of EST has been considerably weakened by the use of the abstract trace element (and other dummy symbols) whose function is a combination of filtering out bad structures and providing a basis for semantic interpretation. Further comparisons will require a more explicit semantics for EST, and proposals for the treatment of a wider range of constructions within the combined Montague-transformational framework.

4.3 Montague grammar when extended and constrained as proposed above offers, if it works, very strong constraints on syntax, semantics, and the link between them. This is accomplished in large part simply by one major shift in the relation of semantics to syntax. Where earlier theories viewed semantic rules as operating on certain syntactic configurations (i. e. P-markers), Montague suggests we view them as operating on derivations (analogous to T-markers). For this we need a concomitant shift to viewing derivations as proceeding bottom-to-top with PS-rules and transformations interspersed. The resulting theory can be viewed equally well as an independently motivatable variant of transformational grammar, with acknowledgements to Montague, or as an independently motivatable variant of Montague grammar, with acknowledgments to the transformational literature. [10]

NOTES

1. See Jackendoff (1975). If Jackendoff is right, the recent 'trace' theory may allow semantic interpretation to be constrained to operate only at end-of-cycle structures, and perhaps even only at surface structure. But the treatment of traces seems to add some of the power of global derivational conditions.

2. For simplicity, I have described only binary-branching constructions; but the syntactic rules in general may have any finite number of input expressions.

3. Reprinted in Thomason (1974). The paper is discussed extensively in Partee (1975a).

4. These points are not the only points of potentially excessive power; the system of syntactic and semantic categories also needs close scrutiny, but that is beyond the scope of this paper.

5. Concatenation will correspond in this system both to the effect of phrase-structure rules and to the transformational operation of sister-adjunction.

6. It may be possible to limit deletion and substitution to cases where the deleted or replaced element is either a specified terminal symbol or a free variable, limiting identity conditions to identity of free variables. Further research is needed on this question.

7. Note that an operation like (iii) is needed to give an explicit statement of such a rule as Quantifier-lowering, which substitutes

an NP for one occurrence of a free variable and a pronoun for all remaining occurrences of the same free variable.

8. The basic constraint on the correspondence between syntactic and semantic rules given in (5) is the primary constraint on the relation between the two components; this constraint could be made even stronger if correlations could be found between the form of particular syntactic rules and the form of the corresponding interpretation rule. E.g. applications of the across-the-board substitution operation, number (iii) in (6), might always be interpreted as variable-binding either by quantification or by λ-abstraction, (ii) and (iii) in (7).

9. I am oversimplifying the derivation a bit at this point; a fuller discussion can be found in Partee (1975b).

10. This paper has benefitted from a great deal of profitable discussion with Emmon Bach and Terence Parsons, neither of whom has any responsibility for any of its defects.

REFERENCES

Chomsky, N. 1965. Aspects of the theory of syntax. Cambridge, MIT Press.

Cooper, R. and T. Parsons. 1976. Montague grammar, generative semantics, and interpretive semantics. In: Partee (1976).

Jackendoff, R. 1975. Tough and the trace theory of movement rules. Linguistic Inquiry 6.437-464.

Katz J. and P. Postal. 1964. An integrated theory of linguistic descriptions. Cambridge, MIT Press.

Lasnik, H. and R. Fiengo. 1974. Complement object deletion. Linguistic Inquiry 5.535-571.

Partee, B. 1973. Some transformational extensions of Montague grammar. Journal of Philosophical Logic 2.509-534. Reprinted in: Partee (1976).

_____. 1975a. Montague grammar and transformational grammar. Linguistic Inquiry 6.203-300.

_____. 1975b. John is easy to please. [Unpublished Mss.] University of Massachusetts, Amherst.

_____, ed. 1976. Montague grammar. New York, Academic Press.

Thomason, R., ed. 1974. Formal philosophy: Selected Papers of Richard Montague. New Haven, Yale University Press.

ON THE THEORETICAL UNITY
OF ETHNOSCIENCE LEXICOGRAPHY
AND ETHNOSCIENCE ETHNOGRAPHIES

OSWALD WERNER
Northwestern University

MARTIN D. TOPPER
Southern Methodist University

0. Introduction. The goal of ethnoscience is to describe in a
theoretically motivated manner the lexical resources of a culture.
Anthropologists have used two theoretical avenues: (1) componential
analysis and (2) lexical/semantic field theory. Werner (1969, 1976)
has discussed the difficulties of the componential approach. Here we
concentrate on the field theoretical approach.

A lexical/semantic field can be viewed as a network. The nodes in
the network are labeled by 'concepts'--the semantic aspects of lexical
items. The edges (lines, or arrows) connecting the nodes to each
other are lexical/semantic relations. These relations and the labeled
nodes represent propositions. Thus a lexical/semantic field is more
accurately described as a network of propositions that contains or expresses the explicit cultural knowledge or world view of a culture.

Anthropologists, linguists, and lexicographers have proposed a
large number of lexical/semantic relations. (The best summary of
these can be found in Evens 1975.) Werner's major theoretical goal--
at least since 1969--has been the reduction of the plethora of relations
to a set of atomic relations. This paper is a continuation of this quest
for a fundamental atomic set out of which the large number of complex, often language specific relations can be constructed.

An ethnoscience ethnography is a method for representing the
microculture of a social system through the language (terminology)
that the members of the system use to talk about their experience in

111

the system. The basic elements of descriptions of cultural experiences are texts. A text can be construed as a linear path selected 'somehow' by the speaker (consultant, informant) through his lexical/semantic network (for problems of path selection see Werner et al. 1975a). Some of these paths can be directly identified with Plans, or more accurately, with Verbal Action Plans, that is, verbal descriptions of particular activities, such as getting up in the morning, baking a cake, chopping wood, making beer, tracking one's horse, planting a field, weaving a rug, and others. Our concept of plan is quite similar to that of Miller et al. (1960). The plan is a representation of guidelines for a series of sequential operations which compose cultural behaviors. We will argue--more convincingly in a subsequent paper-- that all texts are Verbal Action Plans (see section 3).

Here we are first going to explain the relationship of plans to taxonomies of cultural knowledge about culturally appropriate and/or culturally recognized behavior patterns. Every member of a culture has a repertory of plans for behavioral environments which regularly occur and reoccur. Plans may also be developed a priori when an informant enters a strange environment. However, we believe that most cultural behavior is routine and may be adequately accounted for by small alterations in established plans.

Because plans are normally used in response to recurrent cultural environments, they may be seen as coping strategies for cultural environments which Agar (1974) calls 'events' and which Spradley (1971) refers to as cultural 'equivalence classes' of phenomena.

An indispensable part of Verbal Action Plans is the fact that in every Plan the actor has a number of choices that determine the continuity of the activity toward some goal. Almost every node in the path of a Plan is a decision point where an activity may be continued, or aborted and replaced by a new activity. In field work since Topper (1972) we have been using decision table logic (borrowed from data processing) for the elicitation of exhaustive lists of decisions that, for example, Navajos make in order to get through their daily activities.[1] Although we recognized the importance of these decision tables as an eliciting tool that helped us obtain data of great cultural significance, we were, until now, unable to account for either plans or decision tables as part of a unified theory of lexical/semantic fields, that is, ethnoscience theory.

In this paper we are interested in the problem of a theoretically well motivated representation of plans and decision tables which are key tools for ethnoscience lexicography and ethnoscience ethnographies.

After an ethnographer collects his folk-taxonomies, his folk-definitions, his verbal descriptions of plans for action, and fills out decision tables which tell him how informants decide which action they would take under what conditions, he is then faced with a dilemma:

folk-taxonomies and parts of folk-definitions fit well into a theoretical framework; verbal action plans and decision tables do not.

For some time Werner (e. g. 1969) has been experimenting with what we here call the M-T schema (a Modification-Taxonomy schema that will be explained in the next section). In this paper (Section 2) we are attempting to integrate verbal action plans into a more sophisticated M-T-Q schema, where Q stands for the relation of sequential ordering or queueing. We will attempt to incorporate decision tables also. We consider these two steps--theoretical inclusion of plans and decision tables--fundamental for theory and therefore fundamental for the development of better ethnoscience ethnographies, ethnoscience dictionaries, and by extension, of ethnoscience encyclopaedias.

We proceed toward our goal by explaining briefly the M-T schema (Section 1). Then we follow this by expanding it into the M-T-Q schema (Section 2), and by discussing the inclusion of plans and decision tables (also Section 2). In the process we intend to integrate at least one family of complex lexical/semantic relations into the M-T-Q schema. We conclude with a brief review and an indication of the uses of our M-T-Q schema for the analysis of texts and possibly discourse.

1. The M-T schema. In anthropology, following the pioneering work of Frake (1964) and Williams (1966), only Kay (1971) and Werner (e. g. 1972) have continued the theoretical development of generalized lexical/semantic fields. Interestingly, the theoretical notion of a lexical/semantic field, usually equated with memory, is the prevalent view for semantics in the field of Artificial Intelligence (for a summary see e. g. Anderson and Bower 1973). The major differences of the various field or memory representations are to be found almost exclusively in the selection of the set of the lexical or semantic relations. That is, at this stage of development, each researcher has his or her own favorite set. The range rarely exceeds fifty relations; the minimum is below ten. We favor a small set of atomic relations. All complex relations are the result of combinations of lexical items by means of atomic relations.

In order to discuss the set of relations that we want to use in this paper, we commence with practical representations of lexical/semantic fields. In this application we first look at a representation of ethnographic information or the representation of cultural knowledge in lexicographic form. We show later that a representation in lexicographic form or a representation in some yet undefined ethnographic form is or can be a different view of essentially the same system of memory field representation.

For the practical lexicographic (or encyclopaedic) representation of knowledge, the most fundamental relation is that of taxonomy. It is the relation that becomes manifest in natural languages (like English) by sentences such as <u>A is a kind of B</u>, <u>A's are B's</u>, <u>All A's are B's</u>, and others.

The simplest structure of cultural knowledge one can imagine is a cultural domain, defined by some superordinate term, the taxonomic relation, and its subtree graph. Examples are taxonomies of Foods, Plants, or Animals. The topic, or the title for a cultural domain is usually found through a discussion with the consultants (informants), that is, by means of a dialogue or even dialectic, as some have suggested (Watson-Franke and Watson 1975).

After agreement on a high level term that 'stands for' the entire cultural domain, the subsequent elicitation techniques are relatively automatic: we apply question frames. That is, if A is the name of a domain, we formulate a question in the native language (of the members of the culture under study) that would back-translate into English as <u>What kinds of A are there?</u>

The normal human response to such a question seems to be a text, though some anthropologists among some people have been able to train informants to respond by lists. The taxonomic tree structure is then gradually expanded by simply applying the original question frame to more and more specific terms of the same tree. The process ends when the terminal nodes of the taxonomy are reached, that is, when further expansions of nodes become impossible.

We find that the best representation of this kind of a structure is a directed tree graph (Figure 1). The direction of the arrows is a matter of convention. We have become accustomed to drawing them from general to specific nodes. Without further elaboration, the tree graph represents the 'taxonomic aspect' of the cultural domain labeled or titled by (A).

Interestingly, the taxonomic aspect can be elaborated in but one way. All eliciting techniques can be reduced to filling in more detail of the 'content' for each term (node label) of a taxonomy. In actual ethnographic practice one does not necessarily proceed from taxonomy to 'content', but may just as well go from 'content' to taxonomy (Boehm, personal communication). 'Content' in its widest possible sense implies definitions. This is especially true in our case because we take the position that there is no arguable distinction between a definition and an encyclopaedic entry. In other words, there are no minimal definitions (or minimal definitions are trivial) and each non-minimal definition is an open set. No term can ever be 'fully' defined; there is always more left to be said about it.

In Figure 2 we represent the same taxonomic tree which was shown in Figure 1. Each node is now provided with a paragraph of definitions. In our work we proceed usually from taxonomic elicitation to the elicitation of the depicted definitional paragraphs (or pages, or longer

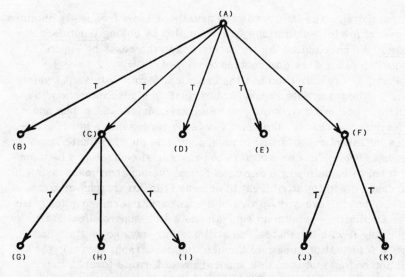

FIGURE 1. The hypothetical directed tree graph of the cultural domain of (A). The parentheses around the A call attention to the fact that the labels are concepts (bundles of attributes) and not the physical shape (vibration of air) of the words, and especially not the objects to which the concepts may refer in the 'outside' world.

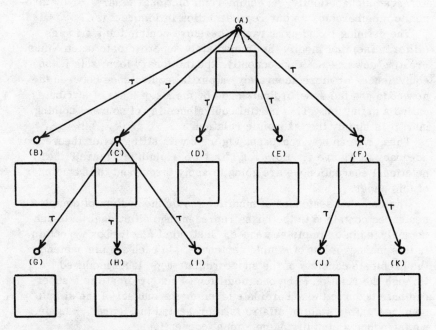

FIGURE 2. The taxonomic structure of domain (A) after the elicitation of folk definitions for each term of the taxonomy. The squares represent paragraphs of texts. In no way should it be construed that the paragraphs are by necessity of equal length. Although an effort should be made to obtain definitions that contain the same amount of the same type of information, this is by the very nature of cultural knowledge actually never the case.

textual units). The information is usually or most frequently obtained by asking for folk-definitions, for example, by asking What does A mean? We have called the text contained in the boxes of Figure 2 'content'. What does this content consist of?

First, every definition has the canonical form: 'P is an A, which . . . .'. The three dots represent the relative clause introduced by 'which'. Following Aristotle, a definition consists of a genus and differentiae. That is, the relative clause represents a set of attributes (differentiae) attached to an appropriate superordinate taxon (genus). The definition asserts the provisional equivalence between the term to be defined (in our case B) and the superordinate term (in our case A) and its attributes (in our case the paragraphs or boxes of text). That is, every definition of a subordinate term--explicitly or often implicitly--sets up an equivalence with a superordinate term by modifying it with attributes. In still another way, no matter what type of information goes into the defining paragraphs (boxes), the relation of that material to a superordinate term is through the relation of modification. Thus, lower taxons are constructed out of superordinate taxons by employing modifiers.

It is therefore clear that the boxed paragraphs are literally 'under' a term to be defined only in a practical dictionary (whether it is arranged alphabetically, as commercial dictionaries are, or by taxonomic membership, as our representation in Figure 2 is).

The defining boxed paragraphs therefore contain the attributes (differentiae) that modify the immediately superordinate taxon--thus creating new nodes. Consequently, the dictionary form sets up an equivalence, or more accurately, a partial equivalence between the new node and the superordinate node by means of a set of attributes called a definition. This partial equivalence is, of course, nothing new; it is simply the taxonomic relation.

Thus, we can now represent Figure 2 with still greater theoretical adequacy in Figure 4. However, first we explain in Figure 3 the notational convention we are going to apply throughout the remainder of this paper.

The complex sentences of modification or the system of complex sentences contained in the boxes representing definitional texts can be analyzed into simple sentences. Instead of a solid box we obtain in this manner a list of simple sentences. In each simple sentence the predicate consists of the superordinate node label modified through the relation M by one modifier. Each predicate is a superordinate taxon to the subordinate taxon or the subject of the simple sentence. This state of affairs is represented in Figure 5. Again, we introduce a simplifying notational convention.

We now replace the many simple or atomic relations of modification (Figure 5a) by two schematic triangles: one containing all M, the other

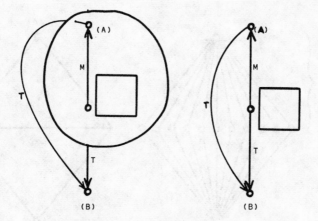

Figure 3a.   Figure 3b.

FIGURE 3. The definitional paragraph represented by the box is a modifier of the
superordinate node labeled (A).   The combination of the two creates a
new node (large egg-shaped line surrounding both) that is taxonomically
related to (B) (Figure 3a).   T is the relation of taxonomy and M the
relation of modification.   Figure 3b shows the simplified notational
convention which we are using instead of Figure 3a.   The direct
taxonomic connection from (A) to (B) we assume as given, and
suppress it in the following for the sake of simplifying our diagrams.

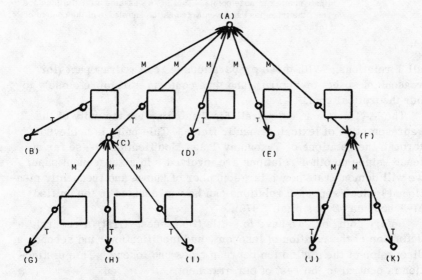

FIGURE 4. This is a theoretically more adequate representation of Figure 2. We have
applied the notational convention exemplified by Figure 3b. (M is modification, T the taxonomic relation.) The paragraph which was before 'under'
(A) modifies a hypothetical superordinate node of (A), is thus outside the
domain of (A), and is therefore omitted.

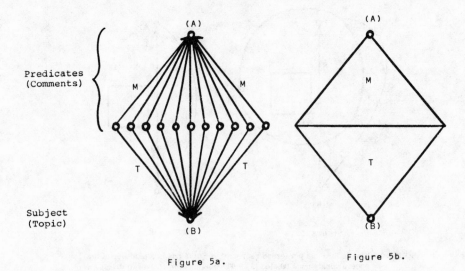

Figure 5a.

Figure 5b.

FIGURE 5. If the content of each box is broken down into very simple sentences we
obtain Figure 5a. We conventionalize this picture for an open set of an
indefinite but large number of modifying attributes by the M and T triangles in Figure 5b. This picture should be interpreted that on the line
dividing the M triangle in 5b from the T triangle, there are an indeterminate number of node points. That is, we assume all definitions are
open: the triangles can be enlarged as the knowledge of the content of
a term grows.

all T relations. With these preparations we can redraw part (for
reasons of space) of Figure 4 and thus conform still more closely to
our theoretical goal. [2]

The M–T schema, as we call Figure 6, implies the unity of the
representation of lexical/semantic fields. This unity is achieved
through the relations of Taxonomy T and Modification M--so far at
least--since no other relations are involved. In a subsequent paper
we will demonstrate how a large number of known and frequently mentioned lexical/semantic relations can be represented in the unified
M–T schema (Evens et al. 1976).

Before going on, we have to settle two issues: first, a general
definition of the relation of taxonomy and modification, and second, a
discussion of the distinction between types and tokens. This distinction is central to the rest of our argument.

1.1 Definitions. Taxonomy T and Modification M are intimately
related to each other. Every word in every language has two aspects.
(1) There is its extension, the set of 'objects' to which it refers.
Thus, the extension of the term <u>animal</u> is the set of all animals in the

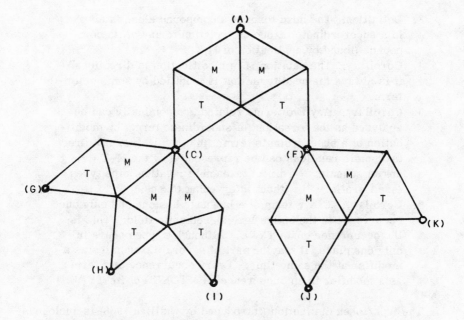

FIGURE 6.   Part of the taxonomy represented in Figure 4 incorporates attribute
fields according to the convention of Figure 3b, combined with the
convention of Figure 5b.   This is a graphic representation of the
M-T schema, or the M-T lexical/semantic field.   The world view
of members of a culture may contain several independent taxonomies.

'real' world.   (2) The intension of a term is the set of attributes necessary for the recognition of the term.   In the case of animals, this is
the set of attributes of all animals and every animal.   Since we do not
distinguish here between some minimal intension distilled from the
large open-ended intension of a term, we include in the intension of a
term all its explicitly and implicitly known attributes (see note 2).
That is, the intension of a term is the total cultural knowledge that
some idealized individual has about the proper application of some
term in some context.   (We have shown (Werner and Matichek 1975)
that context itself is part of a term's intension.)
   The relation M of modification is defined as:[3]

1.   Definition: If two terms are joined by the relation of modifi-
     cation, then the resulting compound term has a larger inten-
     sion and a smaller extension than either of the terms has
     alone.
2.   Corollary: One of the two compounded terms is the head
     term of the compound.

3. Definition: The head term of a compound alone is always
   in a superordinate taxonomic relation to any of its com-
   pounds (found by application of M).
4. Corollary: The relation M of modification is directional:
   it is always the head term that is modified by some other
   term.
5. Corollary: Any two terms related taxonomically can be
   analyzed as the 'creation' of subordinate terms by modification of a superordinate term. In other words, all direct
   taxonomic relations can be represented by the M-T (triangle) schema. (A direct taxonomic relation joins types
   (see Corollary 6) without intervening tokens.)
6. Corollary: Every term of a language has one and only one
   occurrence in the entire lexical/semantic field. This is
   the occurrence of its TYPE. Although a type occurs in
   only one place, it may be part of several taxonomies as a
   modifier at the same time. Every occurrence of a term
   as a modifier is an occurrence as a TOKEN of its TYPE.

The type/token distinction (introduced by Quillian 1968) is analogous
to the occurrence of a word in a dictionary. The word to be defined
is the type. If the word is used in part of the definition of another
word, it is a token. Thus, in our M-T triangles the top and bottom
nodes are always labeled by types because these are taxons in their
'home' taxonomies. The terms appearing as modifiers on the horizontal diagonal of the M-T triangles are always tokens, and therefore
are always away from their 'home taxonomies'. The type-token distinction is perhaps more apparent than real. It is a device for the
representation of the complex interconnectedness of lexical/semantic
fields.

In the remainder of this paper all TYPES are enclosed in round
parentheses, while all TOKENS appear in square brackets. The link
between types and tokens is the TTL or the Type-Token-Link.

2. The M-T-Q schema. In several of our publications (e.g. Werner
1966, Topper 1972) we have taken the notion of Plans (recently also
known as frames for action (Minsky 1974)) from Miller, Galanter, and
Pribram (1960) and applied it to ethnographic elicitation. Subsequently,
we introduced the relation of grading (Casagrande and Hale 1967), or
sequencing, or Q for Queueing. We recognized the relation Q as a
fundamental relation necessary for the expression of temporal and
spatial order and/or sequence. However, we were previously unable
to integrate Plans into the M-T schema.

Our major goal in this paper is to demonstrate the unified structure
of the relations of Taxonomy, Modification, and Queueing. This is the
M-T-Q Schema.

2.1 The Part-Whole relation PW. The bridge between the M-T schema and the relation of Q is the complex or composite relation of Part-Whole or PW. It is usually expressed or made manifest in English by sentences such as: 'B is a part of A', 'A consists of B, . . . , etc.', and in some languages, even 'B is an A-Part'. The question whether the last sentence is acceptable in a language or not appears to us to be a matter of restrictions of style, rather than grammaticality. We feel unabashed, therefore, about using this sentence as our departure toward integration of the complex PW relation with the M-T schema. [4]

First, the relation in the sentences 'B is an A-Part' is clearly taxonomic. That is, due to the transitivity of the taxonomic relation 'An A-Part is a Part', therefore 'B is a (kind of) Part'. Thus, our M-T representation needs to link by the relations of M and T the three constituents of (A), (B), and (Part). We know that (B) and (Part) are directly related taxonomically. From the original sentence it is apparent that (A), or better, its token [A] is a modifier of (Part). That is, (Part) modified by [A] creates (A-Part). Graphically, this may be represented, using the convention of Figure 3b and the type-token distinction, as given in Figure 7.

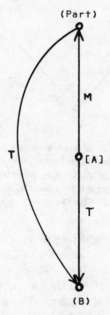

FIGURE 7.   The M-T representation of the complex relation PW or Part-Whole. This relation is manifest in the English sentence 'B is a part of A'. (Note that '"Any part of A" is a (kind of) part'.)

2.2 The representation of plans. We start with a very simple-minded plan. We represent it first by the so-called inverse of Bierman's model (Werner et al. 1974). That is, here we invert the labeling and now symbolize activities by arrows and the relation Q by nodes. This manner of presentation has the advantage that it shows each plan as a definite entity or a closed figure. The contrasting opacity is striking as soon as one shifts to a more standard representation (i.e. plans as node labels and the relation Q as the arrows connecting them; compare Figures 8 and 9).

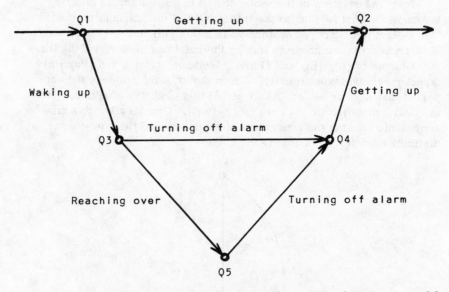

FIGURE 8. The representation of a plan by the inverse of Bierman's model. The arrows represent actions or plans and subplans. The nodes represent the relation Q of sequencing or queueing. Any possible path through the graph is a possible verbal description of the plan 'Getting Up'. The Q nodes are numbered for reference only.

There are three paths through the graph: (1) Q1 to Q2, (2) Q1 to Q3 to Q4 to Q2, and (3) Q1 to Q3 to Q5 to Q4 to Q2. All three are possible descriptions of the plan 'Getting Up'. There are other striking aspects of this graph. 'Getting Up' between Q1 and Q2 represents the most inclusive or the overall level of this plan. The arrow between Q4 and Q2 is also labeled 'Getting Up'. It is the least inclusive or most closely atomic plan representing the actual process of getting out of bed: the transition from wakefulness in bed to the upright (or possibly sitting) position at the commencement of all other daily activities. Similarly, we show between Q3 and Q4 the most inclusive level of 'Turning off

'Alarm'. On the more detailed level below it we have 'Turning off Alarm' again containing only the subplan (not shown) of depressing the alarm's button and retracting arm, before getting up.

The inverse Bierman representation shows the unity and entitativity of a plan very well. Each plan in this representation has a definite but unique entry point and a definite and unique exit. The multiple levels of 'Getting Up' and of 'Turning off Alarm' imply other relations that the diagram of Figure 8 obscures. We turn to a discussion of these to show how plans can be integrated with the M-T schema.

The plan of Figure 8 can be paraphrased in ordinary language. We can verbalize the equivalence of Q1-Q2 with Q1-Q3-Q4-Q2 by 'Getting up consists of waking up and then Turning off alarm and then (actually) Getting up'. Similarly, we can say, 'Turning off alarm consists of Reaching over and (actually) Turning off alarm'. The relationship between the name of the overall plan and its subplans is the relationship of constituency. That is, Q1-Q3 and Q3-Q4 and Q4-Q2 make up or are parts of the overall plan Q1-Q2. In other words, the relationship between the subplans and an overall plan is like parts to the whole or the relation PW. Thus, an alternative representation of the plan in Figure 8 is given in Figure 9 (double arrows represent the Part-Whole relations).

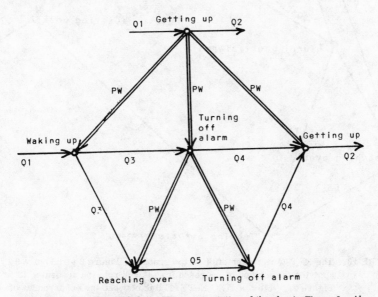

FIGURE 9. The Part-Whole or PW representation of the plan in Figure 8. Although this picture of a plan comes closer to the integration with the M-T schema, it in turn obscures the unity or entitativity of the plan. A permissible sequence for verbal description is now much less clear than it was before.

Figure 9 as it stands is only a stepping stone. By applying the M-T representation of the PW relation from Figure 7 to the graph of Figure 9, we obtain the graph of Figure 10.

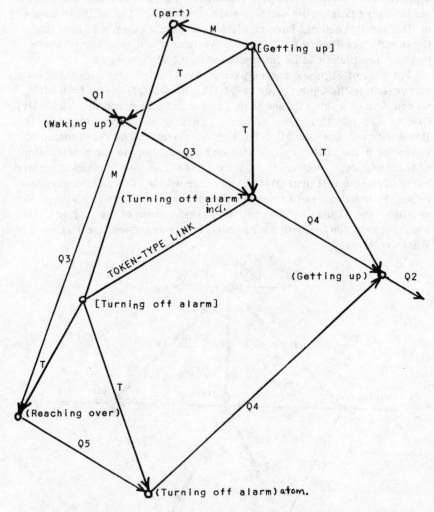

FIGURE 10. The M-T-Q representation of the graphs of Figure 8 and Figure 9 by applying the method of representing the PW relation according to Figure 7. Note the TOKEN-TYPE link between the occurrences of (Turning off alarm) (TYPE) and [Turning off alarm] (TOKEN) as the modifier of (part). We distinguish the more inclusive (turning off alarm) incl. from the more primitive (Turning off alarm) atom.

In this schema (Waking up), (Turning off alarm), and (Getting up) are part [Getting up]; on the lower level of (Reaching over) and (Turning off alarm) are part of [Turning off alarm]. Our intuitions indicate that the type-token relationship ought to be reversed: parts of wholes taken together describe the whole and should therefore be tokens of the types of which they are parts. In other words, all attributes that circumscribe a term should be in the term's token field. In order to understand the anomaly of this graph we look first at the relation between (Turning off alarm) inclusive and the lower, more primitive (Turning off alarm) atomic. The lower/higher distinction is here easily misleading. Upon examination we can demonstrate that (Turning off alarm) incl. has more attributes, i. e. a larger intension and a smaller extension than (Turning off alarm) atom. That is, (Turning off alarm) atom. is a superordinate taxon to (Turning off alarm) incl. (see Figure 11). The striking opposite orientation of the PW and this T relation is shown in Figure 12. This opposition is not a peculiarity of this particular plan. It occurs in all plans where a more inclusive activity bears the same label as a more atomic one: the higher taxon is part of its lower taxon. [5]

The taxonomic relation ((Turning off alarm) incl.) T ((Turning off alarm) atom.) is just like any other taxonomic relation. That is, the superordinate taxon has a smaller intension and a larger extension than the subordinate taxon. This condition is--as we have demonstrated (Corollary 5)--achieved by means of the relation of modification M. The question before us is which tokens are, in fact, modifying the type (Turning off alarm) atom. and thus create the lower, specific taxon (Turning off alarm) incl. The most likely candidate is the atomic plan (Reaching over) immediately preceding (Turning off alarm) atom. This is illustrated in Figure 13.

If the relationship between (Turning off alarm) atom. and (Turning off alarm) incl. is fully explored, it becomes clear that [Reaching over] and [Turning off alarm] atom. must both be parts of (Turning off alarm) incl. But the parts of any 'object' are part of the definition of an 'object'. Thus, both constituent parts of (Turning off alarm) incl. must be attributes modifying (Turning off alarm) atom. If we carry out the logic of this insight we have the still stranger phenomenon that in order to obtain the inclusive plan (Turning off alarm) incl., we must modify (Turning off alarm) atom. by the tokens [Reaching over] and by the token of itself, or [Turning off alarm] atom. The part-whole relation between the inclusive and the atomic plan is precisely the way it should be: between the whole of the type (Turning off alarm) incl. and the atomic constituent plans [Reaching over] and [Turning off alarm] atom. The PW relation is thus firmly established as part of the M-T-Q schema. With this insight the integration of plans into the M-T-Q system is almost complete.

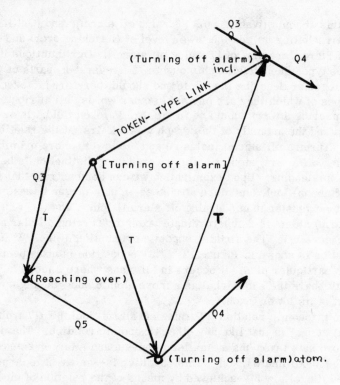

FIGURE 11. Note the striking direction of the taxonomic relation
between (Turning off alarm) atom. as the superordinate
term and (Turning off alarm) incl. The latter has
obviously the larger intension and the smaller extension
and must therefore be the subordinate taxon.

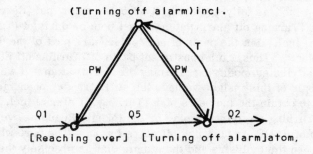

FIGURE 12. The striking opposition of the direction of the PW and
the T relation is even more obvious if we return to the
PW representation. This opposition is always the case
for some parts of all plans. It is never the case for the
PW relation outside of plans.

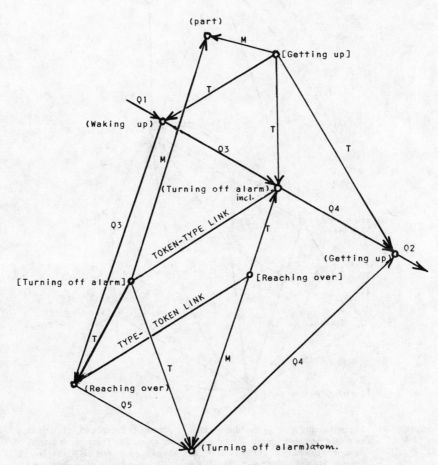

FIGURE 13. Following our definition of the taxonomic relation and its relationship to the relation of modification, every taxonomic node is related to every other node of the same taxonomy via the M-T schema. Thus, we set up the token [Reaching over] as a modifier of (Turning off alarm) atom.

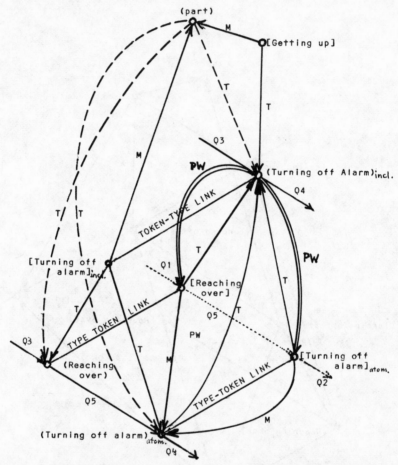

FIGURE 14. By consistently applying the idea of the M–T schema to Figures 10, 11, and 13, we obtain the above graph. (Turning off alarm) atom. and [Turning off alarm] atom. are linked by a TYPE-TOKEN LINK (there is no theoretical distinction between this and a TOKEN-TYPE LINK used in the graph). Quite surprisingly, the token [Turning off alarm] atom. in addition modifies its own type. This also implies that Figure 12 is not quite correct: the part-whole relation needs to be between the type of the inclusive plan and its token parts. The reversed taxonomic relation holds between the type of the superordinate atomic plan and the type of its subordinate inclusive plan. However, there is a taxonomic relation between the token of the atomic plan as a modifier of the type of the atomic plan to (Turning off alarm) incl., but that one has to be read slightly differently than the taxonomic relation shown in Figure 12 (see Figure 13).

We attached the PW arrows always from the types to the tokens as in Figure 14. However, this cannot be done without raising some questions. Our justification of the type-whole and token-parts associ- ation is that the parts of an 'object' represent part of the attribute field in its definition. In other words, they are part of the horizontal diagonal of the M-T triangles and must therefore be tokens linked by the relation M to the superordinate node.

There is, however, a second way of looking at the attachment of the part-whole relation. If we look at entire part-whole systems like ethno-anatomies it is not clear how we could be considering definitions. More adequately, we are looking at a system of types. In other words, PW attachments to both types and tokens are valid.

We are able to generalize this insight for all complex relations. Complex relations attach from a type to appropriate tokens if the com- plex relation is viewed from the point of view of a definition. If the complex relation forms a semantic system or field, it can be also viewed as a relation between types. In complex relations a type par- ticipating in this relation must be therefore attached to both ends of the type-token field (Figure 15).

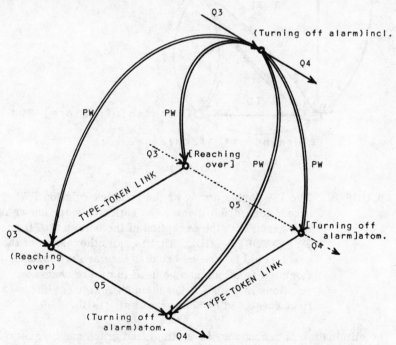

FIGURE 15. The Part-Whole relation has two possible interpretations: (1) From a type to token as the parts. This is the interpretation of the use of the PW relation in definitions. (2) Looking at an entire PW system of, for example, an ethno-anatomy, the relation is between types.

With these insights it can now be shown what the PW relation abbreviates or summarizes. The double arrow of the PW relation stands for the complex structure pictured by all connecting lines or arrows in Figure 16 with the exception of the TYPE-TOKEN LINK (T TL) between (Turning off alarm) atom. and its token, which is part of the plan (Turning off alarm) incl.

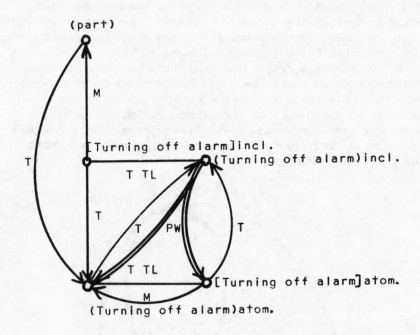

FIGURE 16.   The PW double arrow or the complex relation PW
             stands for or abbreviates the entire network shown in
             this graph with the exception of the bottom T TL or
             TYPE-TOKEN LINK.   That is, all other parts of the
             graph could be erased because they are redundant.
             Complex relations can be used to create chunked
             relations in the M-T-Q schema.   A similar idea was
             first suggested by Schwartz et al. (1970).

The elimination of redundancy by a simplified graph can be generalized to any complex relation of the form '(alpha) is a (kind of) (omega)-
(epsilon)' or '(alpha) is an (epsilon) of (omega)'.

In our example, epsilon is equated with 'part'. It can be equated analogously with 'cause', 'source' (provenience), 'result', possibly 'quantity', and many others.

In the generalized version, the M relation between (alpha) and [alpha] and the T relation (omega)T(alpha) are eliminated. These two relations apply only to special subparts of plans (Figure 17).

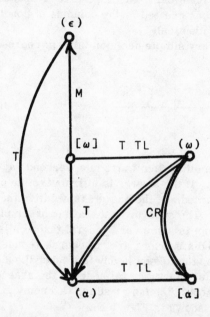

FIGURE 17. The generalized form of one type of complex lexical/ semantic relations. Any relation of the form 'alpha is an epsilon of omega' can be analyzed in this manner. The special feature for parts of plans is that (alpha)M [alpha] and (omega)T(alpha) also apply. Outside the realm of plans those two relations do not apply.

2.3 Decision tables. It has become our custom, especially since Topper (1972), to use decision tables as an eliciting procedure at choice points between plans. These decision tables represent a special variety of TOTE unit: one in which the operation performed is a mental decision activity rather than one in which thought is 'translated' into physical action. Topper solved the problem of representation by introducing into the inverse of Bierman's model (see Figure 8 for an example) choice points as square nodes which referred to carefully elicited decision tables. The decision table, unfortunately, had no theoretical status in the inverse to Bierman's schema.

The theoretical integration of decision tables into the M-T-Q schema is relatively simple. A particular word of a language becomes applicable in discourse if the criteria prescribed by its attributes are met. Analogously, a decision table makes explicit the criteria (conditions or attributes). A particular plan can be performed only if the appropriate set of conditions are met. We maintain that conditions and attributes are identical. That is, the M-T spaces and the semantic field spaces created by the columns of conditions in a decision table are identical.

The following very simple decision table is represented by Figure 18.

Today is weekend	Y	N
Getting up		x
Sleeping late	x	

The conditions are either that today is a weekend day or that today is not a weekend day. If the answer is affirmative the plan (sleeping late) can be performed. If the answer is negative the actor must perform (getting up). The superordinate taxons of the plans (sleeping late) and (getting up) is some very general taxon called (plan) or (action). (Intermediate taxons are, of course, conceivable.) The conditions, that is, the tokens [today is weekend] and [today is not weekend] modify this most general node (in the absence of more detailed knowledge about the plan or action taxonomy). The resulting M-T-Q schema is shown in Figure 18.

Figure 19 illustrates the application of the M-T-Q schema to a more complex decision table. The application is analogous to Figure 18. The decision table represented by Figure 19 is:

Alarm has rung	Y	Y	N	N
Today is weekend	Y	N	Y	N
Getting up (2)	x			
Getting up (1)		x		
Sleeping late			x	
Oversleeping				x

In this decision table Getting up (1) is essentially the plan in our Figure 8. Getting up (2) is a new, unspecified plan for weekends. Oversleeping is not exactly a plan, it is a default. As a result of oversleeping, upon discovery of this fact, some special compensatory plans (e.g. skipping the morning shower and/or breakfast) may be

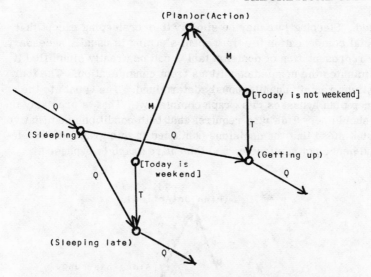

FIGURE 18. The translation of a decision table into the M-T-Q schema. The decision for performing one of two plans depends on the fulfillment of the conditions 'Today is weekend' or its negation. The choice creates a branching at the immediately preceding node labeled (sleeping). The conditions are treated like attributes. The conditions spelled out by attributes have to be met before an action can proceed on one or the other branch.

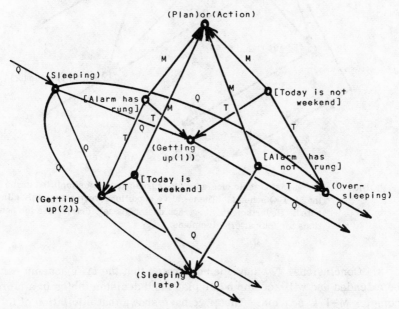

FIGURE 19. The representation of a decision table with 2^2 or four choices in the M-T-Q schema. Larger decision tables can be represented analogously.

activated.   Sleeping late may be similar to oversleeping except that no special compensation for time spent sleeping is usually necessary.

The representation of decision tables can be greatly simplified if one eliminates the negated conditions from consideration.   The four alternatives remain unambiguously determined.   The Q path to the oversleep plan bypasses this graph completely.   That is precisely the way it should be.   This plan requires that both conditions be negative. That must mean that the decisions contained in this graph are irrelevant and hence not applicable, and the entire graph is bypassed.

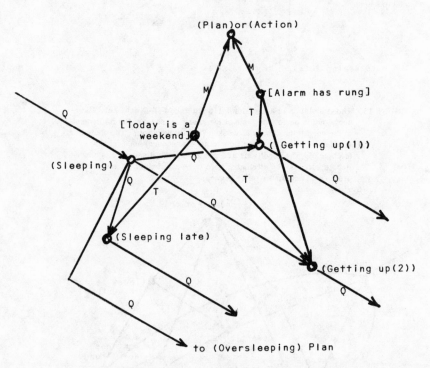

FIGURE 20.   The decision table of Figure 19 represented as a simplified graph in the M-T-Q schema.   The negative conditions were completely eliminated.   Nevertheless, the graph unambiguously determines the conditions for four alternative plans.

3.   Conclusions.   We have demonstrated that the M-T schema can be extended and will accommodate plans and decision tables in a more complex M-T-Q schema.   Thus, we have shown that elicitation of folk-taxonomies, folk-definitions, plans, and decision tables can all be represented within the same theoretical framework.

We claim that ethnographies, just as dictionaries and encyclopaedias, are constructed out of the elicitation of folk-taxonomies, folk-definitions, plans, and decision tables. The only missing ingredient is the dynamic aspects of cultural knowledge. This is folk-logic, the ability to deduce new insights from old knowledge. Werner (1973a), Hamil (1973), and others (most notably Cole and Scribner 1974) have dealt with the problem of cultural logic. These considerations would, however, take us beyond the goals of this paper.

We were less explicit about complex lexical/semantic relations. However, there was at least a hint how some complex relations may fit into the M-T-Q schema. A number of other lexical/semantic relations that have been suggested in the extensive literature on the subject are taken up in Evens et al. (1976).

The integration of plans and decisions into our theoretical schema is particularly relevant to ethnoscience ethnographies, ethnoscience encyclopaedias, and ethnoscience theory. First, it has never been done before. Second, and perhaps more importantly, we hope to make a case in a future publication for the fact that all texts or even dialogues are plans. This can be demonstrated informally. A plan is a series of instructions, i.e. first do this, then that, etc. A text is, analogously, first say this, then say that, etc.

Thus, potentially at least, we have developed the conceptual apparatus (our M-T-Q schema) that integrates folk-taxonomies and folk-definitions with plans and decisions, and by analogy (homology?) to plans and decisions with texts and discourse as well. The full exploration of these ideas remains, for the time being, primarily suggestive and will require considerably more effort in the months and years ahead.

NOTES

This research was supported in part by an NIMH Senior Post Doctoral Fellowship to Oswald Werner. Earlier versions of this paper were presented at the annual meetings of the American Anthropological Association, San Francisco, December, 1975, and at a colloquium of the Committee on Communication and Cognition at the University of Chicago, March, 1976. We are particularly indebted to Martha Evens (of IIT), Madelyn Iris, Bonnie Litovitz, Judy Markovitz, and Raoul Smith (all of Northwestern) for their comments and encouragement.

1. Usually, an event has a name such as the Navajo 'Stomp Dance', a culturally appropriate environment in which it occurs (in this case, a high school or community center gymnasium), and a plan or set of plans which can generate cultural behavior in the environment of the event.

Events and their appropriate plans are related to other aspects of
cultural knowledge in ways which are often very complex. For example, the Navajo taxonomy of types of drinkers has four levels in its
hierarchy (see Topper 1971). On the second level (from the top) five
kinds of drinkers are recognized. All of the categories on the second
level are differentiated from the cover term on the first level through
texts which are added as modifiers. Events and their appropriate
plans form a part of this textual material. For example, the category
ashiike da'ad'laanii 'young men who drink' has as part of its attribu-
tive text a set of plans for appropriate drinking behavior at the event
called a 'stomp dance'. But the category hastoii da'ad'laanii 'older
men who drink' does not. The inclusion of this stomp dance and its
appropriate plans helps distinguish the two categories of drinkers
from one another. It also helps distinguish the ashiike da'ad'laanii
'young men who drink' from the higher level category da'ad'laanii
'drinkers' in general.

This discussion is intended to provide an idea of how plans and
events may be used to form taxonomic hierarchies through the relation of modification. The importance of this becomes clear in Section 1.

2. The intension or the M-T representation of a term can be refined
in a number of ways. The set marked 'a' in the M-T triangles is the
most readily available set of attributes in a given context. The size
of this set is probably of the order of 5 ± 2 attributes (extending somewhat liberally Mandler's (1970) estimate for folk taxonomies). Then

FIGURE 21.

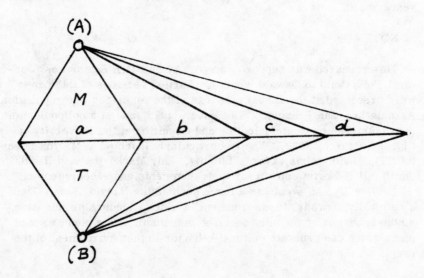

set 'b' can be viewed as the set of all explicitly available attributes, set 'c' as all recognizable but not explicitly available attributes, while set 'd' are all attributes that are not verbalizable or those that are usually not verbalized. Thus, the line between 'c' and 'd' is the boundary between explicit and tacit knowledge.

FIGURE 22.

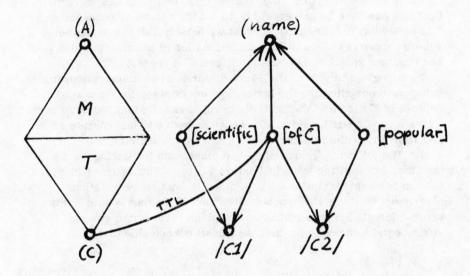

The M-T schema may also be used to explain context (for greater detail see Werner and Levis-Matichek 1975). Context may be viewed as an independent but parallel classification of lexical items. This classification may first determine the location of the partition between sets 'a' and 'b' in Figure 21. That is, context is dynamically controlled by the classification of the sociolinguistic significance of words. Figure 22 captures some of this aspect. It can be interpreted as the M-T version of Chomsky's (1965) 'lexical entry' of the form (C, P) where C is the 'conceptual' part of a term and P the physical or phonological shape of it. The 'conceptual' part (C) is linked by a Type-Token relation to the classification of phonological shapes /C1/ and /C2/, the scientific and the popular form of the same concept.

3. The relations M and T are formally very similar to each other. It is perhaps for this reason that most languages of the world appear to use the same grammatical structure for making both manifest. Both relations may be viewed as types of modification. M is reflexive (a term may modify itself and the result is in M), asymmetrical (if (A)M(B) is in M, then (B)M(A) is not) and not transitive (A)M(B) and

(B)M(C), does not imply (A)M(C)). T is reflexive ((A)T(A) is in T), asymmetrical (if (A)T(B) is in T then (B)T(A) is not in T), and transitive (if (A)T(B) and (B)T(C), then (A)T(C)). The distinction between the two relations is thus only the transitivity of T.

4. We consider the PW relation not to be a universal one. It appears in languages of the world in different guises which do not always translate as 'part-whole' into English. That is, we assume that only simple relations, i.e. the M-T-Q relations, are universal. Complex ones can be universal but do not have to be so necessarily. The particular manifestation of what we loosely call the part-whole relation appears to be a different combination of atomic relations and language specific elements in different languages.

We are grateful to Dr. Rik Pinxten (personal communication) for bringing to our attention the logical system of Stanisľav Lesnievski, especially his logic of the part-whole relation called mereology (from Greek meros 'part'). However, we were unable to incorporate at this time any of the insights of this great Polish logician.

5. The following figures show two plans, one for baking a cake, the other for splitting wood in Eastern Europe (from Werner 1966), each in two representations. Both plans in both representations clearly demonstrate the opposing direction of the part-whole and the taxonomic relation in certain parts of plans. The same state of affairs can be shown to be the case for all conceivable plans.

FIGURE 23.

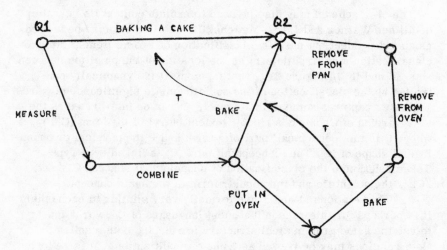

FIGURE 24.

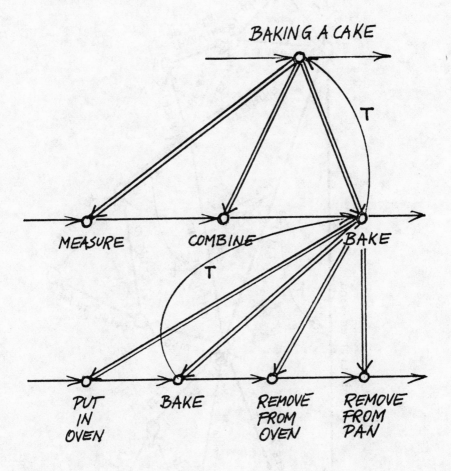

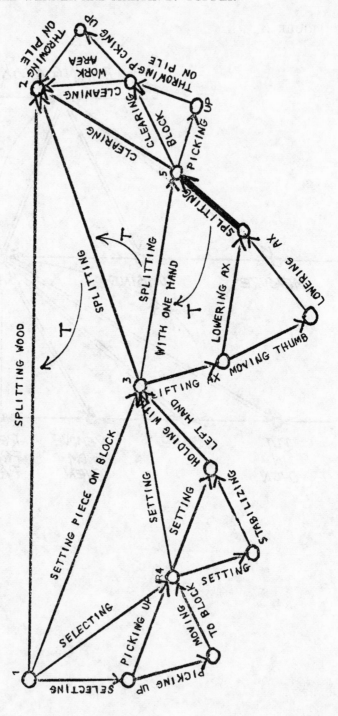

FIGURE 25.

FIGURE 26·

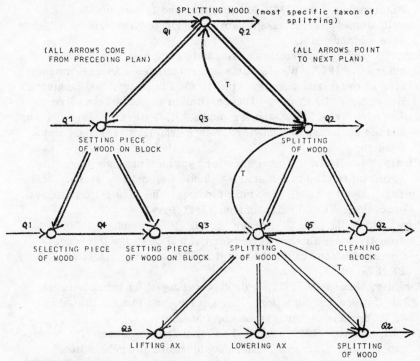

SPLITTING WOOD (most specific taxon of
splitting)

(ALL ARROWS COME
FROM PRECEDING PLAN)

(ALL ARROWS POINT
TO NEXT PLAN)

SETTING PIECE
OF WOOD ON BLOCK

SPLITTING
OF WOOD

SELECTING PIECE
OF WOOD

SETTING PIECE
OF WOOD ON BLOCK

SPLITTING
OF WOOD

CLEANING
BLOCK

LIFTING AX

LOWERING AX

SPLITTING
OF WOOD

REFERENCES

Agar, M. 1974. Ripping and running: A formal ethnography of urban heroin addicts. New York, The Seminar Press.

Anderson, John R. and Gordon H. Bower. 1973. Human associative memory. New York, John Wiley and Sons.

Casagrande, Joseph B. and Kenneth Hale. 1967. Semantic relationships in Papago folk definitions. In: Studies in southwestern ethnolinguistics. Edited by D. Hymes and W. E. Bittle. The Hague, Mouton. 165–193.

Chomsky, Noam. 1965. Aspects of the theory of syntax. Cambridge, Mass., The MIT Press.

Cole, M. and Sylvia Scribner. 1974. Culture and thought. New York, Wiley and Sons.

Evens, Martha. 1975. Semantic representations for Question-Answering Systems. Northwestern University dissertation in Computer Science.

Evens, Martha, Bonnie Litovitz, Judith Markovitz, Raoul Smith, and Oswald Werner. 1976. The M-T-Q schema as universal construction set for complex lexical/semantic relations (working title). In preparation.

Frake, C. O. 1964. Notes on queries in ethnography. American Anthropologist 66:2.132-145 (Romney and D'Andrade).

Hamill, James. 1973. Logic across language boundaries: A Mende case. Manuscript.

Kay, P. 1971. Taxonomy and semantic contrast. Lg. 47.866-887.

Mandler, G. 1970. Words, lists and categories: An experimental view of organized memory. In: Studies in thought and language. Edited by J. L. Cowan. Tucson, University of Arizona Press.

Miller, George A., E. Galanter, and K. H. Pribram. 1960. Plans and the structure of behavior. New York, Holt, Rinehart and Winston.

Minsky, M. 1974. A framework for representing knowledge. Artificial Intelligence Memo No. 306. Cambridge, Mass., MIT.

Quillian, M. R. 1968. Semantic memory. In: Semantic information processing. Cambridge, Mass., MIT Press.

Schwartz, R. M., J. F. Burger, and R. F. Simmons. 1970. A deductive question-answering for natural language inference. Communications of the Association of Computing Machinery 13.167-183.

Spradley, James P. 1971. Adaptive strategies of urban nomads. In: Culture and cognition: Rules, maps and plans. Edited by J. P. Spradley. San Francisco, Chandler.

Topper, Martin. 1971. Alcohol and male adolescence: The Navajo experience. Currently under consideration for publication.

_____. 1972. The ethnography of Navajo daily activities. Northwestern University dissertation in Anthropology.

_____, J. D. Nations, R. Detwiler, and J. A. Stovall. 1974. The ethnography of the day: Some new developments. Manuscript, Southern Methodist University.

Watson-Franke, Maria-Barbara and Lawrence C. Watson. 1975. Understanding in anthropology: A philosophical reminder. Current Anthropology 16.247-262.

Werner, Oswald. 1966. Pragmatics and ethnoscience. Anthropological Linguistics 8:8.42-65.

_____. 1969. On the universality of lexical/semantic relations. Read at the meeting of the American Anthropological Association, New Orleans, November.

_____. 1972. Ethnoscience 1972. Annual Review of Anthropology, 271-308.

_____. 1973a. On the place of the deductive component in memory. Paper read at the Central States Anthropological Society meeting in St. Louis, March.

_____. 1973b. The synthetic informant model. In: Proceedings of the 9th International Congress of Anthropological and Ethnological Sciences. In press.

Werner, Oswald, with W. Hagedorn, G. Roth, E. Schepers, and L.
    Uriarte. 1974. Some new developments in ethnosemantics and
    the theory and practice of lexical/semantic fields. In: Current
    trends in linguistics. Edited by T. A. Sebeok, 12. 1477-1544.
    The Hague, Mouton.
Werner, Oswald, Gladys Levis-Matichek, with Martha Evens and
    Bonnie Litowitz. 1975. An ethnoscience view of schizophrenic
    speech. In: Sociocultural dimensions of language use. Edited by
    Blount and Sanchez. New York, Academic Press.
Werner, Oswald and Gladys Levis-Matichek. 1975. Context and
    memory: Toward a theory of context in ethnoscience.
Williams, G. E. 1976. Linguistic reflection of cultural systems.
    Anthropological Linguistics 8:8. 13-21.

THE REPRESENTATION AND SELECTION
OF COMMONSENSE KNOWLEDGE
FOR NATURAL LANGUAGE COMPREHENSION

CHUCK RIEGER

University of Maryland

Abstract. Plan synthesis and language comprehension, or more
generally, the act of discovering how one perception relates to others,
are two sides of the same coin, because they both rely on a knowledge
of cause and effect--algorithmic knowledge about how to do things and
about how things work. We describe a computer model, based on a
structure called a bypassable causal selection network, which can
organize thousands of small commonsense algorithm patterns into a
larger fabric which is usable by a plan synthesizer and a language
comprehender. And because these bypassable networks can adapt to
context, so will the plan synthesizer and language comprehender. We
describe the theory of the organization, and, insofar as it is of interest, the computer model which implements the theory. We also attempt
to point out some places where learning could be incorporated and,
more generally, to convey some biases in language comprehension
and problem solving. Illustrations are drawn from the children's
story The Magic Grinder. The computer comprehension of this story,
in commonsense algorithm terms, is our current research interest.

0. Introduction. All problems of human intelligence modeling--
including natural language analysis--eventually devolve onto problems
of how to represent and access general world knowledge. It has been
the tradition of most research in natural language to attempt to excise
as much of the world as possible in order to focus on such seemingly
better defined subproblems of the language phenomenon as 'syntax',
'semantics', and 'pragmatics'. Implicit in this approach is the

145

attitude--perhaps 'hope' is a better word--that some components of language are indeed meaningful to study in isolation. I will not attempt here to argue the validity of this point of view one way or the other. Instead, it is the purpose of this paper to propose how we ought to approach the problems of representing and accessing general world knowledge, under the assumption that such knowledge will be useful to all aspects of language analysis.

Specifically, this paper focuses on two issues which seem to be extremely fundamental to any model of human cognitive abilities: (1) a representation formalism which addresses 'static' problems of how to express knowledge about the world in the form of memory patterns, and (2) selection processes, as the primary 'dynamic' component of intelligence. Rather than addressing purely language-related questions, the discussion is aimed at a broader spectrum of human abstract symbol processing which embraces such other so-called intelligent human behavior as 'problem solving', 'story comprehension', and 'learning'.

Although the discussion of representation ought logically to precede the selectional issues, it seems appropriate first to motivate the representation by identifying more precisely what is intended by the term 'selection'. I want to propose that there are exactly two very abstract, qualitatively distinct classes of selection with which any symbol-processing intelligence must ultimately contend:

(1) Strategy selection: an ability to select from among a finite collection of alternative courses of action for achieving some desired goal, based on the context, the goal itself, and a knowledge of what would constitute an 'appropriate' solution, or response.

(2) Thing selection: an ability to select a particular individual for inclusion in some strategy. Things are non-algorithmic concepts like physical objects, other people, word senses, thoughts, etc.

Strategy selection--choosing some algorithmic process to achieve a goal--obviously must be couched upon a very powerful representation of knowledge about cause and effect in the world. If one acknowledges --as I do in the next section--that any individual possesses a very large number of relatively small patterns expressing a teleological knowledge of the world across the broad spectrum of human experience, from tying shoe laces to formulating international political strategies, then the act of selection from such a vast resource of patterns during any act of problem solving or interpretation of event sequences must inevitably play a central role. Hence, in Section 1 a formalism for expressing patterns of cause and effect, and a framework for intelligent selection among them, is proposed.

While algorithm selection relates to notions of best strategy for accomplishing a task, thing selection is the embodiment of an intelligent decision-making component that allows the symbol processor to commit itself to particular objects or concepts during the course of plan synthesis or interpretation. Examples of this kind of selection are somewhat more diverse than algorithmic selection, particularly in the context of a natural language understanding system. Word sense selection during parsing is a very important category of thing selection, where the 'things' range over the possible senses of each word in the sentence being parsed in a given context. Parsing is thus viewable as a multiple act of thing selection. Referent identification--the mapping of an object's external description onto a unique internal concept which represents the object in a model--is another thing selection process that manifests itself during the comprehension of text. In the realm of problem solving, during both plan synthesis and plan execution, the system, having committed itself to a particular strategy, eventually has to commit itself to particular objects in order to carry out the various components of the strategy, e.g. particular hammers, people, insults, and so forth.

If we choose to view intelligence from a perspective that elevates selection to the top of the theory, then it becomes central to any intelligent system that selection be performed in an orderly manner and in as informed a way as possible at every stage. Experience from the Artificial Intelligence point of view has been that failure to acknowledge the importance of intelligent selection at every decision point in any computation can lead to run-time-wise cataclysmic and often theoretically vacuous results. The junk heap of computational models of language is piled high with syntactic parsers which apply no intelligence in selecting parse strategies.

I want to discuss later a computational model of intelligent strategy and thing selection. However, let us first turn to the representational formalism which underlies both forms of selection.

1. CSA representation. The representation formalism is called the Commonsense Algorithm (CSA) representation. The philosophy evident in its structure reflects a specific point of view within AI, namely, that:

(1) a knowledge of cause and effect at all levels of a model is the basis of processes that exhibit intelligent behavior;

(2) such knowledge can be expressed in explicit, decomposable, and rearrangeable patterns which can be treated either as data or as process;

(3) there is a syntax to this knowledge that makes it possible
to perform orderly and evolutionary transformations on it
which amount to forms of 'learning'.

The domain of the CSA representation--the entities which the
representation ties together into cause and effect patterns--consists
of instances of five generic types of event: (1) actions, (2) tendencies,
(3) states, (4) statechanges, and (5) wants.

Actions: forces which originate from volitional internal
commands within 'intelligent' organisms, normally intended
to contribute toward the accomplishment of some state or
statechange (internally or externally)

Tendencies: forces whose origin is not ultimately internal
to a volitional, intelligent organism, and which therefore are
not the product of a 'decision to act'. Tendencies provide a
way of incorporating in the formalism a knowledge of natural
laws (in commonsense terms) which are 'force generators',
and hence action-like, but which are not goal-directed

States: conditions in the world, or internal to the model,
which are not action related, those aspects which remain if
we imagine a totally actorless and tendencyless environment

Statechanges: changes in conditions in the world, or internal to the model, along dimensions which are continuous

Wants: internal states of potential actors which motivate
them to perform actions intended to contribute to the attainment of some other desired state

It is conjectured that these five generic event types are both necessary and sufficient ingredients for capturing all world knowledge of
cause and effect. In the fairly diverse range of cause and effect
knowledge the CSA group has been considering during the past year,
there is no counter evidence to this conjecture. In a sense, however, this is not surprising, since the five categories are quite
abstract.

The other, more distinctive, component of the CSA representation
is its set of approximately 30 links which are designed to express
commonsense cause and effect relationships among instances of
these five generic event categories. By constructing graph-like
patterns of events and links, CSA gives us the ability to represent in
a computer model a fairly detailed knowledge about causality. Some
examples are shown later in this paper.

Eventually, we would hope to be able to assert that there are
exactly N CSA connective links that are necessary and sufficient for
expressing all knowledge about cause and effect, regardless of the

domain of the knowledge. We would furthermore hope to be able to assert that the links correspond closely to culture-independent cognitive primitives. (This is in contrast with theories such as Conceptual Dependency which assert the existence of a small set of primitive actions, or events (Schank 1972). CSA does not seek a set of primitive actions or events, but rather a primitive syntax for knowledge, defined by the links and rules for connecting them.)

It is a key point of CSA theory that the set of connective links be (a) small in number, (b) descriptively adequate for all human knowledge about cause and effect, and (c) universal, perhaps to the extent that they model some level of the genetic endowment of all normal humans. So far, it is clear only that the links in present use satisfy criterion (a)! However, they have survived applications in rather diverse domains (representing a children's story, expressing the operation of physical devices and mechanisms--a reverse trap flush toilet, an incandescent lightbulb, components of a computer, a computer program, to name a few--and expressing some simple principles of social and psychological interaction among people). Because of this, we feel that these links constitute some sort of core for any representation.

The CSA representation is described in this paper only through some examples, with the main goal being to set the stage for the subsequent discussion of selection. Rieger (1975 and 1976a) describe the CSA representation in more detail.

The examples about to be shown are intended to be suggestive of the power of a CSA-like approach and the range of CSA applicability. Bear in mind that, where only one pattern is shown, there are perhaps thousands of companion or alternative patterns in the computer's memory--each dealing with some part of the world, specific or abstract. The idea is to organize the patterns in a manner which causes the higher level memory processes of plan synthesis and language comprehension to see only the most relevant ones at the appropriate times.

Example 1. A very small pattern about locomotion.

Typical of the smallest and most fundamental patterns in CSA are ones such as Pattern 1. This CSA pattern illustrates two of the CSA links and has instances of three of the five generic event types. It is read (by a human!) as follows:

Person X's performance of the 'primitive' action (WALK X) will continually cause a statechange in X's location, SC: (LOCATION X (LOC X) Y), from where he is (LOC X), toward somewhere else, Y, provided that (1) X remains pointed in the right direction, (FACING X Y), and (2) a clear

Pattern 1.

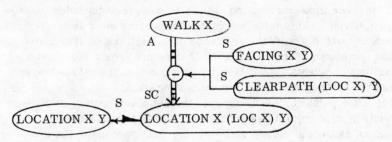

path between X and Y exists for the duration of the activity,
namely, (CLEARPATH (LOC X) Y); eventually, such a statechange in location will reach a distinguished level, in this
case when X finally reaches Y, i.e. (LOCATION X Y).

In this pattern, (WALK X) is an action, SC:(LOCATION X (LOC X)
Y) is a statechange, and (FACING X Y) and (CLEARPATH (LOC X) Y)
and (LOCATION X Y) are states.

The symbol

> GATED CONTINUOUS
> CAUSALITY LINK

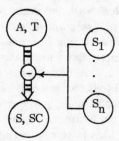

is called the GATED CONTINUOUS CAUSALITY link. This link
specifies that action A or tendency T's continued existence continuously causes state S or statechange SC, provided that other conditions (states) $S_1, \ldots, S_n$ are present throughout A's duration. The
$S_1, \ldots, S_n$ are called GATES, in that they are like valves which control the flow of causality from action to state or statechange. (This
metaphor was inspired by Abelson, as in Abelson 1973.)

The symbol

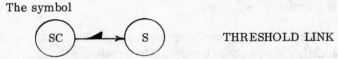

THRESHOLD LINK

is called the THRESHOLD link. This link asserts that statechange
SC eventually reaches some distinguished level S; 'distinguished'
means that the existence of this particular level affects some other

event of interest in the algorithm. In this case, (LOCATION X Y) is of interest because it is the expressed purpose of the algorithm captured by this graph, i.e. to cause X to be located at Y.

In this case, (WALK X) happens to be 'primitive' in the sense that it describes an activity which presumably could be implemented directly, in a context-independent way, by robot engineers. However, the CSA pattern syntax actually allows us to include a reference to another entire CSA algorithm wherever an action is needed. This allows us to use more expressive predicates, while retaining the power to elaborate or define those predicates in terms of other algorithmic patterns.

For example, we may choose to write:

Pattern 2.

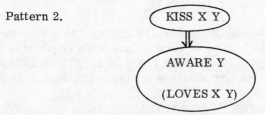

to capture the notion 'kissing is one way to signal affection'. We may then choose either to regard KISS as a primitive, in the sense that our robot engineer could program his robot directly with a KISS reflex, or to define KISS as simply another algorithmic activity which itself is reducible to other CSA patterns. In this case, we would probably define (KISS X Y) to be a compressed way of saying that actor X employed the following strategy:

Pattern 3.

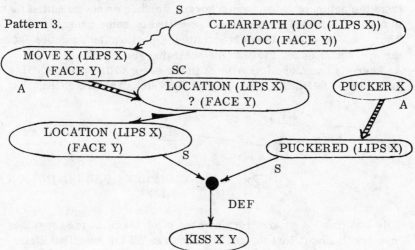

This graph, indexed somewhere else in memory, tells the system that KISS actually refers to a complex goal state consisting of two goals which must be achieved concurrently: X's lips are puckered, and X's lips are in physical contact with Y's cheek. So in case our robot engineer has forgotten to supply us with a KISS primitive reflex, our robot stands a chance of still having a love life!

These KISS patterns reveal two other causal links:

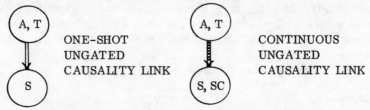

ONE-SHOT
UNGATED
CAUSALITY LINK

CONTINUOUS
UNGATED
CAUSALITY LINK

called the ONE-SHOT UNGATED CAUSALITY link (action A's execution is required only once to achieve state S, and is not required to maintain S), and the CONTINUOUS UNGATED CAUSALITY link which indicates that action A must continually be performed to sustain state S or statechange SC.

Additionally, the CONTINUOUS ENABLEMENT link

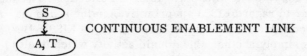

CONTINUOUS ENABLEMENT LINK

has specified that, throughout the duration of action A, state S must remain present to allow A itself to proceed. This notion is distinct from the notion of gates, which govern whether or not an action that is ongoing will achieve the result specified by some causal link. Thus, CSA decouples the prerequisites of performing an action from the prerequisites for the action's achieving some goal.

There is one more link evident in the second KISS pattern. It is called the COMPLEX GOAL DEFINITION link, and is written:

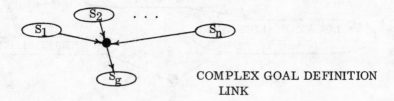

COMPLEX GOAL DEFINITION
LINK

This link couples an arbitrary number of states $S_1, \ldots, S_n$ together in order to assert that the goal S_g requires all the specified states to be in effect simultaneously.

Before proceeding, it seems that a case ought to be made for the utility of such patterns in any system that purports to be a model of human intelligence (as manifest, say, in language comprehension or problem solving). Returning to Pattern 1, we would argue that such a WALK pattern would be quite useful both to a robot that has just been told or has decided for itself to go somewhere: namely, that one alternative is, first, to accomplish a couple of subgoals: (FACING X Y) and (CLEARPATH X Y), then to execute the action (WALK X). This pattern therefore captures one of the possibly numerous strategies for moving from one place to another. In this respect, this and the thousands of other patterns of about this level of complexity comprise the basis of a plan synthesizer's knowledge of worldly cause and effect, e.g. how to go places, how to insult people, how to turn appliances on and use them, how to learn about things.

However, such knowledge as Pattern 1 also bears significance for a robot who is trying to interpret the world and events he perceives around him. If, for example, our robot reads (perceives) 'John turned toward Mary . . .', Pattern 1 would suggest that, since turning toward someone might be intended to achieve a FACING condition, and since a facing condition is part of a WALK pattern, that John just might be getting ready to walk toward Mary, and that John wants to be located at Mary for some reason. Of course, (FACING X Y) may also be a component of a possibly large number of other CSA patterns having nothing to do with going places. Together with this pattern about walking, the collection of CSA patterns in which the condition (FACING X Y) occurs comprises a set of possible interpretations of FACING events.

CSA theory specifies how such a set of alternate interpretations may be searched to yield a context sensitive interpretation of a thought, i.e. to choose one pattern which references a FACING condition above all the rest as an interpretation. (See Rieger 1976a for a discussion of this.) It will simply be pointed out here that knowing the set of CSA patterns in which any given event could participate establishes a framework in which searching for interpretations of perceived events can be carried out.

(The existing computer model can consult its inventory of CSA patterns in order to interpret sentences of English in context. John was mad at Bill. He picked up a rock is a problem which typifies the level of the current program's capabilities. Given these two sentences, the program will consult patterns about hitting and determine (a) that the referent of he in the second sentence is John, and (b) that John was about to propel the rock toward Bill. This is possible because the action of grasping something in the context (a collection of predictions) set up by the first sentence strongly fits into a hitting CSA pattern. Rieger (1976a) describes this mechanism in more detail and a forthcoming report explains the theory at the level of the program which implements it.)

The point to be emphasized, therefore, is that a large collection of CSA patterns such as these we have been illustrating will be one very important source of knowledge that underlies both an ability to plan, o or solve problems, and an ability to interpret, or draw inferences from the continuous bombardment of perceptions.

We are flirting with the tip of an iceberg in discussing CSA representation and search, and I do not propose to dwell on the representation in this paper. However, before proceeding to the selection issues, it will be illustrative to examine two other slightly larger CSA patterns, the intent of the discussion being not to convince, but to support the point of view that CSA-like structures for representing knowledge provide a fairly robust computer representation of human knowledge of cause and effect useful for both language comprehension and problem solving.

The first of the remaining two examples is from the 'people domain', in that it expresses knowledge about how people interact: it is a pattern which describes how to make a contract with another person. The second of the remaining examples is drawn from the physical world. It captures the 'causal topology' of a familiar mechanism, the incandescent lightbulb. (Our current research is leading us along the lines suggested by these two graphs: on the one hand, we are engaged in the representation of the large-scale concepts in a Walt Disney (1975) children's story called The Magic Grinder for the purposes of building a CSA computer model of story comprehension. On the other hand, we are investigating a broad spectrum of man-made mechanisms in an attempt to define and delimit human knowledge about cause and effect in mechanical, electrical, and computational devices. Although it would seem that such different domains as these two would demand different formulations of cause and effect, we are discovering that such is not the case. Indeed, it is the discovery of common patterns and principles which are domain-independent that constitutes the most exciting aspect of the CSA theory.)

Example 2. A pattern expressing the concept of a two-person contract, as motivated by the children's story, The Magic Grinder.

Pattern 4 expresses one general strategy for accomplishing a goal, namely, get someone else to do it by attempting to implant a pattern in his mind which will cause him to behave in the desired way. This single pattern would underlie specific instances of contracts ranging from 'If you shoot yourself, I'll give you a nice funeral' to 'Hughes Aircraft contracted with the government to build 100 jets'.

Pattern 4.

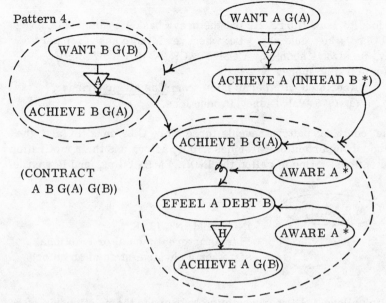

(CONTRACT
A B G(A) G(B))

The pattern reads as follows:

Person A, wishing to accomplish goal G(A), implants a pattern P in B's mind because A believes that if P were in B's mind, B would then do things which would tend to achieve G(A). This pattern to be implanted is: if B achieves G(A), and A is aware of it, such will induce in A a feeling of indebtedness toward B, motivating A to do actions which would tend to accomplish G(B), something A believes B to desire.

Again, a case can be made for the utility of a memory pattern such as this: an intelligence with access to this contract pattern, or one like it, would then be able (1) to make contracts to get its work done, (2) to understand the word contract in some deeper sense, and (3) to understand instances of a contract, or its components during comprehension of, say, a children's story. In fact, the first several pages of The Magic Grinder revolve around this notion of a contract. Any model which 'understands' The Magic Grinder must appeal to this type of knowledge (among others) in order to comprehend why the various characters do what they do at the beginning of the story:

Once there was a poor maid named Minnie. She worked for the greedy Lord Gurr. While he sat in the shade all day, Minnie and her nephews worked in his garden. Minnie picked fruit and vegetables. Morty and Ferdie pulled and cut weeds. At the end of each day, they brought their basket

of food to Lord Gurr. He put the heavy basket on the scale.
'Not bad', he would say. But whenever Minnie asked for her
pay, he always shouted, 'COME BACK TOMORROW!' So
Minnie had no money.

Reprinted with permission from <u>The Magic Grinder</u>.
ⓒ 1975 Walt Disney Productions.

The 'contract' pattern reveals three more CSA links (in fact, the
three most important ones for describing actors and their motivations
and intentions). One is called the INDUCEMENT link, and is written
as:

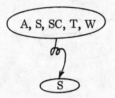

INDUCEMENT LINK
(S is an internal mental or emotional
state, or a physical state of an actor)

This link allows CSA representation to express the relationship of an
external event to internal mental or emotional states which that event
might 'induce' within a perceiver of the event. Thus, for example, to
capture the principle 'If P loves Q and P sees R kiss Q, P might
experience an induced state of feeling jealousy toward R', we write:

Pattern 5.

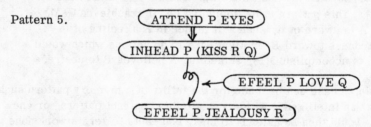

The second new CSA link employed in the contract pattern is written:

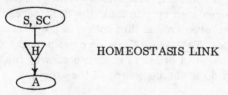

HOMEOSTASIS LINK

and is called the HOMEOSTASIS link. This link ties internal and mental states of a potential actor to predictions about actions he might
perform to compensate for such states. The homeostasis link models
an inherently nonalgorithmic process (i. e. why does some internal
state of a potential actor motivate that actor to perform an action?).

After all, at some point, we must 'cut' the CSA model of cause and effect and say simply, 'because it's the way a human is defined'. However, although the homeostasis link's basis is inherently non-algorithmic, its role in a CSA pattern can be highly algorithmic: if P needs to arouse in Q a feeling of jealousy, some pattern containing a homeostasis link might tell P that one potentially fruitful tactic is to achieve some external event in the world, making sure that Q is aware of it! The point, of course, is that even though the basis of cause and effect in the psychological domain is hard to identify, it can still be described and put to use in algorithmic ways.

The remaining link used in the contract pattern is the so-called ALGORITHMIC MOTIVATION link, written:

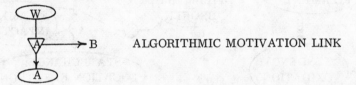
ALGORITHMIC MOTIVATION LINK

and read 'want W motivates the wanter, A, to achieve state S, because A believes another pattern B that tells A that S will directly or indirectly contribute toward the attainment of W'. This link relates actions to intentions via belief patterns, and is hence fundamental to most social and psychological strategies. It provides a linkage between observed or predicted behavior and the underlying belief structures which might account for such behavior. It is a way of explaining behavior in algorithmic terms, in contrast to the homeostasis link which accounts for nonalgorithmic behavior. In the contract pattern, for example, an instance of this link describes how planting a pattern in another's mind might lead to achieving a desired goal of the planter. A future paper will be devoted to a more thorough consideration of this and the homeostasis and inducement links as bases of an 'algorithmic psychological' model.

Example 3. A simple physical mechanism: the incandescent lightbulb.

This pattern would be stored under 'how to cause light to exist' in the larger organization of the memory. It illustrates how CSA represents a 'causal topology' of physical devices, in contrast to their physical layout. We have so far employed the CSA representation to describe articles from the pencil (rather simple physically, rather complex in its causal structure) to the computer (complex in both domains), and it is in this domain of physical devices that CSA seems most complete as it is now defined.

Pattern 6.

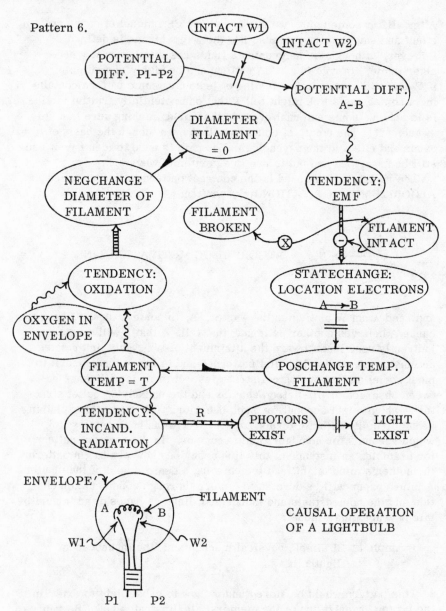

CAUSAL OPERATION
OF A LIGHTBULB

This pattern about incandescent lightbulbs is read roughly as
follows:

A potential difference across P1 and P2 (creating this potential
difference relates to another mechanism description about
switches, stored somewhere else in the memory) is synonymous

with a potential difference across points A and B (referring
to the diagram), providing that wires W1 and W2 are intact.
A potential difference across A and B continuously enables
the tendency EMF (voltage), an actor-like entity. EMF
causes electrons to move from A to B through the filament,
providing that the filament is intact. This current through
the filament is synonymous with an increase in filament
temperature. (Note that the representation allows us to omit
a description of how this occurs if we choose not to describe
the principle of resistance in detail.) This increase in filament temperature eventually results in the filament temperature reaching some threshold T, which then provides continuous enablement to two other tendencies: OXIDATION
and INCANDESCENT RADIATION. INCANDESCENT RADI-
ATION repeatedly causes photons to exist, which is simply
another way of saying that light exists, the primary goal of
the lightbulb's operation. Also, provided there is oxygen
present in the envelope (another continuous enablement required by OXIDATION), OXIDATION, viewed as another
actor, causes a continuous decrease in the diameter of the
filament (eating it away). Eventually, the filament's diameter becomes zero, which is simply another way of saying
that the filament is no longer intact. When this happens,
the causality from EMF that is moving the electrons through
the filament is severed, and the lightbulb shuts down (i. e.
burns out)!

The new link present in this pattern is the ANTAGONISTIC STATE
MARKER, written as:

 ANTAGONISTIC STATE MARKER

This provides a way to highlight feedback loops in CSA patterns. The
interpretation of this link is that the existence of S1 precludes the
existence of state S2, and vice-versa. In other words, S1 and S2 are
descriptions of mutually exclusive conditions. In a sense, this link is
the inverse of the state coupling link. Its role in this mechanism is to
relate (DIAMETER FILAMENT 0) to (FILAMENT INTACT) as antagonistic states.

Once more we ask: what is the utility of a pattern like this which
describes a physical or electrical device? Although this pattern is

indexed (as are all other CSA patterns) from numerous places in the
larger model in which it is stored, one of the primary indexings indicates that operating the incandescent lightbulb is one way to cause
light to exist. Again, such knowledge would be useful either to a plan
synthesizer who itself required light, or to a story comprehender
who was trying to understand a segment of a story where a knowledge
of a lightbulb was central.

But clearly, we wouldn't want this pattern about a lightbulb to make
a nuisance of itself if we were camping in the wilderness and needed
light inside a cave! This rather whimsical observation leads us to the
second part of the paper: selection of strategies and things on the
basis of relevance within a given context or environment.

2. Selection. Imagining that we were to take a 'snapshot' of the
state of an individual's knowledge at some arbitrary point, suppose
that what we saw were thousands of CSA-like patterns containing the
sorts of knowledge about cause and effect that have been suggested
within the CSA representation. Suppose also that we were to see a
large number of nonalgorithmic entities representing concepts and
tokens of concepts which modeled real-world entities such as ANIMAL,
GREEN, JOHN SMITH, and so forth, as well as thousands and thousands of word concepts and their associated word sense concepts.

If we were then to observe any given act of, say, plan synthesis or
language interpretation within the framework evident in this snapshot, we would notice a very remarkable thing: although there are
probably millions of pieces of knowledge, the human, viewed as either
a plan synthesizer, a parser, or an interpreter of algorithmic activity
about him, seems to employ only a startlingly small fraction of this
knowledge in accomplishing his task. Somehow, a knowledge of relevance seems to provide a tremendous filtering service to prevent a
flood of irrelevant mental activity.

The phenomenon is pervasive: the same potent selectional force
seems to be active wherever there is an element of choice involved:
strategy selection, referent selection, 'thing' selection, syntactic
parse rule selection, and word sense selection, to name only a few
of the most obvious ones.

I want to propose that this aspect of human intelligence--this
ability to filter out all but the most relevant knowledge at every point--
is one of the most vital to so-called 'intelligent' behavior, and that,
however it happens, all forms of it have one underlying cognitive
mechanism. The remainder of the paper proposes what this mechanism might look like, and how it might be roughly approximated by a
computer.

Let us return now to consider the observable effects of selection.
In strategy selection, it manifests itself as an agent which masks

most of the overwhelmingly large number of alternative strategies for solving a given problem, making the problem solver 'see' the most appropriate one first, or close to first. For example, let us suppose that P's goal is to go from the kitchen to the living room. Clearly, P will never even consider using a jet plane! Yet, as a pattern for getting places, except for certain relevance conditions, there is no a priori basis for avoiding this pattern. How, therefore, does selection rule out this pattern before the higher levels of the problem solver ever gain access to it?

There is the hint that, stored with every piece of knowledge, there is some sort of 'user's manual' describing the conditions under which the piece of knowledge must be relevant. For strategies involving jet planes, the user's manual would indicate that such strategies are normally most applicable when distances are large, the plan executor has enough money, and so forth. Apparently, it is this knowledge about knowledge with which the selection mechanism must deal, rather than with the knowledge itself. Let us call the knowledge itself 'first-order knowledge', and the knowledge about knowledge 'second-order knowledge.

So before P ever gets to consider the CSA pattern that tells him how to employ a jet to get him somewhere, some second-order knowledge about when this first-order knowledge is relevant apparently informs the selection mechanism not even to present the higher levels of the system with the jet strategies as alternatives. Furthermore, it is this second-order knowledge which must be most sensitive to context, since judgments of relevance are directly a function of the environment in which any activity occurs.

Now, I want to make a point, but must take care not to get carried away. If overstated, the point might read like this:

Any system which makes intelligent selections at every decision point cannot be too far from being an accurate model of a human.

Of course, even if this were true, it would hinge entirely on what 'good decision' means! So a slightly more responsible conjecture is:

Any system that does not make intelligent selection at every decision point cannot be a good model of human intelligence.

A reformulation of this idea would be: It is more often a knowledge about knowledge that makes a system appear intelligent than it is the knowledge itself. Thus, even if our robot has poor strategies for doing things, if it usually selects the best one for each task it attempts, I would still be willing to believe that it is behaving

intelligently. Any system can know some particular strategy for
moving an object. But the system will not appear 'intelligent' unless
it also knows when to apply this strategy in preference to all other
possible strategies. By this standard, my measure of intelligence
is: how well is the system able to select the most relevant strategy
for each given task in a given context. In other words, 'intelligence'
is more a function of second-order knowledge than of first-order
knowledge.

Strategy selection is a rather obvious form of selection. What other
less obvious forms are there? I want to point out three others because,
taken together with the strategy selection, these four forms of selection seem necessary to all forms of human symbolic intelligence.

The other three are: (2) event interpretation selection, (3) word
sense selection during language comprehension, and (4) word choice
during language generation.

We can define event interpretation to be that process which dis-
covers how each perception relates to the context in which it is perceived. For example, how should we interpret the sentence: 'John
shouted at Mary'? Clearly, we ought to 'see' different interpretations
in different contexts: 'John was on the opposite hilltop from Mary.
John shouted at Mary.' vs. 'John was furious that Mary had stayed
out so late. John shouted at Mary' and so on.

The third form of selection, word sense selection, is a well-known
problem in language analysis: it is the process of identifying an internal concept with a word of the language spoken in context. Surprisingly, few computer-based parsers have dealt with problems of
word sense selection; they either defer the problem by focusing on
more syntactic issues, or simply ignore it because the domain of discourse for which the parser is designed permits them to do so, being
narrow in scope--a 'microworld', in the parlance of AI.

Representing the former camp, Marcus (1974) argues that identification of word senses can be bypassed in the initial phases of parsing
since, regardless of the sense, the syntax (e. g. case framework) of
any given word is relatively fixed. If the syntactic component mis-
labels some case because it has ignored the word sense, so be it. It
is nothing more serious than a mislabeling, because a subsequent
semantic process will always know where to salvage the mislabeled
case from the syntactic frame.

Although this point of view bothers me, I have yet to find a counter
example to refute it; in fact, the CSA language front end interface be-
haves in this manner, using a version of Marcus' parser: CSA accepts syntactic case frames with Fillmore-like cases (as in Fillmore
1968), then filters the frames through so-called 'semantic discrimination networks' in order to map the syntax onto the meaning. If, for
example, the sentences are: 'John gave Mary a mean look', 'John

gave Mary a teacup', and 'John gave Mary an idea', by testing the semantic types of the entities assigned to the various syntactic cases by Marcus' parser, the system will map these three thoughts, which look identical in syntactic structure, onto three quite different meaning structures:

(1) (C-INHEAD JOHN MARY (EFEEL JOHN ANGER MARY))
    (John caused Mary to know that he felt anger toward her)
(2) (CSC-POSSESSION JOHN TEACUP JOHN MARY) (John
    caused a statechange in physical possession of the teacup
    from himself to Mary)
(3) (C-INHEAD JOHN MARY IDEA) (John caused some idea
    to be in Mary's mind)

The semantic discrimination networks which interface Marcus' parser to the CSA model also have access to expectancies in the system that are more than semantic, so that a sentence like 'Mary picked the apple' will map onto 'Mary indicated that it was the apple which she wanted' in one context, but 'Mary plucked the apple' in another. A future paper on the CSA language component will describe how this occurs in more detail.

But I would argue that the artificial distinction between syntax and semantics (word sense selection) is not a good one. I personally feel that, although Marcus' parser is perhaps the best-conceived parser around, syntax should not be done all at once as a preprocess, with the result being handed in a lump to semantics, as it is in our current system. Rather, I think a more accurate model of human parsing would be one that starts with semantics, having semantics (e.g. those questions posed by the semantic nets in the existing CSA language interface) call the syntactic component to answer semantically motivated questions such as: 'Is the semantic category of the sentence's direct object "human", "location", or "mental-concept"?. This would amount to 'syntax on demand', yet something a little less radical than the approach to parsing advocated by Riesbeck (1974). The point of this approach is that, while the existence of a syntactic component is still acknowledged, only as much syntax as is required by the meaning extraction process would be dealt with, rather than attempting to construct a complete syntactic analysis before any interaction with semantics. What this has to do with intelligent selection will become clearer in a moment.

The fourth form of selection mentioned earlier, word choice during generation of language, turns out to be an approximate inverse of the word sense selection process, relying on the same knowledge about knowledge that the sense selection process requires.

With this motivation, we ought now to ask: how is knowledge about knowledge to be stored? The requirements of such knowledge are now a little clearer: it must be capable of fueling higher level processes (strategy selection, word sense selection, perception interpretation and word choice during generation) with only the most relevant options, masking all else. During strategy selection, this causes only the most relevant approach to a problem to be seen; during parsing, this causes only the most relevant word sense for each word in context to be seen by the parser as it extracts thoughts from the language.

Let us now return to the user's manual metaphor and suppose that every piece of knowledge has a user's manual. The user's manual for strategies will tell the plan synthesizer which strategy is likely to be most relevant for solving any given goal in a particular context. The user's manual for each word sense will tell the semantics, which are trying to map a syntactic case framework onto a CSA meaning structure, which senses of words to select. How is it that all this 'user information' is coordinated? How is it organized?

The CSA theory proposes that, as each piece of knowledge enters the system, it is dissected into two pieces: the first order knowledge and the second order user's manual. The user's manual is taken apart and integrated into a so-called 'selection network'.

A selection network is an n-way branching discrimination network, consisting of a connected collection of nodes. Each node contains a test and a set of alterative branches to be followed on the basis of the test outcome. Tests in the CSA system are query templates which are presented to the CSA database and deductive components (described in part in Rieger 1976b) as the selection network is 'applied'. Applying a selection network means to consult it, threading a path through pieces of user's manuals which have been implanted in an organized fashion in the network nodes, until a result is reached. A result is, depending on the type of the network, a 'strategy', a 'word sense', or an entity of whatever type it is that is being selected. The purpose of selection networks is to serve as a central unifying structure which will serve as an 'intelligent arbiter'.

Let us now look at two very simple case studies in selection networks. In the first one, we give the CSA system three strategies for moving an object: two dealing with humans, and one dealing with small, graspable objects. The three patterns will roughly approximate the notions of 'walk', 'take a bus', and 'pick it up with your hand':

Pattern 7.

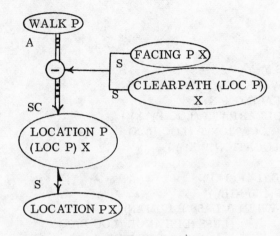

Pattern 8.

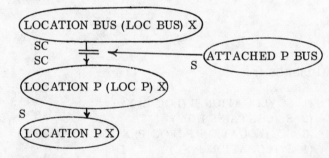

Pattern 9.

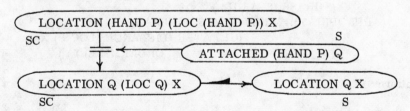

When talking to the CSA computer model, we communicate these patterns to the system as follows:

Pattern 7:

```
($ABS-ALG (
   (NAME *WALK)
   (VARIABLES P X)
   (ACCOMPLISHES 5)
   (EVENTS (1  A (WALK P) )
           (2  S  (FACING P X) )
           (3  S  (CLEARPATH (LOC P) X) )
           (4  SC (LOCATION P (LOC P) X) )
      ·    (5  S  (LOCATION P X) ) )
   (THINGS)
   (LINKS (C-CAUSE (1 4) (2 3) )
          (THRESH (4 5) NIL) )
   (APPROPRIATE-WHEN (CLASS P HUMAN)
                     (LESS (DISTANCE (LOC P) X)
                           ORDERMILE) ) ) )
```

Pattern 8:

```
($ABS-ALG (
   (NAME *GO-BY-BUS)
   (ACCOMPLISHES 4)
   (VARIABLES P X)
   (EVENTS (1  SC (LOCATION B (LOC B) X) )
           (2  S  (CONTAINS B P) )
           (3  SC (LOCATION P (LOC P) X) )
           (4  S  (LOCATION P X) ) )
   (THINGS  (B (CLASS B BUS) ) )
   (LINKS  (S-COUPLE (1 3) (2) )
           (THRESH (3 4) NIL) )
   (APPROPRIATE-WHEN (CLASS P HUMAN)
                     (GREATER (DISTANCE (LOC P) X)
                              ORDERMILE) ) ) )
```

Pattern 9:

```
($ABS-ALG (
   (NAME *GRASP-MOVE)
   (ACCOMPLISHES 4)
   (VARIABLES Q X)
   (EVENTS (1  SC (LOCATION (HAND P) (LOC (HAND P) ) X) )
           (2  S  (ATTACHED (HAND P) Q))
           (3  SC (LOCATION Q X) )
           (4  S  (LOCATION Q X) ) )
```

```
(THINGS (P (CLASS P HUMAN) (RECOMMEND SELF) ) )
(LINKS (S-COUPLE (1  3) (2) )
        (THRESH (3  4) NIL) )
APPROPRIATE-WHEN (CLASS Q PHYS-OBJ)
                    (WEIGHT Q ORDERPOUNDS) ) ) )
```

Selection networks for strategies are cataloged by the primary predicate describing the state of the world the strategy is intended to achieve. In these cases, the predicate is LOCATION. Hence, the user's manuals for all three of these patterns will be synthesized into the (initially empty) AGENT W CAUSES STATECHANGE LOCATION X Y Z strategy selection network. (In CSA, these networks are called 'causal selection networks'.) In a large CSA system, there is a rather complex causal selection network for each state and statechange predicate known to the problem solver.

In the CSA computer model's syntax as seen above, the user's manual is signaled by the keyword APPROPRIATE-WHEN. The information associated with this keyword is in the form of statements about conditions which the variables in the strategy must satisfy, or statements about conditions which must be true (i. e. in the CSA database) at the time the strategy is being selected. The 'appropriate-when' conditions are taken apart and used to construct an initial selection network. How this occurs is a matter of considerable theoretical interest, since we believe it represents a significant form of learning. However, these issues will not be discussed here.

In the example given, the network which results from the synthesis of these three user's manuals looks like this:

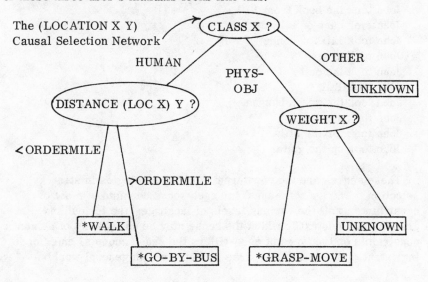

The (LOCATION X Y) Causal Selection Network

Now, whenever the system is confronted with a goal of the form: 'construct a plan wherein agent W causes a statechange in X's location from Y to Z', this causal selection network is called up and 'applied'. The data base and deductive components of the system subsequently see a progression of queries about various features of the W, X, Y, and Z, and about the general state of the world, until the network finally chooses one of the three strategies as most relevant, or determines that it does not have a relevant strategy for the given goal.

Now we have an arbiter, which has been built up automatically from the user's manuals of the various strategies among which it selects. This arbiter is the agent which performs the crucial pre-filtering of strategies for the higher levels of the system. Once the plan synthesizer commits itself to a particular filtered strategy, the strategy communicates a set of subgoals to the synthesizer, and these subgoals evoke recursive behavior for the subgoals identical to the top level behavior. (Actually, there are some other processes which enter the picture as subgoal solutions are constructed. Among such processes are 'demons' which protect a subgoal once it has been solved.)

As a second case study in selection networks, we return to our example of thing selection in which the things are senses of words, and in which the selection is occurring as part of a parsing process. The question is: what is the user's manual for a word sense?

Consider the verb take. Like most verbs, take has a great variety of underlying senses. Some of them are illustrated here.

John took Bill for a ride.
John took the book from Bill.
John took care of Bill.
John took Bill for honest.
John took drugs.
John took the oath.
John took Bill.
John took the green banana.
John took a break.
John took for the hills.
John took up the guitar.

These senses are the counterparts of the strategies in strategy selection. The user's manual for each sense consists of a set of constraints at all the various levels of language: the lexical and grammatical context in which the sense may be used, a set of semantic constraints on the types of case-fillers the sense accepts, and, most important (since it ties the parse process in with general world knowledge and 'deep' comprehension processes), contextual constraints on the types of situations in which the word sense might be used.

For take, an example of lexical environment is: one of the senses of take meaning 'to begin a habitual activity' or 'to reel in' or 'to agree to' (among possibly others) is suggested when the lexical item immediately to the right of take is up. An example of a grammatical rule is: if there is a prepositional phrase beginning with to and specifying a location, then take might have the interpretation 'to move toward rapidly', as in take to the hills. An example of contextual environment is: if the actor associated with the verb take is expected to exhibit selection behavior (e. g. to select which apple to eat), then the sense of take meaning 'to select' is particularly appropriate (as in 'Mary took the green apple').

By applying word sense networks from the bottom up, it should also be possible to generate language. That is, by starting from an internal concept (word sense) that requires expression, and climbing the sense selection network in which that concept appears as a terminal node, the generator would do whatever was required to cause the answers to the network selection questions to be true. Doing so would spell out most of the relevant aspects of the linguistic and conceptual environment surrounding the word thus selected.

A partial word sense selection network for the verb take might look as follows:

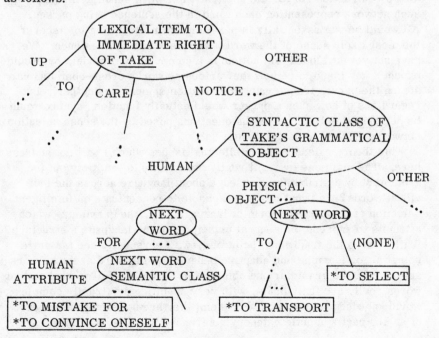

Concerning parsing and language comprehension, the hypothesis I would therefore like to suggest is that most knowledge about language lives in selectional networks such as these, rather than in a traditional grammar. Each word has a number of possible senses, given any snapshot of an individual's knowledge about language, and it is the content and organization of these senses into networks that account for linguistic ability. Put another way, language lives in word senses and in the intertwined user's manuals which result when selection networks are constructed from such a collection of senses. Most of what I like to call 'fancy grammar' is an artifact of this word-sense organization. But it is the organization of word senses around selectional features that is the primary seat of language.

As with causal selection networks, the automatic acquisition and organization of selection networks for word senses is of extremely high theoretical interest, primarily because such structures suggest how a language might be learned, one word sense or one construction at a time--by example, the way I believe my children learn. In other words, I believe that language evolves as a very large collection of individual cases which grow to be organized as word sense selection networks; 'grammar' evolves only as an expediency for answering certain classes of questions posed by networks when they are applied, i. e. when parsing is performed.

A parser which reflected this theory would therefore be little more than a central control for the application of word sense networks, one such network representing each word in the sentence being parsed. All would be run essentially in parallel, each attempting to discover the most likely sense of the word it represents in the sentence. We have not yet developed this notion as a computational model, but would expect a key issue to be how the various networks cross-communicate during the parse, transferring information among one another. But regardless of how such a parser would actually function, syntax would be performed only as far as the questions posed by the sense selection networks demand to perform their job.

This theory raises many intellectual issues which I will not address here. The main one is: is it really reasonable to 'multiply out the grammar' by distributing knowledge about language across the individual words? Is it not more reasonable to concentrate on intelligent selection of the factored form of language, i. e. the grammar, which attempts to express the general principles of the language's structure? While this is the traditional point of view, I personally see far more potential for learning and adaptive behavior in the word sense network approach. The grammar can come later. We often fail to realize that words really are individuals, with very specific, arbitrarily complex world knowledge associated with them; they are not simply members of an abstract syntactic category referenced by some grammar. Why put more emphasis on grammar than anything else? I submit that making grammar central not only is an artificial way to slice through language, but it is also an incorrect way that can lead one into incredibly baroque theories of abstract grammar which have no practical value, in the sense that computational models could be constructed from them. Perhaps by turning the traditional approach to language inside out (which is how I imagine the word sense selection system), things won't be so difficult!

3. Conclusion. Perhaps it is time to pop back up to the surface and conclude. The points of this paper have been twofold: first, that it is important when dealing with language to have a well defined and concise theory of how to represent general world knowledge, and second, that being able to make intelligent selections among alternatives in this knowledge is at least as important as the knowledge itself. Since these two issues pervade all aspects of language understanding and problem solving, they will remain with us for quite a number of years, and perhaps set the stage for theories of how humans learn.

REFERENCES

Abelson, R. 1973. The structure of belief systems. In: Computer models of thought and language. Edited by Schank and Colby. San Francisco, W. H. Freeman.

Disney, Walt. 1975. The magic grinder. New York, Random House.

Fillmore, C. 1968. The case for case. In: Universals in linguistic theory. Edited by Bach and Harms. New York, Holt, Rinehart and Winston.

Marcus, M. 1974. Wait and see strategies for parsing natural language. MIT AI Lab Working Paper 75.

Rieger, C. 1975. The commonsense algorithm as a basis of computer models of human memory, inference, belief and contextual language comprehension. In: Proceedings of the Workshop on Theoretical Issues in Language Processing, MIT.

_____. 1976a. An organization of knowledge for problem solving and language comprehension. Artificial Intelligence, 7.2, Summer.

_____. 1976b. Spontaneous computation in cognitive models. University of Maryland TR 459.

Riesbeck, C. 1974. Computational understanding: Analysis of sentences and context. Doctoral dissertation. Stanford University. AI Memo 238.

Schank, R. 1972. Conceptual dependency: A theory of natural language understanding. Cognitive Psychology 3.4.

LOGIC AND GRAMMAR

GILBERT HARMAN

Princeton University

Abstract. I assume that logic plays a distinctive role in reasoning, that a person's nonlogical views are finitely represented in his mind, and that we can suppose that someone has an infinite number of beliefs only by counting as believed certain logical implications of what he explicitly believes. A theory of the logic of a language will therefore attempt to account for obvious implications by means of logical rules and a finite number of nonlogical axioms. Competing analyses will sometimes be possible, involving different logics and different nonlogical axioms. Considerations of simplicity often favor one competitor over another. For example, it is probably simpler to account for the transitivity of comparative relations by means of a nonlogical axiom than by means of a logic of comparatives in which more or -er than is a logical constant.
Because of the special function of logic, we would expect logical constants to be few in number, relatively fixed, and grammatically distinctive. This suggests that relational predicates, for example, should not be treated as logical constants, and that raises a problem about the status of set theory and the theory of identity. These theories are not normally finitely axiomatized (so they should be included in logic according to our principle of the finiteness of theory) but they are normally stated using relational predicates (which we do not want to count as logical constants). This suggests that we must either finitely axiomatize these theories or else argue that they are somehow implicitly contained in the logic of quantification in ordinary language.

173

An account of the logical forms of sentences[1] in a language L must specify when a sentence is the negation of another (P = not Q), when a sentence is the logical conjunction of two others (P = Q and R), when a sentence is the universal quantification of a (one-place) predicate (P = (x)Fx), and so forth. We might hope that this could be done by appeal to the grammatical structure of sentences of L. Of course, this would not be to identify logical structure with grammatical structure. Not every aspect of grammatical structure will be logically relevant. The distinction between nouns, verbs, adjectives, and prepositions, for example, may well be logically insignificant. To suppose that logical form depends on grammatical structure is not to suppose that logical and grammatical categories are the same. The category 'noun' is a grammatical and not a logical category; 'predicate' is a logical and not a grammatical category. A predicate is, roughly, a sentence with one or more indexed holes in it where proper names or pronouns could go. Similarly, a sentential connective is, roughly, a sentence with one or more indexed holes where sentences could go. In general, a predicate or connective in a sentence need not correspond to a phrase of a single grammatical category in that sentence, for example, the predicate John loves--- in the sentence John loves Mary or the connective ---$_1$ and not ---$_2$ in the sentence John loves Mary and Sally does not love Albert. Still, we must appeal to grammar in order to determine what predicates and sentential connectives are involved in a given example, because grammar tells us what sentences are involved, where names or pronouns might go, and so forth. Grammar might tell us, for example, that the sentence John loves Mabel is involved in examples like the following ones: Mabel, John loves. Sam loves Sally and John, Mabel. Albert loves Mabel, and so does John. Hubert does not love Mabel, but John does. John, but not Hubert, loves Mabel. John is believed to love Mabel. Mabel is loved by John. Mabel is easy for John to love.

One test of a grammar of a language is therefore whether it provides adequate materials for the assignment of logical forms to sentences in a way that accounts for obvious implications. Such an account will also involve rules of immediate logical implication stated in terms of these logical forms and a finite set of nonlogical axioms representing 'meaning postulates' and other more or less obvious or well-known nonlogical principles. I say that only a finite number of nonlogical axioms are allowed because I assume that a person's nonlogical views are finitely represented in his mind. We can suppose that someone has an infinite number of beliefs only if we count as believed certain logical implications of what he explicitly believes. Let us call this the principle of the finiteness of theory and the infiniteness of logic. [2]

The test of the account is this. If speakers take P obviously to imply Q, [3] then there should be a relatively short derivation of Q, using the rules of logic, from P and possibly one or more nonlogical axioms. And, if there is a relatively short derivation like this of Q from P, speakers should find the implication from P to Q relatively obvious. Ideally, we might even hope to be able to account for the degree of obviousness of an implication in terms of the length of the derivation needed and the degree of obviousness of the axioms that have to be used. [4]

Consider, for example, that John is older than Mabel and Mabel is older than Sam obviously implies John is older than Sam. We might begin by supposing that there is an appeal here to an axiom of transitivity for older than: For any x, y, and z, if x is older than y and y is older than z, then x is older than z. The logical rule of universal instantiation applied to this axiom yields: If John is older than Mabel and Mabel is older than Sam, John is older than Sam. Then modus ponens applied to this and the initial premise yields John is older than Sam.

The trouble with this analysis is that it does not show how the implication depends on the comparative construction involved. Other examples: John is wiser than Mabel and Mabel is wiser than Sam implies John is wiser than Sam. John is more intelligent than Mabel and Mabel is more intelligent than Sam implies John is more intelligent than Sam. John is more interested in books than Mabel and Mabel is more interested in books than Sam implies John is more interested in books than Sam. There are an infinite number of implications like these, each requiring a different axiom if the same sort of analysis is given to each. But that is ruled out by our principle of the finiteness of theory.

We might, therefore, try instead to account for all these implications in terms of a special logical principle which says, for example, that x is more F than y and y is more F than z always implies x is more F than z; in other words, whenever a sentence of the one form is true, the corresponding sentence of the other form is also true.

F is here any relative modifier like tall, old, interested in books, and so forth. Strictly speaking, I should say ---$_1$ is tall for ---$_2$, ---$_1$ is old for ---$_2$, ---$_1$ is interested in books for ---$_2$, and so forth, to indicate the relativity. Someone counts as tall only in relation to one or another sort of thing or comparison class. John may be tall for a man but not for a basketball player. Sam may be (relatively) interested in books for a university professor but not for a classicist. In this analysis, then, more is a logical operator that applies to relative modifers, converting them into relational predicates whose arguments are at the same level. Where the relative modifier ---₁ is F for ---₂ relates elements to sorts or sets of elements, the relational predicate ---₁ is more F than ---₂ relates elements to elements.

An alternative analysis treats more as itself a nonlogical relational predicate ---₁ is more than ---₂. In this analysis, x is more F than y has the form A is more than B, where A is perhaps the degree to which X is F and B is the degree to which y is F. John is older than Mabel says, according to this analysis, that the degree to which John is old is more than the degree to which Mabel is old. The implications that we have been discussing are not purely logical implications, according to this analysis. There is no special logical principle involving more as a logical constant; no logic of comparatives. Instead, there is an appeal to general logical principles plus a single nonlogical axiom: For any x, y, and z, if x is more than y and y is more than z, x is more than z.

Now consider the following point. John is older than Mabel and Sam is older than John implies Sam is older than Mabel, but this is slightly less obvious than our original implication, namely, that John is older than Mabel and Mabel is older than Sam implies John is older than Sam. If we are accounting for these implications in terms of a nonlogical axiom, this perceptible difference in obviousness suggests that the axiom in question is more likely to be the one we have already mentioned, for any x, y, and z, if x is more than y and y is more than z, x is more than z, than it is to be this: for any x, y, and z, if x is more than y, and z is more than x, z is more than y. In other words, the former axiom is more likely to be psychologically real than the latter. Our recognition of the slightly less obvious implication appears to depend on a prior recognition that John is older than Mabel and Sam is older than John (logically) implies the same thing in reverse order: Sam is older than John and John is older than Mabel, at which point the relevant axiom is usable. Similarly, if we were to suppose that more is a logical operator, we could take the difference in obviousness as evidence that the psychologically real logical principle is the one previously indicated, namely, that x is more F than y and y is more F than z logically implies x is more F than z, rather than the principle that x is more F than y and z is more F than x logically implies z is more F than y. In either case, we would explain the difference in obviousness as due to a difference in length of derivation.

We have, then, two different analyses, each of which accounts for an infinite number of implications involving the transitivity of the comparative construction. According to the one analysis, these implications are obvious because they are instances of a basic logical principle. According to the other, they are obvious because they depend on an obviously true nonlogical axiom or meaning postulate.

The one analysis takes more to represent a logical constant. The other takes it to represent a nonlogical predicate. How are we to decide between these two accounts?

Well, consider one advantage of the supposition that more is a nonlogical relational predicate, namely, that the same idea works for other uses of more in other contexts. There are more women than men = the women are more than the men. John went to more races than Mabel = the races John went to are more than the races Mabel went to. John loves Mabel more than Sam does = the degree to which John loves Mabel is more than the degree to which Sam loves Mabel. The river is wider than it is deep = the width of the river is more than its depth. In each of these cases more can be treated as representing the same relational predicate; in none can it be treated as representing a logical operator that converts one sort of two-place predicate into another in the same way that, according to the first of the analyses I have considered, it converts old into more old or older.

This suggests, although it does not prove, that more complex and ad hoc principles are needed to assign logical forms to sentences in the analysis that treats more as a logical constant than in the analysis that treats more as a relational predicate. If so, the latter analysis is more likely to be correct as an account of mental reality than the former, since in the latter analysis it is to be expected that more should appear in the various contexts it appears in, whereas this must be seen as purely accidental from the perspective of the former analysis.

I have been saying that in the one analysis more represents a 'logical constant' whereas in the other it represents a 'nonlogical predicate'. In other words, the one analysis requires principles of logic that specifically mention the operator that the analysis takes more to represent, whereas the other analysis does not require principles of logic that specifically mention the predicate that this analysis takes more to represent. The logical constants in an analysis can be identified as those terms that are referred to in the principles of logic according to that analysis. Is there any other way to identify logical constants? If so, that might yield an independent test for deciding between analyses.

Consider the function of logical principles. Let us suppose that they play a distinctive role in reasoning. Then we would expect the principles of logic to have a general application and to be relatively fixed in a way that theoretical principles are not--for it would be logic that determines the implications of our ever-changing theories. Logical constants should therefore not be terms of some special subject matter. Terms like swims or sonic or asteroid should not be logical constants. The logical constants should be few in number and relatively fixed when compared with the many and changing terms needed for theory. We need not suppose that changes in logic are impossible; but we expect such changes to be infrequent and also quite significant if and when they occur, changing our language in a major way. Changes in sociology or physics should not significantly change our language even though such changes add new terminology.

Let us suppose, furthermore, that logical constants are grammatically distinctive. This is not to say that all logical constants belong to the same grammatical category. Obviously, they do not. The one-place sentential connective not is of a different grammatical category from the two-place connectives and and or, and all of these are different from the quantifier any. But let us suppose that there is some important grammatical distinction between any logical constant and any nonlogical term.

Can we make this more precise? We might suppose that logical constants belong to small closed classes whereas nonlogical terms belong to large open classes.[5] This is a promising suggestion, but we must be careful about how it is to be interpreted. The class of prepositions is relatively small and closed, but no one would for that reason want to treat, say, between as a logical constant. Between represents a nonlogical relational predicate, $---_1$ is between $---_2$, relating one thing to a pair of things. We can account for this if we take the logically relevant class of terms to be the class of atomic predicates and not just the purely grammatical class of prepositions. The relevant classes are not purely grammatical classes but are instead classes of atomic members of logical categories: the class of pronouns and proper names, the class of atomic one-place predicates, the class of atomic two-place sentential connectives, and so forth. By this criterion, sentential connectives but not predicates will presumably count as logical constants, because the class of atomic sentential connectives is presumably a small closed class. So, more represents a nonlogical term if it represents a predicate. If more represents an operator that converts one sort of relational predicate into another, it may, by this criterion, count as a logical operator. It will do so if, and only if, the class of atomic operators of this sort is small and closed.

A problem arises when we combine this criterion for logical constants with our previous principle of the finiteness of theory and the infiniteness of logic. The problem concerns the status of set theory and the theory of identity. On the one hand, these theories are normally expressed in terms of relational predicates: the is of identity and the is of set membership. Such predicates cannot be logical constants, according to the suggested criterion. So principles explicitly mentioning them cannot be principles of logic. On the other hand, set theory and the theory of identity are both normally formulated in terms of axiom schemata rather than in terms of a finite set of axioms. Formulated in that way, they count as part of logic according to our principle of the finiteness of theory.

Actually, it is not clear whether either theory is or is not part of logic. Each is sometimes treated as logic and sometimes as theory, although there has been a greater tendency to treat the (weaker) theory of identity as part of logic than to treat set theory (which includes the theory of identity) in this way. Perhaps this ambivalence reflects the apparent conflict in these cases between the principle of the finiteness of theory and the suggested criterion for logical constants.

One way out of this impasse is to opt for a finitely axiomatized set theory and a finitely axiomatized theory of identity. This raises issues that I cannot discuss here.[6] Another way out is based on the observation that the impasse about set theory and the theory of identity arises because of an unsupported assumption that these theories must contain predicates of set membership and of identity, respectively. This is not the only possibility. Wittgenstein suggested a version of quantificational logic in which distinct variables carry an assumption of distinctness of object. For any x there is a y in this version means: for any x there is a y distinct from x. This sort of quantificational logic contains the resources of standard quantificational logic plus the theory of identity. Now it is an open question whether the quantificational logic in ordinary language is more like Wittgenstein's or like the standard logic. Linguists have often remarked, for example, that assumptions about identity and distinctness are often built into certain grammatical constructions. In the following examples, the words the President and Truman cannot be interpreted as referring to the same person:

The President saw Truman in the mirror.
The President decided to wear Truman's jacket.
Truman shaved the President.

Furthermore, in ordinary English, a sentence like everyone loves someone means everyone loves someone else and is not made true (except as a joke) if everyone loves himself or herself. In a similar way, assumptions about sets are built into various grammatical constructions, such as certain uses of plural forms. We do not yet know enough about the sort of quantificational logic that underlies ordinary language to be able to say how much, if any, it contains of a logic of identity and sets.

NOTES

1. Here I use the term 'sentence' as P. T. Geach uses 'proposition' to mean 'a form of words in which something is propounded, put forward for consideration.' In other words, a sentence is an interpreted sentence taken as having a particular grammatical and logical structure, with potential ambiguities resolved, etc.

2. For further discussion of this and other assumptions underlying the present discussion, see my 'Logic of Ordinary Language', to appear.

3. In other words, they suppose that, obviously, P is not true unless Q is. Conversational implicature in Grice's sense is not enough. See H. P. Grice, 'The Logic of Conversation', in Donald Davidson and Gilbert Harman, The Logic of Grammar. Encino, California, Dickenson, 1975.

4. Other things are relevant too, such as one's quickness of mind, the likelihood that one will think of the axioms needed, and so forth.

5. Cf. W. V. Quine, Philosophy of Logic . Englewood Cliffs, N. J., Prentice-Hall, 1970.

6. See 'The Logic of Ordinary Language'.

POLYSEMY AND THE STRUCTURE
OF THE SUBJECTIVE LEXICON

ALFONSO CARAMAZZA AND ELLEN GROBER

The Johns Hopkins University

Abstract. Theories of the structure of the subjective lexicon have
been based almost exclusively on facts about the relations that structure various semantic domains. The basic fact of polysemy has not
been considered in the formulation of models of a mental dictionary.
In this paper we argue that if polysemy is taken into account, as it
must be, a certain class of theories of the structure of the subjective
lexicon are shown to be inadequate. We also present data from
several experiments on polysemy that are consistent with a 'process'
model of meaning representation. In this model it is proposed that
the specific surface sense of a word is determined not by finding a
stored representation of it in memory, but by constructing it from a
core meaning. This general and abstract core meaning representation
is presumed to underlie all uses of a polysemous word. Sets of instruction rules operate on core meanings to produce the various surface senses. The application of an instruction rule is constrained by
the relation that the final semantic representation will have to factual
information a person has stored about the world.

Only in recent years has the issue of the representation of meaning
become a respectable research problem in psychology. Under the
general rubric 'semantic memory', a term coined by Collins and
Quillian (1969), a growing stream of reports have been published
that implicitly or explicitly address the question of the organization
and retrieval of semantic information. Already, the relative merits
of several theories of semantic memory are the focus of a heated
debate (Collins and Loftus 1975; Holyoak and Glass 1975; Smith,

Shoben, and Rips 1974). And, there is even a report in which the author argues that the major theoretical contenders, the set theoretic models and network models, are merely notational variants (Hollan 1975). But, without wanting to minimize the importance of the current debate, it might be profitable to take a step back and ask what properties of lexical use and knowledge should be accounted for by a psychological theory of meaning.

Up to now, experimental work on semantic memory has been based almost exclusively on a single semantic phenomenon: categorization. A typical experimental task is to have a subject decide as quickly as he can whether a noun is a member of a particular category (e. g. true or false--a canary is a bird). It should not be surprising, then, to find that the competing theories account about equally well for the available data. But surely, there are many other things that we know about lexical items besides superordinate and property relations of nouns. What we are proposing, therefore, is that we broaden the scope of our theories by extending our experimental work to other semantic phenomena. By explicitly stating the range of semantic phenomena that a psychological theory of meaning should explain, we might be able to delimit the interesting classes of theories of a mental dictionary. As a first step in this direction it is proposed that we consider polysemy an important phenomenon worthy of the attention of the experimental psychologist.

Before going on to discuss some general aspects of polysemy and experimental work we have carried out, it should be noted that we are not unaware of difficulties involved in broadening the data base for the construction of theories. Clearly, we have the dilemma present in the contrast between the widespread practice of identifying an experimental phenomenon, proposing a model for that phenomenon, and then hoping that by minor modification the model can be extended to cover all relevant phenomena, versus an approach characterized primarily by a logical analysis of the general problem before even engaging in experimentation. Somehow the latter approach is considered suspicious by many experimentalists. Obviously, there are shortcomings to both approaches. The first approach frequently gives the semblance of a rigorous development of knowledge but in fact it can quite easily lead to a situation where considerable effort is expended to construct narrow models that bear almost no relation to our rich cognitive capacities. On the other hand, the second approach can lead to experimental inertia. A judicious balance between these two approaches is clearly what is required. Part of our report is devoted to a demonstration that we can do rigorous experimental work with an ill-defined phenomenon such as polysemy. The paper is broadly divided in two sections. The first part is a brief review of previous work on the problem of polysemy. In this section we rely primarily

on work by linguists and philosophers but we also attempt to relate it
to the question of the psychological representation of meaning. In the
second part we discuss experimental work on polysemy. Here we
rely on work that we have carried out in collaboration with Edgar
Zurif (Caramazza, Grober, and Zurif 1974; Grober 1976).

Polysemy and the representation of lexical items. While the relations that structure various semantic domains have received considerable attention (Caramazza, Hersh, and Torgerson 1976; Miller
1972; Clark 1968; Deese 1965; Fillenbaum and Rapoport 1971; Zurif,
Caramazza, Myerson, and Galvin 1974), there has been little if any
empirical work on the relations among the different senses of polysemous words. The void is somewhat surprising if one considers
polysemy to be as necessary to the study of meaning as are the
semantic relations that exist among words (Ullmann 1957). Moreover,
it is surprising that the rather extensive literature on polysemy in
philosophy and linguistics has inspired so little psychological research.
However, despite all the work by linguists and philosophers, there
seems to be very little agreement on how polysemous words should be
represented in a dictionary. [1] Katz and Fodor (1963) represent a
polysemous word with a given phonological shape and belonging to a
single syntactic category as a single lexical item with one dictionary
entry containing a subentry for each of its recognized senses. Fillmore (1971) suggests that different uses of the same word should appear in a single lexical entry whenever one use results from the extension of the other. For example, the verb load refers to the transfer of objects onto a container, as in the sentence He loaded the bricks
onto the truck. However, the activity of loading results in the filling
of the container. Consequently, the meaning of the verb load has been
extended to include the sense of fill, as in the sentence He loaded the
truck with bricks. It is not clear, however, how the new sense is
assigned. In opposition to a unitary view, McCawley (1968) claims
that there is no a priori reason for grouping items together in a
dictionary. Rather, a lexical item could be a word with one phonological shape, one semantic reading, one syntactic category, or one
set of specifications with respect to grammatical rules. Weinreich
(1966) similarly proposes that a polysemous word have as many entries
in the lexicon as it has meanings.

There are no established discovery procedures available to determine the set of lexical entries required for the correct semantic
description of a word (Weinreich 1962). Whether a given form is one
word with several senses or several words with separate senses is
often decided arbitrarily. There seems to be agreement, however,
on the fact that a word must be assigned as many senses as necessary

to account for the facts about the meanings of sentences in which it occurs.

Although we may want multiple entries for a word, each representing a different sense, we can offer arguments that not all senses need be marked in the subjective lexicon. McCawley (1968) claims that the existence of one lexical item sometimes implies the existence of another. For example, the words for temperature represent not only the temperature ranges but also the temperature sensation produced by wearing an article of clothing. In the sentence This coat is warm, the sensation produced by wearing the coat is implied by its warmth and need not be represented as an additional entry in the lexicon.

Another process whereby one set of lexical items is predictable from another is called 'reification' (Lakoff cited in McCawley 1968). For example, any lexical item denoting a person implies the existence of an otherwise identical lexical item denoting that person's body. For a related example, compare the use of the word poem in the sentence She recited a poem by Keats to its occurrence in the sentence The poem by Keats is on the desk. The former refers to a literary creation while the latter refers to its physical embodiment. Only the former need appear as an entry in the lexicon, the latter is predictable from it. Along similar lines, Weinreich (1966) has proposed a set of 'construal' rules to form new semantic entries by modifying the representation of already existing lexical items. And Bever and Rosenbaum (1971) discuss a production rule that extends the meaning of surface quality adjectives (e.g. colorful) to abstract qualities, as in the phrase the idea is colorful. The extended use need not be part of the lexical entry for the adjective; it can be recognized via the production rule.

In addition to the established senses of words which find their way into the dictionary, the language is replete with metaphorical uses of words which are derivative from their established counterparts. The enumeration of metaphorical uses would show that words can be used intelligibly without being used in any established sense. Instead of listing all the contexts in which a word could be used, it seems more reasonable to find a finite and manageable set of lexical entries that adequately represent the meaning of the word. If we assume that part of the equipment of a mature speaker of the language is the ability to understand new uses of a word by extension or analogy from a focus, then this ability, in conjunction with a small set of lexical entries for a word, should enable a speaker to understand its novel uses.

If we accept the possibility that an empirically determined set of lexical entries could be found to describe adequately the meaning of a polysemous word, we next should consider the form that these lexical entries might take. One method of representing words in the subjective lexicon is by a set of semantic features or components

(Katz and Fodor 1963; Bierwisch 1970; Weinreich 1966; Bendix 1971).
Semantic features, usually mapped as words (+female) or phrases
(+ who is single), decompose the meaning of a word into its basic
concepts. Some linguists maintain that these features are drawn
from a universal set presumed to reflect the perceptual and cognitive
disposition of the organism (Bierwisch 1967; Katz 1967; Chomsky
1965; Clark 1973), while others maintain that they need not have such
a predefined status (Lyons 1968). In any case, these features express the systematic relationships among the various senses of a
word and between that word and the rest of the words in the lexicon;
and, therefore, the degree of similarity between two words can be
easily measured by the number of features they have in common.
The arrangement of the features defining a word forms a loose hierarchy where a feature at the bottom of the hierarchy implies those
features that directly dominate it. This arrangement, however, is
complicated by the fact that some features are cross classified
(Chomsky 1965; Miller 1967). Consider, in this respect, the word
animal. It can dominate branches based both on species membership
and on edibility. Thus, the same lexical entries can be classified in
various ways, each forming a different hierarchy.

A second approach to representing words in the subjective lexicon
is to define the meaning of a word in terms of the meanings of other
words (Weinreich 1966). While definitions would have certain formal
properties in common, they would not be uniquely characterized by
their syntax. Bendix (1971) and Weinreich (1966), both proponents of
this approach, represent the meaning of an item in the form of
schematic sentences or functions which consist of the semantic components necessary and sufficient to distinguish the meaning of the
item from the meanings of other items in the lexicon.

Both approaches have their disadvantages. The feature approach
does not exploit the grammatical resources of the language and may
be required to posit a large number of primitive features, many of
which may occur in the semantic description of only one word. The
definitional approach, on the other hand, less directly demonstrates
the relationship between similar words and runs the risk of circuitous
definitions. [2]

Dixon (1971) suggests a way to minimize the disadvantages of both
approaches by using a combination of the two to form lexical entries.
In this scheme, lexical items can be divided into two groups, nuclear
and nonnuclear. Primitive semantic features define nuclear items
while nonnuclear items are defined in terms of nuclear ones using all
possible grammatical constructions. For example, stare, a nonnuclear verb, could be defined in terms of the nuclear verb look and
the adjective hard through a verb-plus-adverb construction. This
approach has important advantages over the models proposed by Katz

and Fodor and Weinreich. First, in contrast to the feature model of Katz and Fodor, a much reduced number of semantic features which reoccur within the category of nuclear items, is sufficient to capture the relevant facts about lexical meaning. And, secondly, it avoids the problem of circular definitions by explicitly relating synonyms and antonyms to a single nuclear item.

From the preceding, two general notions concerning lexical organization can be isolated. First, it seems reasonable to suggest that only a small set of entries, and in most cases probably a single entry, need be represented in the subjective lexicon to capture the very large set of possible senses that a word may realize in context. And, second, the 'metaphorical' use of words, rather than representing a process distinct from ordinary use, can be taken to represent the normal situation in assigning different senses (meanings) to words. That is, given a single (or small set of) very general and abstract meaning representation(s) of a lexical item and the cognitive process of creation by extension or analogy, which roughly corresponds to what linguists have variously called construal rules, reification processes, or production rules, an indefinite set of senses can be generated in different contexts. Our empirical investigations were an attempt to demonstrate that the different senses of a word can be captured in this manner; that is, by a very general abstract meaning representation which precludes having to store all the many possible senses realized by a word in various contexts.

Before turning to our data, one other issue warrants brief consideration, namely, the form of the relation between meaning and context. It is obvious from the foregoing that we favor the autonomy of lexical meanings. Unlike certain philosophers and linguists (Walpole 1961; Bogulowski 1970; see Antal 1963 for other references) who maintain that words have meaning only derivatively--contextualists--we accept the autonomist's position that a lexical item has a meaning 'nucleus' or 'core' (Wiggins 1971; Antal 1961, 1963) that is independent of any context--and further, that this nucleus underlies all uses of that lexical item.

Experiments on polysemy: (1) the meaning of line

The first set of experiments we carried out were devised to tap adult speakers' intuitions about the relations holding among the various senses of a polysemous word. The work we are summarizing here made use of 26 senses of the word line (see Table 1), but we have since analyzed 40 senses of the word run with essentially identical results. In the first three experiments we had different groups of subjects: (a) make judgments of the acceptability of the word line in the sentence context; (b) make judgments of how similar to the

TABLE 1. Sentences for line.

(1) Ford is coming out with a new line of hard tops.

(2) I am no longer in that line of business.

(3) He had come from a line of wealthy noblemen.

(4) They came to two different conclusions using the same line of reasoning.

(5) Sam owned the local bus line.

(6) When the curtain rose for the second act, Bob could not recall his opening line.

(7) She said it was a line from Keats.

(8) He began to type the first line of his paper.

(9) When you arrive in New York, please remember to drop me a line.

(10) The tailor would line the coat with fur.

(11) The rich man was able to line his pocket with money.

(12) We wanted to line the street with people.

(13) We were told to line up.

(14) Line your paper for writing.

(15) Sergeant Jones would bring him into line.

(16) We built a fence along the property line.

(17) There was no turning back; they had crossed the enemy line.

(18) The children were playing in the direct line of fire.

(19) The judge had to draw a line between right and wrong.

(20) I pulled on the line with all my strength.

(21) The workman broke through to the gas line.

(22) The shortest distance between two points is a straight line.

(23) We were told to draw a line under the title of the book.

(24) When he frowned, a line formed across his forehead.

(25) The road was flanked by a line of trees on either side.

(26) As I examined the wall of the cave, I could clearly see a line of iron ore.

subjects' general understanding of line was the sense expressed in a particular sentence (typicality measure); and (c) produce as many sentences with different senses of the word line as they could.

Interestingly, the two most frequent uses for line ((13) and (22)) also received among the highest ratings on acceptability and typicality. The correlations between frequency and acceptability and frequency and typicality are $r = .63$ and $r = .40$, respectively. Both correlations are significantly different from chance ($p < .001$ and $p < .05$, respectively).

The results obtained in these experiments permit several interesting conclusions. The first is motivated by the pattern of high correlations among the three tasks used. More specifically, it is based on the observation that sentences (13) and (22) were not only the most frequently produced ones but also those that received the highest acceptability and typicality ratings. It is our contention that this situation is not an accidental one, but that it is a direct consequence of important properties of the conceptual structure of <u>line</u>. That is, it does not appear unreasonable to suggest that the communality in sense realized by <u>line</u> in these two sentences comes very close to capturing what we have called core meaning: in the present case, what might be termed the quality of UNIDIMENSIONAL EXTENSION.[3] It seems likely that it is precisely this core meaning that is stored in the psychological representation for the meaning of <u>line</u>. This view allows a fairly natural explanation of the results thus far.

Taking first the production data, it seems plausible that a subject generates a specific sense or instance of <u>line</u> by accessing the core meaning and generating a context consistent with it. By this reasoning, it follows that the most frequently generated senses (in the experimental task used) should be exactly those that are close to the core meaning of the item. Senses that deviate substantially from the core meaning should be produced only very infrequently. Similar explanations to that given for the production data can be given for the acceptability and typicality data. Thus, sense-instances that are close to core meaning should receive high acceptability and typicality ratings, lower ratings should go to sense-instances that deviate further from the core meaning. That is, a subject assigns a rating by first computing a distance value between the specific sense-instance and the core meaning, and then mapping this internal metric onto the experimental scale. The results in the first three experiments, then, are generally in agreement with our view that to capture the meanings of polysemous words it is sufficient that the subjective lexicon store a single (or at most a very small set of) meaning representation(s).

Can the data we have presented also be reconciled to the notion that all senses are directly represented in the lexicon? Not unless complex ad hoc performance mechanisms are included in this alternative. However, before discussing specific details, let us consider a general objection that can be raised against this latter view. We can present the objection by way of an example. Imagine that we are trying to implement a computer system that can understand English. One part of the system is a lexicon that contains sense-instances of the words of the language. Obviously, one of the questions we must answer early in our endeavour is just how many and which senses to store in the lexicon. We doubt that there is a reasonable answer to this question. That is, there are quite clearly very many different senses for every common English word. And, furthermore, the actual number of senses cannot be determined: we can always construct a new sentence context such that a word will have a new though perhaps only very slightly different sense. But even if this problem could be circumvented, there remain others. For example, suppose that we find a heuristic for determining a cut-off point such that we represent only and all the 'important' senses of a word. One obvious problem that arises is how the machine will determine which of the potentially very large number of stored senses is the relevant one for a proper interpretation of the incoming sentence. Another even more serious problem with this approach is the following: given that we have arbitrarily excluded certain senses from the lexicon, what happens when our machine encounters a sentence containing a word which has a sense that is not represented in the lexicon? Clearly, the computer will fail to give a correct interpretation of the sentence. Therefore, if the system is to meet the very minimum of requirements, it must, in principle, represent all sense-instances of a word, a highly unlikely, if not unattainable achievement. At this point it might be proposed that in addition to storing 'important' senses, we add to the machine a component that can compute the new sense value of a word from its context and store this new information for future use. However, if we were to accept this suggestion, then we are left with what is essentially a modified view of our original proposal whereby each new sense-instance is constructed from an abstract core representation. On this basis, then, the original hypothesis is the stronger one.

Returning, however, to the hypothesis that all senses are represented in memory specifically in the light of our data, the question arises as to why there should be differences in production frequency among sense-instances? We might explain the observed frequency distribution by suggesting that access of specific senses is not random but ordered. That is, sense-instances are stored and accessed according to some principle such as order of acquisition, language use, frequency, etc. Some psychologists have in fact proposed just such explanations to account for certain distributional properties of lexical items in general (Conrad 1972, Wilkins 1971, Loftus 1973). But even if so, why should acceptability ratings not be arbitrary with respect to any one particular sense and why should there be a substantial correlation between frequency of production and acceptability? One possible answer is that when seeking correspondence to the sense-instance of a given experimental sentence, subjects tend to give lower acceptability ratings to sentences that require a longer search through the stored list of senses. In a similar fashion, we can also account for the nonarbitrariness of the observed typicality ratings: namely, subjects give higher typicality ratings to senses retrieved early in their search and lower typicality ratings to senses retrieved later. But if so, then we must hypothesize that senses are stored and accessed in terms of their 'representativeness'; i. e. their storage is ordered from most typical to least typical. In sum, what emerges is a proliferation of ad hoc mechanisms specifically tailored to fit each new set of facts.

We have additional evidence that our proposal for a single core meaning underlying all senses of a polysemous word is a plausible one. Our evidence comes from two other experimental studies. In the first of these two studies, the evidence is in the form of a cluster analysis and multidimensional scaling of similarity judgments among the senses of <u>line</u>. The other source of evidence is a correlational analysis of typicality ratings to major senses with typicality ratings to a general sense of <u>line</u>.

Both the clustering and scaling analyses revealed five major groupings of the twenty-six senses of <u>line</u>. The spatial representation displayed in Figure 1 gives a graphical account of the sequence of mergings for the hierarchical clustering solution embedded in the spatial solution obtained from the scaling analysis (see Caramazza, Grober, and Zurif 1974, for a detailed discussion of procedures). The important fact to note here is that the clusters that emerge from the analyses can be given clear descriptions.

FIGURE 1. Combined spatial-hierarchical representation for senses of <u>line</u>.

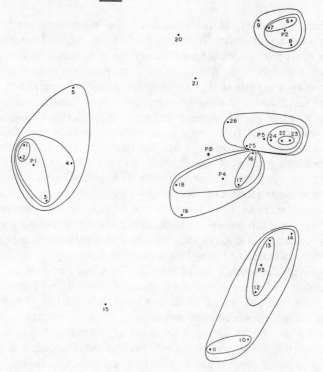

Cluster 1, comprised of sentences (1), (2), (3), and (4) (and marginally, (5)), suggests a sense of line that might be labelled a SEQUENCE or ORDERING OF CONSTRUCTS. Thus, in sentences (1) and (2), line is used to indicate KIND OR TYPE. In sentence (3) it denotes a CONSECUTIVE SEQUENCE OF ANCESTORS, and in sentence (4) it refers to a SEQUENCE OF THOUGHTS. Cluster 2 represents a grouping of sentences (6), (7), (8), and (9), and the sense of the line found here can be described as a CONTINUOUS SEQUENCE OF WORDS. In sentences (6) and (7), and to a lesser extent (8), the words have a formal status, while in sentence (9) they do not. The sense of line in the third cluster, formed by sentences (10), (11), (12), (13), and (14), does not have the same conceptual unity as the other four. In sentences (10) and (11), line denotes the FILLING or COVERING of a surface by ARRANGING objects in a CONTIGUOUS FASHION. [4] In sentences (12) and (13) people are ARRANGED IN A SERIES OF ROWS, while in sentence (14) it is MARKS that are ARRANGED IN ROWS. Cluster 4 (sentences (16), (17), (18), and (19)) indicates a BOUNDARY or DEMARCATION that may or may not have a physical existence. The BOUNDARY in sentences (16) and (17) does, while in sentence (18) it does not. Sentence (19) involves a DEMARCATION between moral constructs or categories. The fifth cluster (sentences (22), (23), (24), (25), and (26)) represents a sense of line that denotes a CONCRETE and CONTINUOUS MARK. This sense is most clear in sentences (22) and (23), where a distance is traced out by a MARK. In sentence (24) a wrinkle in the skin is the thing that resembles a MARK. In (25) it is a continuous row of trees and in sentence (26) it is a seam of iron ore. Sentences (20) and (21) were clustered at the final stages of the program and together with sentence (15) were unstable with respect to their positions in the two solutions. Our results, then, suggest the existence of five conceptually distinct clusters (major senses) which can be clearly labelled. In addition, and consistent with our earlier discussion, it seems that the labelled clusters share the common semantic concept of EXTENSION. However, it should also be noted that although the semantic description of the clusters includes the concept of EXTENSION, the saliency of this concept in their description quite likely varies from one cluster to another. Thus, not only does each cluster reflect this core meaning, but each cluster can also accommodate an independent characterization. In turn, the sentences which comprise each cluster reflect in some measure a common meaning of this cluster in the same way that each cluster reflects the core meaning of the concept line.

The last study in this series is a more direct experimental test of the notion that the various senses of line can be considered as relative deviations from a common core meaning. The specific procedure we used was a simple one. We obtained typicality ratings for each of the twenty-six senses to a prototypical sense for the five clusters and then correlated these ratings with the typicality values of each sense to the general sense of line (experiment 2). The relevant results can be briefly summarized. First, it was noted that there was an asymmetry in the specific typicality ratings. That is, we found relatively low mean typicality ratings to prototypical senses for clusters 1 and 2, and a relatively high mean rating for cluster 5. This suggested to us that the shared meaning of cluster 5 is quite general (or close to the core meaning of line), while those of clusters 1 and 2 are more specific or relatively distant from the core meaning of line.

A prediction follows from this asymmetry. If the typicality ratings from experiment 2 are correlated with the typicality ratings for each of the five prototypes, these correlations should preserve the linear order of the grand means for the prototypes. That is, the correlation between general typicality ratings and the ratings for prototype 5 should be the highest, while the correlations between general typicality and prototypes 1 and 2 should be the lowest, with prototypes 3 and 4 falling in intermediate positions. This would suggest that the notion of EXTENSION which we claim underlies all meanings of line is more central to the sense of cluster 5 than to either of the senses denoted by clusters 1 and 2. Put differently, while all sentences appear to reflect a core meaning for line, those comprising clusters 1 and 2 seem, in addition, to have a more forceful independent component than those comprising the other clusters. Similar arguments were used by Clark and Begun (1971) to determine core meanings of sentence subjects in English. The results of the correlation analysis appear in the first line of the matrix in Table 2. The sense which correlated highest with the general typicality ratings was MARK (cluster 5) followed by BOUNDARY (cluster 4) and ARRANGEMENT

TABLE 2. Correlations between general typicality and specific typicality ratings.

	G	S5	S4	S3	S2	S1
G	1	.48	.46	.23	.03	-.31
S5		1	.64	.30	-.28	-.39
S4			1	.19	-.08	-.36
S3				1	-.33	-.21
S2					1	-.06
S1						1

From Caramazza, Grober, and Zurif (1974).

IN A SERIES (cluster 3). The sense described by a SEQUENCE OF WORDS (cluster 2) was uncorrelated, while the sense denoted by KIND (cluster 1) had a moderately negative correlation.

The remaining rows of the matrix in Table 2 indicate how the specific typicality ratings for each of the prototypes correlated with one another. There was a very high positive correlation between the sense of MARK and BOUNDARY. This is due to the close agreement in the ratings for their corresponding prototypes, reflecting the likelihood that clusters 4 and 5 (BOUNDARY and MARK, respectively) both load heavily on the core meaning of line, with little additional information. The linearly decreasing trend in the correlations between general typicality and specific typicality of the first row of the matrix is repeated in the remaining five rows of the matrix. One inversion occurred between the correlations of cluster 3 with clusters 2 and 1. I take the overall pattern of correlations to be a quantitative measure of how essential the core meaning of the concept line is to each of the senses which represent its meaning. The notion of EXTENSION is most central to the meaning of clusters 4 and 5, and is somewhat obscured by other information in clusters 1 and 2.

The combined results from these five experiments have led us to suggest that the meaning of a polysemous word--all words--must be captured on two levels. The first is the core meaning level. In the case of line, it would appear that this underlying semantic thread can be labelled EXTENSION. The second level consists of the set of conceptually salient senses that represent those meanings of line that occur in actual language use. This view of polysemy is superficially similar to a treatment of the lexeme over by Bennett (1973). According to Bennett, the features which distinguish among the senses of the word are contextually determined and thus are not part of its 'inherent' meaning. The notion of SUPERIORITY has the same status in his analysis of over as the notion of EXTENSION has in our analysis of line.

However, in our analysis, even though the core meaning is considered sufficient to represent an underlying unification for the different senses of line that people can distinguish, we feel that the subjective lexicon also uses information of a more specific kind. That is, in a manner somewhat analogous to the distinction between nuclear and nonnuclear terms proposed by Dixon (1971), the subjective lexicon contains--in addition to the abstract definition or core meaning of line--a set of specific 'instructions' (or features) that allow the generation of other senses of a polysemous word. It should be emphasized that these senses are not viewed as constituting separate lexical entries: to produce any of the 'surface' senses we always access the core meaning and apply instruction to generate specific sense-instances.[5] Thus, for example, starting with the core meaning of line, the first set of presumed instructions produces a less general sense that corresponds roughly to the abstract meaning of one of the five clusters. Thereafter, the application of subsequent instructions produces the 'surface' sense that we encounter in a specific context. As an example of how the instruction rules may operate, consider the two sentences The judge had to draw a line between right and wrong and We built a fence along the property line. The two senses of line in these sentences both indicate a DEMARCATION or BOUNDARY and, in fact, belong to the same cluster. They differ, however, in that in the first instance the BOUNDARY is an abstract one, while in the latter it has a physical representation. In our model, therefore, the derivation of these two senses will share the same instruction rules up to the point where BOUNDARY is specified. At that point the instruction rule for sense one may be characterized as 'REALIZE BOUNDARY CONCEPT AS ABSTRACT' while that for sense two is 'REALIZE BOUNDARY CONCEPT AS CONCRETE'.

One advantage in treating individual senses as derived by a set of instructions applied to a core meaning is that it permits the application of 'fuzzy' (Lakoff 1973) instructions. That is, an instruction may read as 'REALIZE BOUNDARY CONCEPT AS SORT OF CONCRETE' to capture part of the sense of line in the sentence There was no turning back, they had crossed the enemy line. In this way a fairly natural and internally motivated procedure is available for producing and interpreting the usually fuzzy natural language concepts.

A final point about our overall results. Nowhere in our results did we obtain support for a distinction of senses on the basis of form class. We take this null result to suggest that just as all the senses of a polysemous word are generated from a single core meaning, so the different grammatical forms are generated from the same core by instruction rules analogous to those for generating different sense instances. Thus, for example, the sense of line in the sentence Line your paper would have among others the instruction rule 'REALIZE MARK CONCEPT AS VERB'. This view departs from the position presented in Katz and Fodor (1963). We feel, however, that in addition to the data we have presented, there is ample support for this position both in the psychological and linguistic literature.

First, with respect to the psychological literature, it has been observed that, unlike semantic category membership, grammatical form is not a psychologically salient dimension either in inducing clustering in free recall tasks (Cofer and Bruce 1965; Hamill 1973) or as a release from Proactive Inhibition (Wickens 1972). This, together with the data we have presented, suggests that, at least on psychological grounds, grammatical form may be a derivative property of a fairly superficial sort. Further evidence in support of our claim is available in the linguistic literature. Here we refer to that large body of

literature which has been concerned with the nondiscreteness of grammatical categories (Bolinger 1961; Carden 1973; Anderson 1974;
Quirk 1965; Ross 1972). Thus, considerable evidence is accumu-
lating that such categories as Noun, Verb, Adjective, Noun Phrase,
etc. may not be discrete categories after all, but that they should be
considered as varying along a continuum of membership to a category.

Experiments on polysemy: (2) A test of two semantic memory
models. At the beginning of this paper we alluded to a current controversy on the issue of how to represent semantic information in memory.
The controversy has revolved around the question of which class of
models, network (Quillian 1968, 1969; Collins and Loftus 1975; Rumelhart, Lindsay, and Norman 1972; Anderson and Bower 1973; Holyoak
and Glass 1975) or set-theoretic (Meyer 1970; Schaeffer and Wallace
1970; Smith, Shoben, and Rips 1974), best handles an increasing body
of experimental data on semantic processing. In this section we evalu-
ate these two classes of models in light of semantic facts about polysemy. The first part is devoted to some general observations on how
these two classes of models might account for polysemy. The second
part is based on direct experimental work to test these models
(Grober 1976). For purposes of exposition we are concentrating on
the two most clearly articulated models from these two classes of
theories: the Teachable Language Comprehender (Quillian 1969;
Collins and Loftus 1975) represents the network models; the Feature
Comparison Model represents the set-theoretic models. Any conclusions we may reach on these two specific models can be generalized
to the class of network and set-theoretic models.

The Feature Comparison Model represents word meanings as sets
of features. It differs from the familiar Katz-Fodor theory in that
Smith et al., following Lakoff (1973), distinguish between 'definitional'
and 'characteristic' features. The former are features that are essential in determining class membership, for example, those properties
of dog that make it a member of the class mammal; the latter are un-
important in this last respect and are particular to the lexical items
under consideration, perhaps the fact that dogs are friendly animals.
A further property of this model is that defining and characteristic
features are to be considered as a fuzzy-set of features (see Hersh
and Caramazza 1976, for a review and experimental investigation of
specific claims of fuzzy-set theory). We take this last property to be
an important one, but it does not figure prominently in their actual
process model. Without getting into processing characteristics of
this model at this time (we are going to do so when reviewing the experimental data), we could ask whether it can adequately cope with
facts about polysemy. As far as we can determine, the only way this
model could account for polysemy is by listing separately under each

phonemic matrix for a word all the senses of the word. But we have already argued in the preceding section that this cannot be the case. The problem with this model is that it was originally designed to handle a specific set of facts--primarily, categorization into superordinate categories--and it does very well at that. As a general model of semantic memory, however, it is inadequate.

The Teachable Language Comprehender of Quillian has the opposite difficulty: it is not specific enough. This last model was originally designed to handle disambiguation and only later (Collins and Quillian 1972) was it extended to cover other semantic facts (in particular, categorization). Word meanings in this model are represented by connecting pathways of labelled relations among lexical nodes in a network. This model allows as many readings of a polysemous word as are necessary since we can always trace an alternative path among nodes. Our objections to this model are two. First, we do not see how it can differentiate between homonymy and polysemy. Second, there is no principled way to capture the relative semantic distance of polysemous senses from a core meaning. Clearly, this model can be identified with the contextualist tradition where any meaning, given a context, is appropriate. We find this position to be untenable.

But these models are not only inadequate at the general level we have discussed thus far; they also fail specific experimental tests. In a series of experiments Grober (1976) has used polysemous words to test specific processing aspects of these models. We will now briefly review these experiments.

The experimental procedures used were simple ones. In all the experiments subjects were to decide as quickly as they could whether a definition applied to a word. The word can be taken to correspond to the superordinate concept in other categorization tasks (e. g. animal) and definitions of specific senses of that word to members of that superordinate category (e. g. dog). For each of two senses of a word such that one sense was clearly typical and the other atypical, she constructed definitions. In the first experiment the subject was first shown a word and half a second later a definition appeared on a screen in front of the subject. The task of the subject was to depress a button if the definition captured one of the senses of the word shown previously. The dependent variable was Reaction Time. There were several independent variables, but I discuss only two: dominance--that is, whether the sense was a typical or atypical one; and degree of polysemy, where degree of polysemy was determined by word frequency and number of entries in a standard English dictionary.

For the verification task described above, both set-theoretic and network models predict that the more typical sense of the polysemous word should be verified faster than the less typical sense. Table 3 presents mean Reaction Times for the effect of typicality. As can be seen from column 1 of this table, there is a substantial effect due to dominance. When typicality is entered as a covariate in an analysis of covariance (correlation between typicality ratings and Reaction Time, $r = .52$), the effect of dominance is completely eliminated (column 2 of the table). Though this result does not help falsify either model, we report it for two reasons: first, to show that the task is a sensitive one, and second, to support the contention that we can think of senses of a polysemous word as having different semantic distances from a core meaning.

TABLE 3. Mean RTs for the effect of dominance.

Dominance level	Mean RT	Adjusted mean RT
Dominant meaning	1.485 (.23)	1.657 (.08)
Nondominant meaning	1.860 (.34)	1.689 (.08)
Note: Standard deviations are in parentheses. From Grober (1976).		

The second independent variable--degree of polysemy--can, however, be used to choose between the two models as they make different predictions. In the case of set-theoretic models, degree of polysemy should have no effect on Reaction Time since the factor that determines whether a positive or negative response is made is the overall semantic similarity between the underlying general concept and the definition. In contrast, degree of polysemy should be an important determinant of Reaction Time in network models since it is related to the length of the search process needed to find an appropriate pathway. In the reasoning of Collins and Loftus (1975) there is a limited amount of activation and the more meanings that are primed, the less each is primed. Consequently, there should be less activation for each sense of a highly polysemous word than for a less polysemous word. This would result in slower Reaction Time for highly polysemous words. In fact, however, Grober did not obtain an effect for degree of polysemy (see Table 4). We take this null result to support set-theoretic models and against network models. In a second experiment this temporary advantage of set-theoretic models was quickly eliminated.

TABLE 4. Mean RTs partitioned by word frequency and number of dictionary entries.

	Word frequency		Dictionary entries	
	High	Low	Many	Few
Dominant meaning	1.469	1.476	1.502	1.450
Nondominant meaning	1.824	1.795	2.076	1.812
From Grober (1976).				

As pointed out earlier, the critical factor in determining Reaction Time in the Feature Comparison Model is the semantic similarity (or distance) between the superordinate category and a particular member of that category. If the semantic distance between a category concept and a member is either very large or very small, that is, if the semantic relatedness value falls above a critical value C_1 or below a critical value of C_0, then a fast Reaction Time is executed. If, on the other hand, the semantic relatedness value falls somewhere between C_1 and C_0, a second comparison stage is executed where more deliberate comparisons of shared features are made. The execution of this second stage results in a slower Reaction Time. The relative number of second stage comparisons for a given set of stimulus items depends in part on the nature of false items: if the semantic similarity of false category-member pairs is always high, the task of discriminating true from false items becomes difficult, leading to a greater number of cautious second stage comparisons; if, instead, the semantic similarity for false items is very low, then they can easily be rejected on first stage comparisons only. A consequence of this latter case should be that a subject can preset C_1 low enough to respond for true items always on the basis of first stage comparisons. Now, since the typicality effect in the Feature Comparison Model is explained on the basis of a mixture of first and second stage processing and since in this latter case we have eliminated second stage processing, we should similarly eliminate the dominance effect. In contrast, the network models do not make this prediction.

Grober performed an experiment where she controlled the nature of false items. In Table 5 are presented mean Reaction Times for dominance levels separately for related and unrelated false-item blocks. The interaction predicted by the Feature Comparison Model did not obtain. Thus, these results are consistent with network models and not with set-theoretic models.

TABLE 5. Mean RTs and percent errors for true items in experiment 2.

Semantic relatedness	Dominance level	Mean RT	% Errors
Unrelated	Dominant meaning	1.302 (.23)	2.4
	Nondominant meaning	1.562 (.37)	9.4
Related	Dominant meaning	1.422 (.26)	2.8
	Nondominant meaning	1.600 (.34)	14.9

Note: Standard deviations are in parentheses.
From Grober (1976).

We are in the situation, then, that both network and set-theoretic models fail in fairly specific processing aspects. And this is in addition to more general objections to structural properties of these models.

Conclusion. We have argued that short of representing all possible senses of a word in memory, a theory of meaning cannot account for the basic facts of polysemy. Given, on the one hand, an indefinite number of different senses for common English words, and on the other hand, the fact that native speakers deal easily, naturally, and consistently with a wide range of surface realized senses, it seems unreasonable to suggest that meanings are assigned to sounds by searching through a list of senses until the appropriate one is found. That is, it seems unlikely that what is stored is a list of pairs $w_1, s_1; w_2, s_2; w_3, s_3; \ldots w_4, s_i; \ldots w_i, s_1;$ where w is a phonological matrix and s a semantic feature matrix. This latter approach may be a good first approximation to a static and essentially incomplete description of what it is a speaker of a language knows about lexical items, but it certainly could not do as a basis for a model of language comprehension and production.

The alternative we are suggesting is a 'Process' view of meaning (Parisi and Antinucci 1970; Rumelhart and Norman 1975).[6] As we have already briefly indicated, specific sense values are not determined by finding a stored representation; rather they are computed. Admittedly, we are still quite vague as to the actual processes involved but a general outline can be given.

There are three basic components involved in our Process theory of meaning. The first is a linguistic dictionary that contains a list of sound-meaning pairs: the sound part of the pair is a phonological matrix; the meaning part, a conceptual representation corresponding to what we have called a core meaning. These core meanings will vary in degree of abstractness, being essentially determined by the degree to which they allow polysemy; the more polysemous (e.g. run), the more abstract the representation, while the less polysemous (e.g. tachistoscope), the less abstract the representation. A likely form for these representations is a semantic tree specifying an n-place predicate.

The second component consists of a set of instruction rules. These rules are somewhat analogous to the transformations in a generative semantics grammar. Instruction rules are of the form 'REALIZE X AS Y' where X and Y correspond to semantic representations. Several different instruction rules can be applied on a core meaning, and all surface senses require the application of at least one instruction rule. That is, core meanings do not have direct surface representations.

Instruction rules operate on trees to produce new trees. An example of how an instruction rule might work can be shown by deriving part of the sense of line in draw a line under the title of the book. One of the components of meaning of this sense of line is that it has unidimensional extension. Thus, we would have the instruction 'REALIZE EXTENSION AS UNIDIMENSIONAL EXTENSION'. A further aspect of the meaning of the sense of line under discussion is that it is visually perceptible. Adding this component would result in 'REALIZE UNIDIMENSIONAL EXTENSION AS VISUALLY PERCEPTIBLE', and so on until a specific surface sense has been realized.

It might be noted that our instruction rules could be thought of as 'features'. We have no objection to this terminology and, in fact, a feature or componential analysis would form the basis for identifying what instruction rules are stored in this second component. But we have chosen to use instruction rules instead of features for two reasons: first, because we want to emphasize the dynamic aspect that we would like to see introduced in theories of meaning; and second, because we want to allow complex instructions to be executed such as, for example, the 'fuzzy' instructions discussed earlier.

The third component is an encyclopedic dictionary. In this dictionary is stored all the factual information a person has about the word. Both denotative and connotative aspects of meaning are represented in this dictionary: it is essentially a map of world knowledge. One important function of this component is to act as 'regulator' or, to borrow yet another term from generative semantics, as a source of 'derivational constraints'. That is, the application of an instruction rule is constrained by the relation that the final semantic representation will have to a segment of the cognitive map or entry in the encyclopedic dictionary. Thus, for example, in the derivation of surface senses of line, the instruction rule 'REALIZE X AS MULTIDIMENSIONAL', where multidimensional is greater than two dimensions, will be blocked since the encyclopedia will not accept as meaningful the final semantic representation. Hence, by the reasoning we are developing, encyclopedic knowledge plays a direct part in the explication of a semantic theory.

NOTES

1. We use 'dictionary' with systematic ambiguity to refer both to an internalized mental repository of lexical knowledge and to the usually alphabetized collection of words and their definitions.

2. Bierwisch (personal communication) argues that there is no substantial difference between the two approaches, claiming that the feature approach need not posit an indefinite number of features and that the definitional approach may well show direct sense relations among words. However, insofar as each of these two approaches has been formalized, the potential disadvantages we have listed cannot, in principle, be ruled out.

3. This term was suggested to us by Charles Osgood (personal communication).

4. It may be noticed that sentences (10) and (11) are the only ones that seem to implicate more than Unidimensional Extension and it was because of these two sentences that we initially adopted for core meaning the concept of EXTENSION unmodified by 'unidimensional'. The consequence was that we made the core representation more abstract and inclusive than was perhaps warranted. There are reasons why we may want to separate (10) and (11) from the other senses. That is, we may want to consider line in (10) and (11) to be a homonym of line used in the other sentence contexts. There is, of course, no clear-cut procedure for distinguishing polysemous from homonymous instances of a word. One way is to rely on the intuitions of native speakers of the language. Another more mechanical procedure is to use philological considerations judiciously (see Zgusta 1971 for a discussion on some of these issues). By using aspects of the etymology of line and morphological characteristics of derivative grammatical forms, Bolinger (personal communication) criticizes our lumping the senses of (10) and (11) with the other twenty-four senses. He points out that even though all senses of line are ultimately related to the word for linen, the historical derivation of the sense of (10) and (11) differs from the

others. The sense in (10) and (11) is directly related to the word linen in that linen was a primary lining material. Also, he comments on the fact that the derivative noun form of line in (10) and (11) is not line but lining. Obviously, these considerations are not sufficient to decide whether we have a case of homonymy or polysemy, but they could be considered symptomatic of deep differences. We are now inclined to agree with Bolinger (a similar observation was made by Osgood). However, since the question is really an empirical one, and since our earlier treatment and its theoretical underpinnings are affected only minimally, we have decided to retain the original analysis and discussion.

The distinction between homonymy and polysemy is a necessary one since it forms the basis for accessing core meanings. Thus, two homonyms will have different core meanings while polysemy results from the application of different instruction rules to a single core meaning. It would be a basic principle in the theory that the semantic distance between any pair of acceptable senses generated from a single core meaning (polysemy) will always be smaller than the distance between any pair of senses generated from different core meanings (homonyms), irrespective of the number of instruction rules applied.

5. The view we are presenting here, namely, of generating surface senses from abstract deep representation, is somewhat similar to a proposal by Binnick (1965). Although Binnick did not deal directly with polysemy (he concentrated primarily on motion verbs), there are striking parallels between his suggestions on how to account for surface lexical items and the views we have presented in this paper. Thus, for example, he claims that it is probably sufficient to have the three basic, nonderived verbs be, go, and come in order to transformationally derive all other locative and motive verbs. Quite clearly, Binnick's basic verbs are roughly analogous to our core meanings, while his transformations have rough correspondence to our 'instruction' rules. However, neither Binnick's view nor the one we are outlining is yet sufficiently developed to show differences in the two approaches clearly. One obvious but perhaps trivial difference is that the application of transformations in Binnick's system results in different morphological representations, whereas in our work we are talking only of semantic changes; the morphology remains the same.

6. We are not really sure of the Rumelhart and Norman position. On one hand, they assert that they view meaning as a process and on the other hand, they want to represent all senses directly in the lexicon. Obviously, they must be using 'process' in a different way from the way we are using it.

REFERENCES

Anderson, J. R. and G. H. Bower. 1973. Human associative memory. Washington, D. C., Winston and Sons.

Anderson, L. B. 1974. Distinct sources of fuzzy data. In: Towards tomorrow's linguistics. Edited by R. W. Shuy and C.-J. N. Bailey. Washington, Georgetown University Press.

Anglin, J. 1970. The growth of word meaning. Cambridge, The MIT Press.

Antal, L. 1961. Sign, meaning, context. Lingua, X, 2. 211-219.

_____. 1963. Questions of meaning. The Hague, Mouton.

Bendix, E. H. 1971. The data of semantic description. In: Semantics: An interdisciplinary reader in philosophy, linguistics, and psychology. Edited by D. D. Steinberg and L. A. Jakobovits. Cambridge, The University Press.

Bennet, D. C. 1973. A stratificational view of polysemy. In: Readings in stratificational linguistics. Edited by A. Makkai and D. Lockwood. Alabama, University of Alabama Press.

Bever, T. G. and P. S. Rosenbaum. 1971. Some lexical structures and their empirical validity. In: Semantics: An interdisciplinary reader in philosophy, linguistics, and psychology. Edited by D. D. Steinberg and L. A. Jakobovits. Cambridge, The University Press.

Bierwisch, M. 1967. Some semantic universals of German adjectives. Foundations of Language 3. 1-36.

_____. 1970. Semantics. In: New horizons in linguistics. Edited by J. Lyons. Baltimore, Penguin Books.

Binnick, R. 1968. On the nature of the lexical item. In: Papers from the Fourth Regional Meeting, Chicago Linguistic Society. Edited by B. J. Darden and C.-J. N. Bailey.

Bogulowski, A. 1970. On semantic primitives and meaningfulness. In: Sign, language, and culture. The Hague, Mouton.

Bolinger, Dwight L. 1961. Generality, gradience, and the ALL-or-none. The Hague, Mouton.

Caramazza, A., E. H. Grober, and E. B. Zurif. 1974. A psycholinguistic investigation of polysemy: The meanings of LINE. Unpublished manuscript. Baltimore, The Johns Hopkins University.

Caramazza, A., H. Hersh, and W. Torgerson. 1976. Subjective structures and operations in semantic memory. Journal of Verbal Learning and Verbal Behavior 15. 103-117.

Carden, G. 1973. Disambiguation, favored readings and variable rules. In: New ways of analyzing variation in English. Edited by C.-J. N. Bailey and R. W. Shuy. Washington, Georgetown University Press.

Chomsky, N. 1965. Aspects of the theory of syntax. Cambridge, The MIT Press.

Clark, E. V. 1973. What's in a word? On the child's acquisition of semantics in his first language. In: Cognitive development and the acquisition of language. Edited by T. E. Moore. New York, Academic Press.

Clark, H. H. 1968. On the meaning and use of prepositions. Journal of Verbal Learning and Verbal Behavior 7.421-431.

_____ and J. S. Begun. 1971. The semantics of sentence subjects. Language and Speech 14(1).34-36.

Cofer, C. N. and D. R. Bruce. 1965. Form-class as the basis for clustering in the recall of nonassociated words. Journal of Verbal Learning and Verbal Behavior 4.386-389.

Collins, A. M. and E. F. Loftus. 1975. A spreading-activation theory of semantic processing. Psychological Review 82.407-428.

Collins, A. M. and M. R. Quillian. 1972. How to make a language user. In: Organization of memory. Edited by E. Tulving and W. Donaldson. New York, Academic Press.

Conrad, C. 1972. Cognitive economy in semantic memory. Journal of Experimental Psychology 92.149-154.

Deese, J. 1965. The structure of associations in language and thought. Baltimore, The Johns Hopkins University Press.

Dixon, R. M. 1971. A method of semantic description. In: Semantics: An interdisciplinary reader in philosophy, linguistics, and psychology. Edited by D. D. Steinberg and L. A. Jakobovits. Cambridge, The University Press.

Fillenbaum, S and A. Rapoport. 1971. Structures in the subjective lexicon. New York, Academic Press.

Fillmore, C. F. 1971. Types of lexical information. In: Semantics: An interdisciplinary reader in philosophy, linguistics, and psychology. Edited by D. D. Steinberg and L. A. Jakobovits. Cambridge, The University Press.

Grober, E. J. 1976. Polysemy: Its implications for a psychological model of meaning. Unpublished Ph. D. dissertation. The Johns Hopkins University.

Hamill, B. W. 1973. A study on form-class clustering in free recall using overt suffixes. Paper presented at the 81st Annual Convention, American Psychological Association, Montreal.

Hersh, H. and A. Caramazza. 1976. A fuzzy-set approach to quantifiers and vagueness in natural language. Journal of Experimental Psychology: General (in press).

Katz, J. J. 1967. Recent issues in semantic theory. Foundations of Language 3.124-194.

_____ and J. A. Fodor. 1963. The structure of a semantic theory. Lg. 39.170-210.

Hollan, J. D. 1975. Features and semantic memory: Set-theoretic or network model? Psychological Review 82. 154-155.

Holyoak, K. J. and A. L. Glass. 1975. The role of contradictions and counterexamples in the rejection of false sentences. Journal of Verbal Learning and Verbal Behavior 14. 215-239.

Lakoff, G. 1973. Hedges: A study in meaning criteria and the logic of fuzzy concepts. Journal of Philosophical Logic 2. 450-508.

Loftus, E. F. 1973. Category dominance, instance dominance, and categorization time. Journal of Experimental Psychology 97. 70-74.

Lyons, J. 1968. Introduction to theoretical linguistics. Cambridge, The University Press.

Macnamara. J. 1971. Parsimony and the lexicon. Lg. 47(2). 359-374.

McCawley, J. D. 1968. The role of semantics in a grammar. In: Universals in linguistic theory. Edited by E. Bach and R. T. Harms. New York, Holt, Rinehart and Winston, Inc.

Meyer, D. E. 1970. On the representation and retrieval of stored semantic information. Cognitive Psychology 1. 242-299.

Miller, G. A. 1967. Psycholinguistic approaches to the study of communication. In: Journeys in Science--Small steps--Great strides. Edited by D. Arm. Albuquerque, University of New Mexico Press.

_____. 1972. English verbs of motion: A case study in semantics and lexical memory. In: Coding processes in human memory. Edited by W. Melton and E. Martin. Washington, V. H. Winston and Sons, Inc.

Parisi, D. and F. Antinucci. 1970. Lexical competence. In: Advances in psycholinguistics. Edited by G. B. Flores d'Arcais and W. J. Levelt. Amsterdam, North Holland Publishing Company.

Quillian, M. R. 1968. Semantic memory. In: Semantic information processing. Edited by M. L. Minsky. Cambridge, Mass., The MIT Press.

_____. 1969. The teachable language comprehender: A simulation program and theory of language. Communications of the ACM 12. 459-476.

Quirk, R. 1965. Descriptive statements and serial relationship. Lg. 41. 205-217.

Ross, J. R. 1972. The category squish: Endstation Hauptwort. Chicago Linguistic Society 8. 316-328.

Rumelhart, D. E., P. H. Lindsay, and D. A. Norman. 1972. A process model for long-term memory. In: Organization and memory. Edited by E. Tulving and W. Donaldson. New York, Academic Press.

Rumelhart, D. E. and D. A. Norman. 1975. The active structural network. In: Explorations in cognition. Edited by D. A. Norman and D. E. Rumelhart. San Francisco, W. H. Freeman and Company.

Schaeffer, B. and R. Wallace. 1970. The comparison of word meanings. Journal of Experimental Psychology 86. 144-152.

Smith, E. E., E. J. Shoben, and L. J. Rips. 1974. Structure and process in semantic memory: A featural model for semantic decisions. Psychological Review 81(3). 214-241.

Ullmann, S. 1957. The principles of semantics. Oxford, Basil Blackwell and Mott, Ltd.

Walpole, H. 1961. Semantics: The nature of words and their meanings. New York, W. W. Norton and Company, Inc.

Weinreich, U. 1962. Lexicographic definition in descriptive semantics. In: Problems of lexicography. Edited by F. W. Householder and S. Saporta. Bloomington, Indiana University.

Weinreich, U. 1966. Explorations in semantic theory. In: Current trends in linguistics, volume 3. Edited by T. A. Sebook. The Hague, Mouton.

Wickens, D. D. 1972. Characteristics of word encoding. In: Coding processes in human memory. Edited by W. Melton and E. Martin. Washington, V. H. Winston and Sons, Inc.

Wiggins, D. 1971. On sentence-sense, word-sense and difference of word-sense. In: Semantics: An interdisciplinary reader in philosophy, linguistics, and psychology. Edited by D. D. Steinberg and L. A. Jakobovits. Cambridge, The University Press.

Wilkins, A. 1971. Conjoint frequency, category size, and categorization time. Journal of Verbal Learning and Verbal Behavior 10. 382-385.

Zgusta, L. 1971. Manual of lexicography. The Hague, Mouton.

Zurif, E., A. Caramazza, R. Myerson, and J. Galvin. 1974. Semantic feature representation for normal and aphasic language. Brain and Language 1(2). 167-187.

SEMANTICS IN SPANISH LANGUAGE CURRICULA

FRANCES M. AID

Florida International University

0. Introduction. What I have to say on the relevance of semantic analysis to the teaching of Spanish is the product of research and practice; it is both report and prognosis. It may seem strange to question the role of meaning in second language pedagogy, since language, after all, is supposed to be a system and a process for exchanging meaningful utterances. It seems to me that there are at least two reasons why the question of semantics in language pedagogy is interesting right now. First, because semantics has come on the scene as a strong challenge to the syntactic bias in linguistic theory; and second, because the goal of second language learning, linguistic competence, has been restated as communicative competence. I would like to suggest that applied semantics lies at the interface between linguistic competence and communicative competence with respect to second language curricula and instructional activities.

1. Applied linguistics. A generation ago American foreign language teaching was subject to the influence and authority of structural linguistics, a tradition in which semantics had little prominence. The products of structural linguistics were pedagogical theory and curricular materials that championed the principles that the 'what' of language teaching was the structure of the target code, and that the 'how' of language teaching was intensive practice of the structured sound patterns and grammatical patterns of that code. The applied linguists of that generation took themselves very seriously: they had an obligation to language teachers as interpreters of linguistic research, guides to curriculum development, and promoters of certain methodologies and techniques. Subsequent development of generative grammars has

207

raised questions and challenged beliefs about foreign language curricula
and instructional techniques. However, the primary influence of
generative syntax has been a clarification and reinforcement of the
notion that the goal of the learner is the acquisition of a linguistic
competence.

Today the position of the applied linguist is much less secure,
though no less important. It may be more realistic. He knows that
among competing theories of language and of language acquisition none
is adequate, most are embryonic. The field of language pedagogy has
gone through several cycles of reaction against the trends of the last
generation. Ironically, without the previous generation we would be
even less enlightened than we are about what language is, how it is
acquired, and what instructional approaches are effective; yet the
most stimulating discussions today in language pedagogy in many
cases have little to do with linguistics. And so we ask, what is the
role of the contemporary applied linguist in second language teaching?

Albert Valdman has answered the question several times:

> Applied linguistics is concerned with two main activities: first,
> the preparation of pedagogical grammars, that is, the formu-
> lation of statements about the structure of particular languages
> that can be readily utilized for the preparation of teaching
> materials; second, filtering recent research in all areas of
> linguistics to make insights from the field accessible to the
> classroom teacher (1974:67).

Given the plurality of models of grammar confronting us, it is wise to
note Valdman's view of the pedagogical grammar:

> A pedagogical grammar is more than the simplified version of
> a scientific description of a language: while a scientific gram-
> mar will adhere consistently to a single model of description
> and will strive for the greatest simplicity and elegance com-
> patible with noncontradictory and rigorous presentation, a
> pedagogical grammar will use whatever grammatical theory
> proves most useful for a specific aspect of the structure of
> the language (1966:xxi).

It is to Valdman's second point that I will direct the remainder of
this discussion: the role of the applied linguist is to raise the con-
sciousness of the language teacher, to share as much as possible of
what contemporary linguists are finding, to pass on everything he
knows about language. While theoretical linguists of various positions,
conflicting or compatible, continue to develop their models of language, they are turning up valuable information on how language is

used and how it is structured. Teachers and learners know we have
not told them enough yet. Teachers are faced with inadequate textbooks, fragmentary analyses of language, and the demands of the
learners' everyday needs in the classroom. The applied linguist has
to be eclectic and opportunistic, to share everything he can find with
the language teachers. I submit that he will discover the new research
in semantics of particular significance to the newly stated goal of
second language learning, communicative competence.

2. Communication. Prominent in the second language teaching
profession today is the claim that the goal of linguistic competence in
language learning is inadequate. The restatement of the goal as the
acquisition of communicative competence as articulated by Sandra
Savignon has attained wide acceptance: linguistic competence:

> . . . may be defined as the mastery of the sound system and
> basic structural patterns of a language . . . Communicative
> competence may be defined as the ability to function in a
> truly communicative setting--that is, in a dynamic exchange
> in which linguistic competence must adapt itself to the total
> informational input, both linguistic and paralinguistic, of one
> or more interlocutors (1972:8).

The ability to discriminate and pronounce the sounds of a language,
and to produce grammatical sentences is not necessarily the same as
to initiate speaking and to interact in a social setting.
It is curious that at the same time that instructional programs and
learning activities are being developed to facilitate the goal of communicative competence, on all sides courses are appearing such as
'English for Business', 'Spanish for Medical Personnel', and the like,
all under the aegis of 'language for special purposes'. It seems to
imply that there has been something wrong with the 'purpose' of
standard second language courses. Perhaps the problem, in part,
has been the restricted goal of linguistic competence.
To deal with the question of the 'ability to function in a truly communicative setting', it is useful to consider the various social functions of talking. These have been identified as 'informational', conveying information, 'expressive', conveying feelings or attitudes,
'directive', influencing the behavior or attitudes of others, 'aesthetic',
creating an artistic effect, and 'phatic', talking to maintain social
bonds (Leech 1974:67-68). Learning materials and activities designed for mastery of the linguistic system may often neglect these
several social functions of talking. Practice of grammatical patterns
and rehearsal of conversations are just not the same as having to get
certain information across to a listener, meeting a need to express

one's psychic states, getting people to do specific things through speaking, or establishing social bonds through the games a society plays with its small talk.

It is also worth considering the process of first language acquisition in terms of the social functions of talking. Young children are impressively expressive and directive through intonational patterns and a most limited grammar and lexicon. It has been observed that when they first speak they imitate talking, not language. They seem to talk to learn. Rehearsal in the second language classroom is frequently practice of language rather than practice in talking. As a step toward authenticity in second language activities, Long suggests 'the organisation of the immediate learning environment so as to allow learners to adopt roles commonly associated with the communicative functions of language' (1975:219). Language learners need to have the opportunity to imitate the talking and the social interaction of their target culture. This clearly upgrades the teacher from the drillmaster function, even permits him to follow the advice of Postman and Weingartner in Teaching as a subversive activity: 'Prohibit teachers from asking any questions they already know the answers to' (1969:138).

3.0 Applied semantics. I have stated that semantic analysis often applies at the interface between linguistic and communicative competence. That is, certain semantic structures occur in concurrence with specific communicative functions.

3.1 Ser and estar. In applying Chafe's rules of semantic formation to Spanish copula sentences, I hoped to show that all occurrences of the Spanish copula forms ser and estar could be predicted in terms of the selectional and derivational features of the predicate in a clause. I found this to be true in all cases except one class of estar sentences (Aid 1973a; 1973b). Simple state predicates generate the ser copula in surface structure; experiential state predicates generate ser with Object nouns, estar with Experiencer nouns; locative state predicates generate estar; and all derived resultative predicates generate estar.

However, outside the regularity of this system, we find a use of estar that is situationally sensitive, independent of the selectional features of the predicate. This use of estar, although very frequent, is restricted by extralinguistic parameters. For example, if you are writing a geography book and are describing deserts, you may say in Spanish los desiertos son secos 'deserts are dry'. That is the way they are. But if you go to a desert and experience the dry winds, you are likely to say in Spanish el desierto está seco 'the desert is dry'. In the two sentences 'desert' means 'desert' and 'dry' means 'dry'. The predicate seco has the same selectional features in each case.

The difference lies in the purpose of the speaker's utterance: with the estar sentence the speaker is sharing his own perception rather than conveying a possible generalization. One produces this kind of sentence in reference to immediate experience, not in absentia.

Consider another example. If you are writing a guide to Spanish cuisine and are describing soups, say caldo gallego and gazpacho, one of which is served hot and the other cold, you might explain that caldo gallego es caliente and gazpacho es frío. Since both are delicious, you might recommend to your reader that las dos son muy buenas. But if you are served one of these soups you will respond to the experience remarking that está caliente, or está frío, or está muy bueno. Ordinarily a person responding to these sensations will comment with an estar sentence. However we formalize the ser/estar contrast in a semantic analysis, the choice of one or the other reflects a difference in communicative function. The speaker uses estar when reacting to experience of the thing described. (Compare English verbs that occur in a verb + adjective structure such as look, feel, taste, seem, smell, sound.)

The predicates seco, caliente, frío, and bueno are the same whether they occur with ser or estar, but the occurrence of the latter marks a difference in the communicative act. If the language learner is to acquire a communicative competence, if he is to be able to 'function . . . in a dynamic exchange in which linguistic competence must adapt itself to the total informational input', then we have to provide him with situations in which he has to react verbally. This is not the same as practicing patterns or rehearsing conversations in which other speakers' reactions are expressed. Rehearsal of talk is just not the same as immediate verbal response to experience.

3.2 Indirect objects. Investigation of the semantic formation of sentences through a dependency model such as Chafe's, wherein the verb is central and its selectional features determine the number of nouns in a clause as well as their semantic roles, or cases, puts an interesting light on the functions of indirect objects in Spanish sentences. We are not concerned in this instance with the morphological dative (le) that is required with certain verbs (gustar, faltar, parecer, etc.) but with the form when it occurs in a sentence that may also have a direct object.

If we observe the correspondence between semantic structures that certain verbs generate and their surface structure organization, we find that three general verb sets form sentences in which three nouns may occur, and often, therefore, sentences having syntactic structures with two objects. There are verbs of communication: tell, ask, warn, explain, answer, show; verbs of exchange: give, steal, accept, deliver, lend; and verbs of transport and placement: take,

move, bring, send, put, remove. With verbs of communication the
indirect object noun is the receiver of information; with verbs of exchange it is the gainer or loser in the transaction; with verbs of transport and placement it is the locative source or goal. The neat regularity of this system suggests some useful and practical implications
for second language vocabulary learning and the acquisition of lexical
competence (Aid 1974; Richards 1976).

Beyond the scope of the system in which the selectional features of
a verb account for the accompanying nouns, we find in Spanish pro-
lific use of what is morphologically and syntactically identified as the
indirect object, but which occurs in the sentence in accord with decisions of the speaker, independently of the dependency structure of
the verb. This indirect object may be categorized as a Beneficiary
noun of a higher predication. It refers to an entity that profits or
loses with respect to the event predicated in a lower proposition. It
is a device whereby a speaker can indicate that the events he relates
have in some way affected himself or the participants in his narration.
Sometimes these Beneficiary nouns occur in a hierarchy such that
the speaker may indicate the effect on himself as well as on the
participants in the event.

Consider an example. Ese bobo se me bebió media botella de ron
'the fool drank (himself) half a bottle of rum (on me)'. In this sentence the verb beber 'to drink' forms a semantic structure with Agent
and Object nouns. The 'involved' entities which surface as indirect
objects (one or two) are subject to the speaker's option. They are
proper to the expressive function of language. Practice of these linguistic structures makes little communicative sense unless the
speaker-learner is in fact expressing his own involvement, or that of
an observed participant, in the event. Although grammatically the
indirect object form is like the second object that is generated with
verbs of communication, exchange, and transport, its communicative
function is totally different. So, I submit, is its incorporation into
the learner's communicative competence (cf. Bull 1965; Lamadrid
et al. 1974).

3.3 Indicative and subjunctive. Semantic treatments of the subjunctive in Spanish point out yet another aspect of language teaching
in which authenticity in learning activities is important for the acquisition of a communicative competence (cf. Bolinger 1974; Terrell
and Hooper 1974). Bolinger asserts that the theory of performatives
in language is essential to the understanding of the indicative/sub-
junctive oppositions in the Romance languages. In Spanish, the
significance of the modes is semantic: 'they represent two ways of
looking at reality, one intellectual and the other attitudinal . . . the
performative theory puts a foundation under what we know intuitively'

(1974:469). According to Bolinger, the performative analysis supports the traditional treatment of the indicative mode as the mode of reporting, of conveying 'intelligence' about the real world. The performative is formalized in Spanish by means of the indicative mode, which makes it explicit that an utterance is intended to convey stored information. When the function of talking and the intent of a speech act is expressive, attitudinal, or directive, rather than only informative, Spanish formalizes the nonreporting function by means of the subjunctive mode, which signals that the utterance is not governed by 'I say to you' . . . but by an alternative posture of the speaker toward the hearer, e.g. 'I hypothesize . . . I doubt . . . I regret . . . I request'.

To internalize the indicative/subjunctive system it would appear that the student of Spanish needs an opportunity to perform different kinds of speech acts: to assert and inform; to direct and request; to hypothesize; to contradict or deny; to express various attitudes within contexts where these various functions of talking correspond with his own communicative needs, to psychological realities.

3.4 Tú and usted. The morphology of the Spanish second person pronoun system presents only moderate difficulty to the second language learner, and really does not profoundly challenge the ingenuity of the teacher. It is true, of course, that the system is more complex in Spanish than in English. There is the surface structure case system in which there are forms for the functions of subject, indirect object, direct object, reflexive object, and prepositional object. In addition, Spanish employs at least two different sets of forms, depending on the relationship between speaker and addressee, the familiar second person set and the formal second person set. The choice of form is subject to dialect variation. There are also plural forms, and among some forms gender distinctions. There is person-number agreement marked in corresponding verb suffixes. The speaker of English finds that his handy you corresponds to tú, te, ti, vos, vosotros, vosotras, os, usted, le, lo, la, ustedes, les, los, las, se, and sí.

Once prepared with this morphosyntactic apparatus, the learner must deal with the social networks in which the familiar/formal sets operate, a network that tends to vary considerably among Hispanic speech communities. Sociolinguistic descriptions of these networks, such as the studies underway among speakers in New York City and Mexico City (Keller 1974; 1975), represent research in social meaning that bears on the question of communicative competence.

The use of tú and usted in communicative situations may serve to assert, establish, maintain, or resist social relationships among participants in conversation. It appears that for communities where relatively rapid social change is taking place, for example, in some Hispanic communities in the United States, traditional textbook generalizations about the boundaries of familiar/formal usage are vastly inadequate. Nevertheless, it is precisely in these communities that the teaching of Spanish as a second language has the most immediate practical applications. The use of the language to establish social relationships will be a very important component of the learner's communicative competence.

Among Cuban Americans in South Florida, where the use of tú has a relatively wide scope in comparison to some other Hispanic groups, there is among young people a mixing of the two forms of address that may come as a surprise to the newcomer. To deal with the rules of speaking, one needs to know the social parameters of reciprocal and nonreciprocal usage of the second person forms (Keller 1975:85). In Miami, a speaker must also know that there is a regular mixed usage, specifically, the insertion of the conversation fillers tú sabes and tú entiendes 'you know' regardless of the familiar/formal relationship expressed in the context of conversation. For example, Profesora, usted puede (formal) prestarme el libro, tú sabes (familiar), el libro que me enseñó (formal) el otro día . . . Whether the purist wants to teach or participate in this usage or not, he had better be at least prepared to interpret it. And for the learner, communicative competence clearly involves more than linguistic proficiency in the morphosyntactic apparatus.

4. Conclusion. Much of today's linguistic research deals with meaning in language, in language structure and language use. The questions raised in the study of semantics frequently lead the linguist to consider a sentence in its discourse, and meaning in its communicative context. It appears that the meaning that leaks over the boundaries of a sentence is often a clue to the communicative function of an utterance. In turn, second language acquisition is seen to have as a goal not only linguistic competence, but communicative competence as well.

However, as Leech cautions, despite current rapid developments in semantics, 'we are still a very long way from turning the discipline from a would-be science into a science' (1974:361). The same must be said with regard to the study of language acquisition and language pedagogy. Nevertheless, while research continues, as new insights are shared, the applied linguist need not suspend activity to lament the conflicts and kinks in theoretical linguistics. He had better tell the language teachers everything he can about what language is, how it is acquired, how it functions in communication, so that the teachers can make effective decisions about methods and techniques. Hopefully, the point of view and the examples presented here will facilitate communicative competence in the talk between applied linguists and second language teachers.

REFERENCES

Aid, Frances M. 1973a. Semantic structures in Spanish: A proposal for instructional materials. Washington, D.C., Georgetown University Press.
_____. 1973b. The semantic formation of Spanish copula sentences. In: The University of Michigan Papers in Linguistics 1.2. Ann Arbor, University of Michigan Press.
_____. 1974. Semantic universals in instructional materials. TESOL Quarterly 8.53-64.
Applegate, Richard B. 1975. The language teacher and the rules of speaking. TESOL Quarterly 9.271-281.
Bolinger, Dwight. 1974. One subjunctive or two? Hispania 57.462-471.
Brown, H. D. 1975. The next 25 years: Shaping the revolution. In: New directions in second language learning, teaching, and bilingual education. Edited by Marina K. Burt and Heidi C. Dulay. Washington, D.C., Teachers of English to Speakers of Other Languages.
Bull, William E. 1961. A visual grammar of Spanish. Los Angeles, University of California.
_____. 1965. Spanish for teachers. New York, The Ronald Press.
Chafe, Wallace L. 1970. Meaning and the structure of language. Chicago, The University of Chicago Press.
Grimshaw, Allen D. 1973. Rules, social interaction, and language behavior. TESOL Quarterly 7.99-115.
Hymes, Dell. 1967. Models of interaction of language and social setting. Journal of Social Issues 23.8-28.
_____. 1974. Foundations in sociolinguistics. Philadelphia, University of Pennsylvania Press.
Keller, Gary D. 1974. La norma de solidaridad y la de poder en los pronombres de tratamiento: Un bosquejo diacrónico y una investigación del español de Nueva York. The bilingual review/La revista bilingue 1.42-58.
_____. 1975. Spanish tú and usted: Patterns of interachange. In: 1974 colloquium on Spanish and Portuguese linguistics. Edited by William G. Milan, John J. Staczek, and Juan C. Zamora. Washington, D.C., Georgetown University Press.
Lakoff, Robin. 1975. Linguistic theory and the real world. Language Learning 25.309-338.
Lamadrid, Enrique, William E. Bull, and Laurel A. Briscoe. 1974. Communicating in Spanish. Boston, Houghton Mifflin Company.

Leech, Geoffrey. 1974. Semantics. Baltimore, Penguin Books.
Lehrer, Adrienne. 1975. Talking about wine. Lg. 51-901-923.
Long, Michael H. 1975. Group work and communicative competence in the ESOL classroom. In: New directions in second language learning, teaching and bilingual education. Edited by Marina K. Burt and Heidi C. Dulay. Washington, D.C., Teachers of English to Speakers of Other Languages.
Paulston, Christina Pratt. 1974. Linguistic and communicative competence. TESOL Quarterly 8. 347-362.
Postman, Neil and Charles Weingartner. 1969. Teaching as a subversive activity. New York, Dell Publishing Company.
Richards, Jack C. 1976. The role of vocabulary teaching. TESOL Quarterly 10.19-32.
Rivers, Wilga, Milton M. Azevedo, William H. Heflin, Jr., and Ruth Hyman-Opler. 1976. A practical guide to the teaching of Spanish. New York, Oxford University Press.
Savignon, Sandra. 1972. Communicative competence: An experiment in foreign-language teaching. Philadelphia, Center for Curriculum Development.
_____. 1974. Talking with my son: An example of communicative competence. In: Careers, communication, and culture in foreign language teaching. Edited by Frank Grittner. Skokie, Illinois, National Textbook Company.
Tarone, Elaine, Merrill Swain, and Ann Fathman. 1976. Some limitations to the classroom applications of current second language acquisition research. TESOL Quarterly 10.19-32.
Terrell, Tracy and Joan Hooper. 1974. A semantically based analysis of mood in Spanish. Hispania 57.484-494.
Valdman, Albert, ed. 1966. Trends in language teaching. New York, McGraw-Hill.
_____. 1974. Grammar and the American foreign language teacher. In: Student motivation and the foreign language teacher. Edited by Frank Grittner. Skokie, Illinois, National Textbook Company.

THEMATIC MEANING, WORD ORDER, AND INDEFINITE ACTOR SENTENCES IN PORTUGUESE

MILTON M. AZEVEDO

University of California, Berkeley

Abstract. In Portuguese, the sequence of surface elements NP_1 VP NP_2 parallels both the unmarked linearization of participant roles (that is, actor-(verb)-goal) and the least marked distribution of communicative dynamism (that is, theme-transition-rheme). This parallelism of participant roles and thematic meaning accounts for the tendency speakers have to interpret the surface sequence NP_1 VP NP_2 as standing for the sequence of syntactic functions subject-(VP)-direct object, in which the actor/subject is thematic and the verb and the goal/direct object are rhematic.

A semantic actor specified as [indefinite] is ipso facto thematic and carries a very small degree of communicative dynamism, and a semantic configuration containing such an actor may be actualized in the surface structure as a sentence in which the actor is represented by the indefinite pronoun se. Two surface patterns are possible, namely, (a) NP_{goal} VP + se and (b) VP + se NP_{goal}. Since the general tendency of the language is for the element containing the highest degree of communicative dynamism to be placed at the end of the sentence, where it will receive sentence stress to indicate its rhematic status, the choice between patterns (a) and (b) depends, theoretically, on the relative distribution of communicative dynamism between VP and NP_{goal}. In other words, VP is rhematic in (a) and thematic in (b).

If pattern (a) is chosen, however, the preposed NP will tend to be interpreted as the subject, by virtue of homonymy with a sentence expressing either a reflexive action or a reciprocal one. The conflict

217

between these unintended interpretations and the requirement that the rhematic verb be placed at the end of the sentence can be solved by means of the substitution of an agentless passive for the sentence with the indefinite pronoun se, whenever such ambiguity is likely to occur. Consequently, these two sentence types are in partial complementary distribution and should not be presented as being functionally interchangeable in all cases, as is commonly done in Portuguese textbooks.

One of the general conclusions that can be drawn from what has been said at these meetings is that the relationships between semantics and language instruction are varied and susceptible of being studied from several different angles. If approached from the point of view of applied linguistics, that study can be regarded as a powerful means of identifying and explaining target language problems which, for one reason or another, pose special difficulties to learners.

Identification and explanation of troublesome learning points are of course only part of the task of the applied linguist, who must also utilize his findings in the formulation of teaching procedures, which include both classroom techniques and the preparation of pedagogical grammars for teachers and designers of instructional materials. [1] The present paper may be regarded as a research report preparatory to the organization of one such pedagogical grammar, although not as one intended to describe or even suggest specific teaching techniques or exercises.

A great deal of recent research carried out under different frameworks has contributed to clarify the forms of the rules and the characteristics of the processes whereby surface patterns are derived from deep structures. However, the question of motivation of the language user's choice among alternative surface arrangements has received less attention than it seems to deserve. It is reasonable to think that, if we are interested in language as a process of communication, the relationships between apparently equivalent surface sequences and the semantic encoding of linguistic messages ought to be studied just as carefully as problems concerning the generation of sentences.

This paper is intended to explore, from a semantic point of view, the relationships between thematic meaning and word order in Portuguese with regard to two types of sentences. One of these is analyzed as containing a transitive verb associated with a goal noun forming a semantic configuration that is realized in the surface structure as an agentless passive. The other contains, besides a transitive verb and a goal noun, a semantic actor which, because of its rather unique semantic specifications, is represented in the surface structure by the unstressed third person pronoun se, which indicates that the semantic actor is indefinite or indeterminate. For brevity's sake, constructions of the latter type will be referred to as 'indefinite se sentences'.

The approach adopted in this study takes into account three levels of language structure. [2] The syntactical level has to do with grammatical functions such as subject, object, agent of the passive, etc., as well as with the relationships that obtain among these functions. Word order rules and other syntactic restrictions operate at this level. The level of semantic relations involves the organization of matrices of features such as [human] and [animate], as well as the organization of semantic configurations involving participant functions such as actor, goal, beneficiary, and so on. The third level has to do with thematic meaning, recently defined by Leech as being 'what is communicated by the way in which the message is organized in terms of order and emphasis' (1974:26). The relationships that concern us at this level are directly linked to the relative degree of informativeness of each sentence element, and to the possibilities of linearization of semantic material that are reflected in different patterns of word order in the surface structure.

Thematic meaning has to do with the relative importance of each sentence element for the intended message as a whole. Although contemporary work in semantics has been concerned mainly with conceptual meaning, a few linguists have given some attention to thematic meaning as well. One may cite, for example, the brief treatment of it by Leech (1974), as well as Chafe's (1970) analysis of the relationships between new and old information and word order. Some of the most fruitful work on thematic meaning, however, has been carried out by members of the Prague school of linguistics such as Mathesius, Daneš, Firbas, and Vachek, to whose research we owe the two allied concepts utilized in this study, namely 'communicative dynamism' (CD) and 'functional sentence perspective' (FSP).

By FSP is meant a general principle which controls the linearization of sentence elements according to their degree of CD, a variable characterized by Firbas as 'the extent to which the sentence element contributes to the development of the communication, to which it "pushes the communication forward", as it were' (1966b:270). According to this view, sentence elements are distributed, depending on their relative degree of CD, among three general areas, namely the theme, the transition, and the rheme. As regards the theme, it should be pointed out that, although Mathesius 'defines the theme as "that which is known or at least obvious in the given situation"' (Firbas 1966b:268), its main characteristic lies in the fact that its elements, whether containing new or old information, carry 'the lowest degree of CD within the sentence' (Firbas 1966b:272). Thematic elements set up a frame of reference which serves as background for displaying the new information contained in the rheme, which is defined as 'that which the speaker states about, or in regard to, the theme' (Mathesius, apud Firbas 1966b:277). This means that the rheme includes what is predicated about the theme; rhematic elements have the highest degree of CD in the sentence and thus constitute the very core of the message.

The principle of FSP allows us to classify the semantic elements of a sentence along a continuum ranging from theme to rheme, that is, from less important, or subsidiary information to more important or new information. [3]

Application of the concept of FSP requires that sentences be considered as inserted in a discourse rather than in isolation. It is not possible to decide about the relative CD of the elements of isolated sentences, for the same surface structure may carry different arrangements of FSP according to how a given sentence fits into its discourse context. For instance, the elements of a sentence like (1) may be analyzed in different ways, depending on the context defined by a preceding question. For example:

(1) Answer: A minha filha casou
           'My daughter got married.'
(2) Question: E a sua filha?
           'And what about your daughter?'
(1a) A: theme = a minha filha   [-new]
     rheme = casou   [+new]
(3) Q: E que é que a sua filha fez?
     'And what did your daughter do?'
(1b) A: theme = a minha filha   [-new]
            PAST   [-new]
            PERFECTIVE   [-new]
     rheme = casar   [+new]
(4) Q: Por que você está tão triste?
     'Why are you so sad?'
(1c) A: theme = a minha filha   [+new]
     rheme = casou   [+new]

In answer (1c), though both the theme and the rheme carry new information, the latter has a higher degree of CD.

The basic requirement of the principle of FSP is that sentence elements be arranged in an order of increasing CD. [4] In general terms, this means that sentence material is usually arranged in a theme-rheme sequence. However, the final patterning of a sentence is not determined by FSP alone, but rather by the interplay of constraints operating at each of the three levels of sentence structure mentioned above. The actual organization of an utterance also depends on language specific rules of word order and grammatical function.

In the remainder of this paper we shall analyze some of the means whereby the linearization of sentence elements in Portuguese accommodates the distribution of CD in which rhematic elements follow thematic ones.

Marked and unmarked sentences

The unmarkedness of the sequence subject-verb-object (S-V-O) is suggested by the fact that, ceteris paribus, speakers of Portuguese tend to interpret the first NP of a sentence following the pattern

(5) NP_1 VP NP_2

both as functioning as the subject and as containing the semantic actor of the sentence, as for example in (6) and (7). The second NP, in turn, is normally interpreted as functioning as the direct object and as containing the semantic goal. This tendency accounts for the semantic oddness of sentence (8), which only in special registers (see below) might be considered as conceptually synonymous with (6). It also accounts for the fact that sentence (9) is perceived as syntactically anomalous, due to the lack of agreement between the verb and the first NP.

(6) O canibal devorou o missionário.
    'The cannibal devoured the missionary.'
(7) Os canibais devoraram o missionário.
    'The cannibals devoured the missionary.'
(8) O missionário devorou o canibal.
    '? The missionary devoured the cannibal;' 'The cannibal devoured the missionary.' (in special registers)
(9) ? O missionário devoraram os canibais.
    'The cannibals devoured the missionary.' (only in special registers)

This tendency is even more noticeable in sentences in which one of the NP's is an inanimate noun, as in examples (10) through (13). Whereas the first two offer no difficulty of interpretation, sentence (12), if interpretable at all, would receive a figurative meaning--for example, something like 'that house ruined my father'. Sentence (13), however, strikes one as semantically ill-formed, for the verb construir 'to build' requires an animate actor, whereas casa 'house' is inanimate.

(10) Meu pai destruiu aquela casa.
'My father destroyed that house.'
(11) Meu pai construiu aquela casa.
'My father built that house.'
(12) ?Aquela casa destruiu meu pai.
'?That house destroyed my father.'
(13) ?Aquela casa construiu meu pai.
'?That house built my father.'

The sequence O-V-S does occur in Portuguese, but it is usually
restricted to special registers (such as emphatic speech, poetry, and
oratory), and special devices are often used to signal the syntactic
status of the first NP. For example, in sentences (14) and (15) the
direct object is introduced by the preposition a, and in sentences
(16) and (17) it is signalled by the presence of the redundant unstressed pronoun o ~ no 'him'.

(14) Ao missionário devorou o canibal.
'prep + the missionary [goal] + devoured [sg] + the cannibal
[actor]'
(15) Ao missionário devoraram os canibais.
'prep + missionary [goal] + devoured [pl] + the cannibals
[actor]'
(16) O missionário, devorou-o o canibal.
'the missionary, devoured [sg] + him + the cannibal
[actor]'
(17) O missionário, devoraram-no os canibais.
'the missionary, devoured [pl] + him + the cannibals
[actor]'

Another possible variation in word order consists in using the
sequence O-S-V, with or without a redundant object pronoun, as in
examples (18) through (20).

(18) Aquela casa, o meu pai construiu.
'That house, my father built [it].'
(19) Aquela casa, o meu pai a construiu.
'That house, my father + it + built'
(20) Aquela casa, o meu pai construiu ela[5]
'That house, my father built it.'

These are marked patterns--marked for emphasis, if you will--
in which the thematic goal/direct object is shifted to the beginning of
the sentence so that the elements carrying more CD may appear in
the rhematic position. The goal/direct object is thus announced to

the hearer as being what the message is all about; and it is worth
noticing that it is usually set off from the rhematic elements by
means of a pause, which may be indicated by a comma in ordinary
writing, as in examples (16) through (20).

The preceding analysis confirms the view that in unmarked styles
the pattern NP$_1$ VP NP$_2$ is decoded as signalling the sequence S-V-O.
If NP$_2$ is null, the pattern NP V is interpreted as representing the
sequence S-V, a tendency which, as we shall see, has several consequences for the distribution of agentless passives and indefinite se
sentences.

Indefinite actors

Let us now consider sentences (21) through (23), the first of which
involves the indefinite se whereas the other two are agentless passives.
They exemplify sentence types derived from similar but not identical
semantic configurations, like those shown in diagrams (24) and (25).

(21) Estudou-se a lição.
'studied [3d p. sg., + past] + [+pro, +indef, +hum] + the
lesson'
(22) A lição foi estudada.
'The lesson was studied.'
(23) Os ovos foram botados.
'The eggs were laid.'

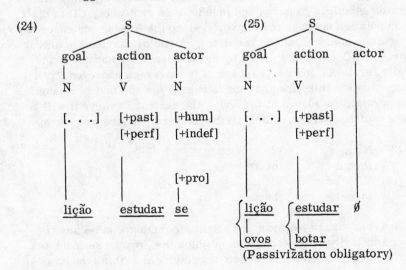

(Passivization obligatory)

The basic difference between these two configurations is the
feature [+human] which appears in the specification of the actor in

diagram (24). This feature requires that the verb be specified as
[+human], a requirement which accounts for the fact that sentence
(23) has no counterpart with the indefinite se. Thus, example (26)
is semantically anomalous and grammatically ill-formed because it
breaks that restriction by associating a non-human action such as
botar ovos 'to lay eggs' with the human actor implicitly signalled by
the indefinite se. [6] However, as long as actions considered specifically non-human are not involved, the two sentence types are
semantically equivalent, insofar as conceptual meaning is concerned,
and thus they may be used interchangeably.

(26) *Botaram-se os ovos.
      'laid [3d p. pl, +past] + [+pro, +hum, +indef] + the eggs'

Word order and thematic meaning

To recapitulate: the sequence S-V-O corresponds to the least
marked distribution of CD, that in which the actor/subject is thematic and the goal/object is rhematic. [7] If, however, a different
distribution of CD obtains at the semantic level of thematic meaning,
it may be reflected in the surface structure by means of other syntactic arrangements, the purpose of which is to place the rhematic
element in a position where the stress of the noun will coincide with
sentence stress. If the actor is rhematic, it may be placed at the
end of the sentence by means of the passive transformation. [8] As
regards agentless passives and indefinite se sentences, CD is distributed between the goal and the verb, since the former sentences have
no actor to speak of; and in the latter, the actor carries the lowest
degree of CD, as is suggested by the fact that its identification is
totally irrelevant for the purposes of the message conveyed. [9] Of
those two elements, the goal and the verb, the one that is rhematic
will normally be placed at the end of the sentence, where it will receive sentence stress. The possible surface patterns are, then,

(27) NP$_{goal}$ VP   + se
      theme   rheme
(28) VP + se   NP$_{goal}$
      theme   rheme

However, these patterns are potentially ambiguous because of
their similarity to constructions in which the pronoun se indicates
that the action is either reflexive or reciprocal. This type of ambiguity is less likely to exist in sentences patterned after (27), such
as examples (29) through (30), than in those patterned after (28), such
as (31) through (32). The reason for this is that in the former

sentences the NP is interpreted, by virtue of its position, as being the subject, and consequently the pronoun se tends to be interpreted either as reflexive (29) or as alternatively reflexive or reciprocal (30).

(29) O prisioneiro enforcou-se.
   'The prisoner hanged himself.'
(30) Os prisioneiros libertaram-se.
   'The prisoners freed themselves/each other/one another.'
(31) Enforcou-se o prisioneiro.
   (a) 'The prisoner hanged himself.'
   (b) 'hanged [3d p. sg., +past] + [+pro, +hum, +indef] +
      the prisoner'
(32) Libertaram-se os prisioneiros.
   (a) 'The prisoners freed themselves/each other/one another.'
   (b) 'freed [3d p. sg., +past] + [+pro, +hum, +indef] +
      the prisoners'

In sentences like (31) and (32), by virtue of not being in the normal subject position, the noun phrase may be interpreted either as a rhematic actor (31a, 32a) or as a rhematic goal (31b, 32b).

There are several ways of avoiding this type of ambiguity. One of them, which is extremely widespread in spoken Brazilian Portuguese, consists in assigning to the NP in (31b) and (32b) the function of direct object, rather than subject, as required by normative grammar rules, thus making it possible for the verb to remain in the singular even when that noun phrase is in the plural, as in (33):[10]

(33) Libertou-se os prisioneiros.
   'freed [3d p. sg., +past] + [+pro, +hum, +indef] + the
   prisoners'

Reflexivity

The verbs used in our examples of se sentences so far share a semantic characteristic represented by the feature [+reflex], whose effect in the semantic characterization of a verb consists in making it potentially reflexive; or more precisely, if you will forgive the neologism, reflexizable. If we use a [-reflex] verb in a reflexive construction, the result will be an anomalous sentence like those of examples (34) and (35). Other verbs that are essentially [-reflex] are massacrar 'to massacre', fuzilar 'to execute (by a firing squad)', aprisionar 'to take prisoner', assassinar 'to murder', and so on.[11]

(34) O escravo indultou-se.
      'The slave granted himself a pardon.'
(35) A menina raptou-se.
      'The girl kidnaped herself.'

Since the reflexive interpretation of these verbs is restricted, there is a tendency to avoid using them in sentences with pattern (27), unless, of course, the NP is in the plural and a reciprocal action is meant. Otherwise, the only interpretation that can be attributed to sentences like (34) and (35) is that involving an indefinite se; but this reading clashes with the fact that the word order in these cases parallels that of the unmarked sequence S-V-O. An alternative would consist in using pattern (28), thus having:[12]

(36) Indultou-se o escravo.
      'granted [3d p. sg., +past] a pardon + [+pro, + hum, +indef] + (to) the slave'
(37) Raptou-se a menina.
      'kidnaped [3d p. sg., +past] + [+pro, +hum, +indef] + the girl'

TABLE 1. Distribution of features in agentless passives and indefinite se sentences.

			verb			
			rhematic		thematic	
			+refl	-refl	+refl	-refl
goal	+anim	sg.	1	5	9	13
		pl.	2	6	10	14
	-anim	sg.	3	7	11	15
		pl.	4	8	12	16

(Numbers refer to examples in Table 2)

This solution, however, may not be satisfactory if the verb is rhematic; for in this case the distribution of CD would have to be indicated by displacing the sentence stress away from its normal, unmarked position on the last word of the sentence, so as to have it coincide with the stressed syllable of the verb. This is a possibility, but there is always the danger that the resulting sentence may sound contrastive when this is not the speaker's intention.[13]

We see, then, that there are several restrictions that limit the use of the indefinite se. Some of the grammatically possible patterns tend to be avoided, for reasons having to do either with the feature [-reflex] or with the possibility of undesirable synonymy with reflexive or reciprocal homonymous sentences. As a result, some functional gaps

TABLE 2. Correlations between agentless passive and indefinite se sentences.

Examples	Semantic interpretation	Passive equivalents
X (1) O soldado matou-se. X (2) Os soldados mataram-se.	Reflexive (also reciprocal in #2) interpretation imposed by word order bars the indefinite se interpretation.	(1) O soldado foi morto. (2) Os soldados foram mortos.
X (3) Este livro se vende facilmente. X (4) Estes livros se vendem facilmente.	Indefinite se interpretation masked by figurative reflexive interpretation.	(3) Este livro é vendido facilmente. (4) Estes livros são vendidos facilmente.
X (5) O escravo indultou-se. X (6) Os escravos indultaram-se.	'? The slave granted himself a pardon.' '? The slaves granted themselves a pardon.'	(5) O escravo foi indultado. (6) Os escravos foram indultados.
X (7) O comboio tocaiou-se. X (8) Os comboios tocaiaram-se.	'? The convoy ambushed itself.' '? The convoys ambushed themselves.'	(7) O comboio foi tocaiado. (8) Os comboios foram tocaiados.
(9) Matou-se o soldado. (10) Mataram-se os soldados.	Indefinite se and reflexive (also reciprocal in #10) interpretations possible; passives serve to disambiguate.	(9) O soldado foi morto. (10) Os soldados foram mortos.
(11) Vendeu-se o livro. (12) Venderam-se os livros. (13) Indultou-se o escravo. (14) Indultaram-se os escravos. (15) Tocaiou-se o comboio. (16) Tocaiaram-se os comboios.	Indefinite se in all cases.	(11) O livro foi vendido. (12) Os livros foram vendidos. (13) O escravo foi indultar. (14) Os escravos foram indultados. (15) O comboio foi tocaiado. (16) Os comboios foram tocaiados.

are created in the list of theoretically possible patterns shown in Table 2, where the gaps are indicated by the letter X.

These gaps occur precisely in the cases in which the verb is rhematic, that is, when it carries more CD than the associated NP. A solution for this difficulty is provided by the use of agentless passives instead of the less than adequate indefinite se sentences. In all other cases, there is total equivalence in FSP between the two sentence types, which may be used interchangeably.

The severest restriction to the use of the indefinite se results from the conflict between the features [rhematic] and [-reflex], especially if the goal noun is [-anim], as in examples (7) and (8), Table 2. A sentence like O comboio tocaiou-se 'the convoy ambushed [3d p., sg., +past] + se' is very difficult to interpret as an indefinite actor sentence because of the order of its elements, and it evidently has no possible reflexive interpretation. If the goal is [+anim], as in examples (5) and (6) in Table 2, we have the same problem as regards actor indefiniteness and the reflexive and reciprocal readings involve semantic contradictions.

A lesser restriction exists in the case of [+reflex] verbs associated with inanimate goals. In this case, there is a conflict between the reflexive interpretation suggested by the sequence (27) and the semantic impossibility of having an inanimate noun perform an action upon itself. This conflict can only be solved by means of a figurative interpretation of the action, and this is exactly how sentences such as (3) and (4) in Table 2 and (38) and (39) below are interpreted:

(38) Este livro se vende facilmente.
  'This book sells itself (i.e. is sold) easily.'
(39) Estes livros se vendum facilmente.
  'These books sell themselves (i.e. are sold) easily.'

Finally, if the verb is both [+reflex] and [+rhematic] and the goal noun is [+anim], as in cases (1) and (2) in Table 2, the unwanted reflexive interpretation is avoided by using an agentless passive instead of pattern (27).

It appears, then, that agentless passives and indefinite se sentences are in partial complementary distribution, that is, they are functionally equivalent in some cases but not in others, at least insofar as the unmarked distribution of CD and the unmarked (that is, non-contrastive) placement of sentence stress are concerned.

Conclusion

The analysis I have presented shows that there is no reason to think of indefinite se sentences as involving a special use of a reflexive pronoun, for there is nothing reflexive about these constructions. The essential condition for reflexivity is the co-occurrence of two identical NP's in the semantic roles of actor and goal, respectively-- a condition which is not fulfilled in the semantic representations of indefinite se sentences. For similar reasons, it is descriptively inappropriate to refer to the latter as a kind of passive, for passivization is a grammatical rather than semantic concept which has to do solely with the occurrence in the surface structure of the auxiliary ser 'to be' in association with the past participle of an action verb.

The fact that two sentence types may often be used interchangeably does not mean that they are equivalent syntactically. Indefinite se sentences constitute a unique type of constructions with well-defined semantic and syntactic characteristics, and any attempt to regard them as variants of other sentence types can only serve to complicate the description of the language.

This analysis also provides a formal basis for the intuitively correct view that the pronoun se has exactly the same function in sentences like (40) through (43) as in those generated by the semantic structure represented in diagram (24). This means that there is no reason to assign different interpretations to the function of se in otherwise identical sentences such as (42) and (43), which differ from each other only in that the former, but not the latter, has a goal noun in its semantic structure. 14 The verb in the latter is of course intransitive.

(40) Trabalha-se muito aqui.
     'One works a lot here.'
(41) Vive-se bem nessa terra.
     'One lives well in that land.'
(42) Aqui estuda-se.
     'Here one studies.'
(43) Aqui estuda-se grego.
     'Here one studies Greek.'

As regards pedagogical applications, this analysis provides the theoretical justification necessary for teaching indefinite se sentences as a separate type of construction, rather than in terms of either reflexive or passive counterparts. Once both se sentences and agentless passives have been mastered by the learners, the next step should involve teaching their distribution in the language. As regards this, clarification of the relationships of partial complementary distribution that exist between the two sentence types would contribute to make the learners aware of the role of word order in the distribution of thematic meaning and as a means for avoiding the potential ambiguity created by the existence of homonymous surface patterns.

Post scriptum

One of the drawbacks (or advantages--it is all a matter of point of view) of working with Portuguese is that one often duplicates parts of analyses worked out for other Romance languages, particularly for Spanish. The present paper is no exception to the rule, for it owes a good deal to Lozano's (1970) lucid study of the indefinite se in Spanish. Lozano's framework is basically the standard theory of transformational grammar and has therefore a syntactic orientation; nevertheless, he states, about the features animate/nonanimate and human/nonhuman, that 'although this may appear to be a semantic classification, it has syntactic consequences' (1970:452). This remark seems to suggest that a purely syntactic analysis is not powerful enough to unravel the problem. Part of Lozano's solution consisted in assigning to se the function of subject;[15] in turn, the semantic goal was seen as being 'realized as a pseudo-subject in the surface structure' (p. 454), hence the agreement between this element and the verb.

In a recent application of Chafe's (1970) model to Spanish, Aid (1973) develops a general analysis which explains indefinite se sentences in Spanish in terms of a rule called 'se focus', which is defined as 'an obligatory deep structure inflection for verbs that undergo a Decausative derivation. Its function is to mark a verb root that normally requires a causative relation as having to do with a Process going on without reference to any cause' (Aid 1973:89). Verb agreement with the semantic goal (or 'semantic object', in Aid's terminology) is described as a matter of 'surface form only' (p. 81).

With minor modifications, both Lozano's and Aid's analyses may be applied to Portuguese with results consistent with the premises inherent in their theoretical frameworks. Some of the conclusions that necessarily follow from this application, however, I find less than satisfactory as regards the semantic characterization and the syntactic function of se.

If we accept that se is the surface subject, we are faced with what would be the only case of a morphological unstressed pronoun functioning as such. While this solution is by no means absurd, it would add to the description of Portuguese an exception which, for the sake of descriptive elegance if for nothing else, had better be avoided.

As regards grammatical function, Aid's interpretation of <u>se</u> as a subject substitute[16] seems more adequate. The same cannot be said, however, of her contention that the occurrences of <u>se</u> 'in these sentences do not function as pronouns, as there is no noun in the semantic structure to which they correspond' (Aid 1973:81). I think that it is both possible and desirable to postulate an actor noun in the semantic structure of these sentences, as indicated in diagram (24), for it is undeniable that there is an actor in these constructions, and actors in Portuguese, as well as Spanish, are usually nouns or pronouns. That noun, however, is incompletely specified semantically, and because of this it is obligatorily marked as [+pro] and realized in the surface structure as a pronoun.

If <u>se</u> is not the true subject and the goal noun surfaces as a pseudo-subject, the inevitable conclusion is that indefinite <u>se</u> sentences have no subject. This interpretation would not be possible in the framework of standard transformational grammar, in which a rule like S⟶NP VP necessarily generates the partial structure (44),

(44)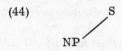

which defines the function of subject.[17] In the approach followed in the present study, however, there is no absolute requirement to the effect that an actor must be accounted for in the deep structure of every sentence, even when it has no surface manifestation.[18] My position on this matter is that the syntactic function of the pronoun <u>se</u> consists simply in indicating that the actor is indefinite; <u>se</u> is, if you will, a subject substitute, but it alternates in this function with the other pseudo-subject, that is, the semantic goal. The majority of sentence types of Portuguese do have a subject, speakers vacillate in their interpretation of which surface element should be assigned that function. When the goal is regarded as such, the agreement rule that produces sentences like (32) is applied automatically; when the goal is interpreted as an object, the function of subject is assigned to <u>se</u>, the agreement rule does not apply because <u>se</u> is not marked for plural, and a sentence like (33) results.

NOTES

1. For a characterization of the role of applied linguistics in foreign language instruction, see Politzer (1972).
2. The elements necessary for the characterization of this view of language can be found in works by Chafe (1970), Daneš (1966), and Halliday (1970).

3. Thematic and rhematic elements are joined by transitional ones, which according to Firbas 'rank above theme . . . and below rheme' (1965:170) as regards their degree of CD. The characterization of these elements is not a simple matter, and since it is not essential to the present study, the examples given here will be analyzed in terms of theme and rheme only. On the characterization of transition in FSP, see Firbas (1959); a discussion of problems of transition in relation to verbal tense may be found in Firbas (1965); on non-thematic subjects, see Firbas (1966a).

4. Firbas attributes this requirement to 'the character of human thought and . . . the linear character of the sentence' (1964:115).

5. The use of the third person subject pronouns ele (-s), ela (-s) in the function of direct object is extremely common in colloquial Brazilian Portuguese.

6. The indefinite se may be used with typically non-human actions if a figurative meaning is intended, but this is the exception that confirms the rule. For example, the humor of a sentence like Pasta-se muito bem no restaurante universitário 'one grazes very well at the university restaurant' is created precisely by the clash between se and the non-human action expressed by the verb.

7. A similar situation obtains in English: 'In what may be called the "least marked" instances, a surface structure subject carries the old information of a sentence' (Chafe 1970:212).

8. For an explanation of this function of the passive transformation in English, see Chafe (1970:219f). The sequence

$$\text{goal}^{NP}\text{subj} \quad VP_{pas} \quad \text{prep} + \text{act}^{NP}\text{agent}$$

is the unmarked passive pattern in Portuguese. Word order rules allow several variations of this sequence, as shown by Azevedo (1973).

9. This is a simplification, for we are not taking into account the possibility of other elements (such as adverbials) being present.

10. This is Rodrigues Lapa's interpretation. In his excellent analysis of the problem, he states, regarding this ambiguity, that 'there was some confusion, which the language managed to avoid in a simple way: instead of making the verb plural, as determined by the [grammar] rules, it made it singular, as if it were an impersonal verb . . . the reflexive pronoun [i. e. se] was considered equivalent to an indefinite pronoun such as alguém 'someone', uma pessoa 'a person'. This is an ingenious device which does not go against the spirit of the language . . . however, this construction, used in the popular language, is not accepted by grammarians . . .' (Rodrigues Lapa 1970:146, translated by M. M. A.). Another very insightful traditional analysis of the problem may be found in Said Ali (1966).

11. The distinction between [+reflex] and [-reflex] verbs does not always hold in figurative language. Thus, <u>ele se massacrou ao barbear-se</u> 'he massacred himself while shaving' is perfectly well formed, as is also <u>o escravo indultou-se por seu bom comportamento</u> 'the slave granted himself an indult for his good behavior', meaning something like 'the slave managed to get himself an indult on account of his good behavior'.

12. As in the case of examples (21), (26), (31b), (32b), and (33), so also in (34) and (35), I have glossed sentences with the indefinite <u>se</u> in the most literal way possible in order to emphasize relevant semantic and grammatical features. If those glosses were intended to indicate equivalent constructions in English, sentences with the indefinite pronoun <u>one</u> might have been used. Thus, for (36) we would have 'one granted the slave a pardon', and so on in the other cases.

13. This type of contrast may be illustrated by the sentences <u>RAPTOU-se a menina</u> vs. <u>RESGATOU-se a menina</u>, i.e. 'The girl was KIDNAPED' vs. 'The girl was RESCUED'. (Capitals indicate contrastive stress, which coincides with sentence stress.)

14. Some traditional grammarians characterize sentences like (40) through (43) as being all passives (Pereira n. d.:320-21; Bueno 1944:382-83). Others make a distinction between the use of <u>se</u> as a passivizing element, variously called a 'pronoun' or a 'particle', as in (43), or as a marker of subject indeterminacy, as in the other three examples (Almeida 1967:204-05; Brandão 1963:315-19). A few deny that <u>se</u> has a passivizing function and characterize it as a marker of subject indeterminacy in both cases (Lacerda 1966:77-78; Said Ali 1966:89-91).

15. 'We conclude that the indefinite <u>se</u> as distinct from the reflexive <u>se</u> is a subject' (Lozano 1970:454).

16. The relevant rule of subject selection in this case would be (Aid 1973:107):

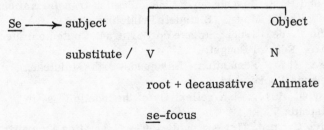

17. Cf. Jacobs and Rosenbaum (1968), Chapter 10.

18. In this view, therefore, there is no need to postulate a dummy deep structure actor for impersonal verbs that refer to atmospheric phenomena such as <u>chover</u> 'to rain', <u>trovejar</u> 'to thunder', and the like.

REFERENCES

Aid, Frances M. 1973. Semantic structures in Spanish: A proposal for instructional materials. Washington, D.C., Georgetown University Press.

Almeida, Napoleão Mendes de. 1967. Gramática Metódica de Língua Portuguêsa. São Paulo, Edição Saraiva.

Azevedo, Milton M. 1973. On passive sentences in English and Portuguese. (Dissertation Series, No. 54). Ithaca, N.Y., Cornell University Latin American Studies Program.

Brandão, Cláudio. 1963. Sintaxe Clássica Portuguêsa. Belo Horizonte, Imprensa da Universidade de Minas Gerais.

Bueno, Francisco da Silveira. 1944. Gramática Normativa da Língua Portuguêsa, Curso Superior. São Paulo, Edição Saraiva.

Chafe, Wallace L. 1970. Meaning and the structure of language. Chicago, The University of Chicago Press.

Daneš, František. 1966. A three-level approach to syntax. Travaux Linguistiques de Prague 1.225-240.

Firbas, Jan. 1959. Thoughts on the communicative functions of the verb in English, German, and Czech. Brno Studies in English 1.39-63.

_____. 1964. From comparative word order studies. Brno Studies in English 4.111-126.

_____. 1965. A note on transition proper in functional sentence analysis. Philologica Pragensia 8.170-176.

_____. 1966a. Non-thematic subjects in contemporary English. Travaux Linguistiques de Prague 2.239-256.

_____. 1966b. On defining the theme in functional sentence analysis. Travaux Linguistiques de Prague 1.267-280.

Halliday, M. A. K. 1970. Language structure in language function. In: New horizons in linguistics. Ed. by John Lyons. Harmondsworth (Middlesex), England, Penguin Books, Ltd.

Jacobs, R. A. and P. S. Rosenbaum. 1968. English transformational grammar. Waltham, Mass., Blaisdell Publishing Co.

Lacerda, Eulício F. de. 1966. Sintaxe do Português Contemporâneo. Rio de Janeiro, Editora Pongetti.

Leech, Geoffrey. 1974. Semantics. Harmondsworth (Middlesex), England, Penguin Books, Ltd.

Lozano, Anthony G. 1970. Non-reflexivity of the indefinite se in Spanish. Hispania 53:3.

Pereira, Eduardo C. n.d. [1st ed. publ. 1907] Gramática Expositiva, Curso Superior. (19th ed.) Rio de Janeiro, Cia. Editora Nacional.

Politzer, Robert L. 1972. Linguistics and applied linguistics: Aims and methods. Philadelphia, The Center for Curriculum Development.

Rodrigues Lapa, M. 1970. Estilística da Língua Portuguêsa (6th
  ed.). Rio de Janeiro, Livraria Acadêmica.
Said Ali, Manoel. 1966. Dificuldades da Língua Portuguêsa, Estudos
  e Observacões (6th ed.). Rio de Janeiro, Livraria Acadêmica.

COMMUNICATIVE LANGUAGE TEACHING AND THE DEBT TO PRAGMATICS

CHRISTOPHER N. CANDLIN

University of Lancaster

Abstract. There has been considerable recent interest in applied linguistics in the development of so-called 'communicative' or 'functional' syllabuses. These differ from existing language learning syllabuses in having a base in speech acts rather than grammatical structure. This paper characterizes such syllabuses, paying attention to the problems involved in such a speech-act base, particularly concerning the question of discreteness in definition of such acts, and the need to look at overall discourse structure rather than only at individual units. This extension raises theoretical and descriptive questions of the relationship of semantics to pragmatics, and the possible need to draw insights for applied linguistics from 'nonlinguistic' subjects such as ethnomethodology, with alternative views of the notion 'rule of discourse'.

1. Although inevitably too short and too summary, this paper is concerned with enumerating a number of problematic areas in discourse analysis, thrown up in the course of applied linguistic research into the design and realisation of what have been called communicative syllabuses. As an exploration I hope that it will also serve to exemplify one interpretation of applied linguistics as a discipline, namely, that of a two-way channel between descriptive accounts of language and pedagogical practices. It is two-way, in that syllabuses for language learning not only derive in some sense from accounts, but also serve to modify them in that while organising the presentation of data about language we are inevitably concerned with the nature of the described data themselves. It is an exploration since, as we all know, there is only

recently concern for suprasentential analysis, and that on the whole more from outside linguistics than within it. It might even be theoretical, in the sense that while engaged in the practical job of devising syllabuses, particularly in this terra incognita, we are all the time taking decisions which imply a view of what we consider language as communication to be, and hence, however unstated and inexplicit, we are doing theoretical work.

Over the last five years or so in Britain, applied linguists have at last been concerned with the only proper goal of a language learning syllabus, that of leading a learner to be able to communicate and understand in a foreign language not only the meaning contained within grammatical structure, but also the range of meaning which lies outside the surface form, meaning as the communication of information which is negotiated between speakers and hearers in the context of their talk and against a backdrop of their beliefs. The 'at last' is only significant in that it was Firth who looked in the thirties to conversation as the place to find out how language 'works'; the wheel has come round. The present concern is with relationships in discourse, the connections between an utterance and its interpreters, and it is here that linguists like Kempson (1975) plead for an abandonment of the conflation of semantics and pragmatics, shunting the explanation of how language is used for communication into the latter, 'whose status within an overall theory of language is still unclear', while keeping the former to the proper bailiwick of determining referential rules. It is from a desire to establish a framework within which to interrelate semantic interpretation and pragmatic use that the applied discourse analysis of current language learning syllabuses is theoretically crucial, even if accounting for the accomplishment of communicative competence entails probable rather than categorial rules and compels an appeal to other disciplines than linguistics. This interrelation begins from the assumption that we cannot accept that all aspects of meaning will find their clues in sentences.

2. It would be outside the bounds of this paper (and indeed our present state of knowledge) to specify all these clues, but it is perhaps worthwhile to set down the areas of enquiry commonly accepted among applied linguists as contributing to the study of discourse, and which are drawn on in the development of communicative syllabuses for language learning.[1]

    A. Studies in textual cohesion (especially the work of Halliday and Hasan, the Prague School)

    B. Studies in language function (Jakobson, Hymes, Halliday, Ervin-Tripp)

C. Studies in speech act theory (Austin, Searle, Sadock, Gordon, and Lakoff)
D. Studies in sociolinguistic variation (Labov, Bailey, Bickerton, Fasold)
E. Studies in presuppositional semantics (Kempson, Vennemann, Grice)
F. Studies in interaction analysis (Bales, Argyle)
G. Studies in ethnomethodology and face-to-face analysis (Goffman, Sacks, Garfinkel, Schegloff)
H. Studies in the ethnography of speaking (Hymes, Gumperz)
I. Studies in process analysis (Wunderlich, Rehbein, and Ehrlich)
J. Studies in discourse analysis (Sinclair and Coulthard)

It is already clear, even from this bald list, that we are having to take a rather wide focus if we are going to make sense, even only partially, of the ways we employ to diminish the apparent unpredictability of what we mean to each other when we engage in interaction. Equally clearly, we can expect that individual designers of language learning syllabuses will only take certain of these contributing areas into account, and will reflect the lack of unanimity among proponents or seek to enforce consensus at the price of delicacy. As we shall see, the link between 'form' and 'function', the relationship between 'sentence' and 'speech act', and the collapsing of different sizes of discourse unit are all cases in point. Nonetheless, it is possible, in a general way, to identify the syllabus designers that I have been referring to as accepting a distinction between sentence meaning and utterance meaning, as seeking to reflect both the cohesiveness of text and the coherence of discourse, and as viewing a language learning progression as a movement towards interactive competence. It is not surprising, though this is not my concern here, to note that such views redefine methodology from 'telling' to 'interpreting', and in the search for audiences, involve this wider view of linguistics in current issues of social concern.

3. Perhaps because of the appealing nature of these views to a fraternity professionally engaged in communication, we have seen in the last five years an explosion of language teaching materials, all claiming allegiance to 'content' (sometimes to the apparent abandonment of 'form') and sharing Silva's (1975) conviction

. . . that it is of the utmost importance to offer the learner the language he will need to participate as speaker-hearer in real acts of communication. An organisation of language teaching determined by the semantic choices the speaker is expected to make will turn the language learning into an activity which is meaningful and relevant to the learner.

With some caveat about the term 'semantic' here, this reasonably represents what a number of us have been saying and practising for some time, [2] not only with secondary school students in mind, but with an increasingly differentiated audience in academic study or work situations. Acronyms such as ESP (which in the context of negotiating what we think we mean might well have the alternative readout), EOP, and EAP, programmes for Asian laundry workers and for casualty doctors communicating with patients, would all subscribe to the quotation; the unfortunate matter at present is that they do so in confusing ways.

The following are brief examples from some such applied linguistic approaches to the theme. I have selected them not out of any spirit of destructive criticism, nor out of any wavering from the essential rightness of the theme of the quotation, but as a vehicle to show, on the one hand, this 'widening of the view of meaning' which I referred to earlier, and on the other, to show later where we should direct our research intention. The examples are all chosen from syllabuses concerned primarily with oral/aural skills, rather than with reading or written communication. This is not intended to imply that syllabuses concerned with the latter cannot share the premises of communicative teaching indicated earlier; indeed, much of the applied linguistic impetus for this investigation of discourse has come from scholars concerned with just these skills (Allen and Widdowson 1974; Widdowson 1973; Selinker and Trimble 1968, 1972: for further references see the British Council ETIC bibliography referred to in note 2).

EXAMPLE 1 (extract only).

David Wilkins. 1972. An investigation into the linguistic and situational content of the common core in a unit/credit system. Strasbourg, Council of Europe.

A. Semantico-grammatical categories
 1. Time
    a. Point of time
    b. Duration
    c. Time relations
    d. Frequency
    e. Sequence
    f. Age

2. Space
   a. Dimensions
   b. Location
   c. Motion
3. Case
   a. Agentive   e. Locative
   b. Objective   f. Factitive
   c. Dative   g. Benefactive
   d. Instrumental
B. Categories of communicative function
   1. Argument (i. e. categories relating to the exchange of information and views)
      a. Information asserted c. Disagreement
         and sought   d. Denial
      b. Agreement   e. Concession
   2. Emotional relations (i. e. expression of response to events usually involving interlocutor)
      a. Greeting   d. Flattery
      b. Sympathy   e. Hostility
      c. Gratitude

EXAMPLE 2 (extract only).

Tom Jupp and Sue Hodlin. 1975. Industrial English. Heinemann.

Language functions	Language forms
Listening to, repeating and passing on information and messages	message formulae reported speech
apologizing	phrases with <u>sorry</u>
asking for an explanation about something wrong asking for attention and acknowledging it	various question forms politeness phrase: <u>thank you</u> <u>for</u> explaining vocabulary: job faults
simple use of the telephone for business: approaches, identification, essential information	revision including names <u>can</u> questions

EXAMPLE 3 (extract only).

Brian Abbs and Ingrid Ferm. Starting Strategies. Longman (forthcoming).

Interpersonal communication
Asking for and giving things
Agreeing to do things
Asking people to do things
. . .
. . .
Asking for and giving permission
Arranging to meet somebody
. .
. . .
Asking for and giving description
Asking if somebody is present
Comparing people and countries
. . .
. . .
Asking for and giving reasons

EXAMPLE 4 (extract only).

T. F. Johns. 'Materials for seminar discussion strategies'. 1975.
Unpublished ms. University of Birmingham, Department of English.

Units
amplificators   explanation
contradiction   consequence
counter   prefaces and suppletion
restriction

EXAMPLE 5 (extract only).

Christopher Candlin, Clive Bruton, and Jonathan Leather. 1976
(forthcoming). Doctor-Patient Communication Skills. Medical
Recording Service Foundation, Chelmsford.

Module: INTERROGATE

Instructional goal: To be able to interrogate the patient about the
occurrence of his injury or the development of his complaint.

Instructor notes: 1. Illustration.

Below is a tapescript of the taped extracts from consultations that you play to the learners to illustrate what an INTERROGATE is. Each INTERROGATE is underlined.

D: What's happened
P: Morning doctor I've had an infection in this ear and it's swollen but it's coming down a bit now the soreness has gone away but it's very wet inside here
D: How long have you had this
P: It'll have been about a fortnight now

Instructor notes: 2. Recognition.

Below is a tapescript of the taped extracts from consultations that you play to the learners. In this exercise the INTERROGATES are not underlined, and the learners have to try to recognise and underline them as they occur.

D: Hello
P: Good morning doctor
D: What's happened to you then
P: Well er a week last no last Thursday night I was painting inside the toilet and I er slipped you know and in falling struck around here on the toilet seat it's been painful ever since so I thought I'd better come and see you
D: How far did you fall
P: Oh not far a foot or two maybe
D: I see and what is this pain like
P: Hard to say really it's there most of the time though

Instructor notes: 3. Discussion.

a. After the doctor has greeted the patient at the outset of the consultation he then tries to get broad background information about the patient's complaint by means of an ELICIT. At this stage he may need to obtain more details about, for example, the time, manner and place of the accident, or the time and manner of the onset of the complaint and the development of the symptoms. He will use an INTERROGATE to extract this more detailed information.
b. The ELICIT is used to get broad background information from the patient. The INTERROGATE, on the other hand, focusses on what the patient says, and is used to fill in the gaps in the information that the patient has provided.

c. Thus the INTERROGATE differs from the ELICIT in that the
realisation of it depends on the information given by the patient.

If we examine the examples, I believe we can see this widening view
of the scope of meaning that I was referring to earlier. Taking the
Wilkins example (and seeing it as part of a blueprint for syllabus design rather than an actual product for a particular group of learners),
there is a sharp distinction drawn between what he calls 'semantico-
grammatical categories', and 'categories of communicative function'.
The first set are reasonably familiar, as Widdowson (1973) points out.
They are close to the basic semantic categories of a grammar made
plain by Jespersen (1924) and are present in language learning syllabuses, though with the important difference in organisational terms
that syntactically varied realisations of, say, Time, Place, Quantity
are not presented in each case as alternatives to the learner as a
conscious procedure of syllabus design. Wilkins' second set is less
homogeneous; it again harks back in part to Jespersen (see his categories of Jussive, Compulsive, Obligative, etc., all having an element of 'will' in them), but it also includes items like Agreement and
Denial. To these Wilkins attaches a number of syntactically varied
realisations, following the distinction between sentence and speech
act drawn by Austin and Searle. At the same time, there exists a
macro-category of 'Argument', subsuming, for example, Agreement
and Concession, and apparently implying a higher-order discoursal
unit.

If we look now at the second example, from Jupp and Hodlin, we
can recognise some of Wilkins' second category items, like 'apologis-
ing' and 'asking for explanation', but we also notice a discoursal development in that the item 'asking for attention and acknowledging it'
is obviously not prime; it implies at least two 'moves' in an 'exchange'
(using the terms nontechnically). Furthermore, the reference to an
item: 'simple use of the telephone for business: approaches, identification, and essential information' not only brings in 'outside' features such as channel of communication, but again refers to a quite
large discoursal unit, some kind of 'transaction' (again used nontechnically).

With the third example from Abbs and Ferm, there is much more
homogeneity on the surface, in that with the possible exception of
'Comparing peoples and countries', all items would fit into Wilkins'
second set; yet there is still the difficulty that 'arranging to meet
somebody' is expandable from a single utterance See you at eight
then ? into a lengthy exchange, depending presumably on the degree
of coyness met with. We are beginning to meet with a problem to
which we shall return later, that of the size of unit in discourse, and
the match to be made with language form.

The example from Johns (number 4) differs from the others in that it is linked to an explicit audience in a nominated setting: that of postgraduate students who have to interact in seminars. Influenced by studies in ethnomethodology, particularly the concept of 'turn-taking', we can see Johns' units as being of a different order from either of the two Wilkins' sets. Johns looks at the whole discourse of the seminar and examines the 'turns' that participants take, and the strategic problems interaction poses; when and how to interrupt, to counter, to contradict. These items are not the semantic categories of a sentence grammar; they are categories of discourse and are, we presume, expounded by some of Wilkins' second set, in that for example, by disagreeing I can counter, and by agreeing I can amplify. Nonetheless, again in Johns we can see difference of order, in that my explanation might also be my counter, or to use another of Johns' terms, my repair move.

The final example, Candlin, Bruton, and Leather (number 5) shares some of the features of Johns in that the audience of doctor and patient is specified and the setting of the casualty consultation is central to the materials. Without going here into the detailed specification of the casualty consultation as an event (see Candlin, Bruton, and Leather 1974, 1975, and forthcoming), the item INTERROGATE is not only a functional activity of the doctor which has a number of possible realisations, it also has a place in the transaction which is the whole consultation. INTERROGATES are recognised therefore not only by their communicative value, in terms of 'seeking more detailed information' but also by their position after the general inquiry of an ELICIT. They derive part of their meaning as INTERROGATES from their position in the discourse. Furthermore, and this is perhaps more of a methodological point, the example illustrates the stance taken towards meaning in the materials; meaning is seen as something to be 'discovered' and discussed. There will be occasions when the value in question will not be immediately clear--where, for example, an utterance or part of an utterance will be multifunctional and it is necessary to proffer a number of variant interpretations: 'I think we'll just give you a couple of jabs' simultaneously realises a DIRECT to the nurse and an ACTION-INFORM to the patient, with REASSURing overtones (our metalanguage).

The syllabuses or categorisations of language exemplified here are representative of what at present are confusingly referred to as 'notional' or 'functional' or 'communicative' syllabuses (the terms chosen to present alternatives to a grammar-based syllabus of a structural type). Looking at the gradual development of discourse in the examples we have chosen, the reason for the alternative labelling becomes clear. It relates to meaning being seen as having varying numbers of levels and also, in a sense, to the size of the discourse unit you are focussing on. As an interim clearing-up operation, at least as far as the labels are concerned, I suggest (see Candlin, Kirkwood, and Moore 1975; Leech and Svartvik 1975) that we regard meaning as being composed of a number of levels or layers. Any utterance can have a first layer of notional meaning peeled off, referring here to the basic semantic categories of Time, Place, and Quantity found earlier in Wilkins' semantico-grammatical categories. Here we notice indefinite and future time, particular quantity, and so on, realised by certain choices in the formal structure of the surface grammar. A second layer could be that of the referential meaning of the utterance, where Austin's locutions and propositions of the truly semantic kind are to be found. Here, as Leech and Svartvik point out, interrogatives always mean questions. Thirdly, however, we need to place the utterance (a 'real' utterance now) in someone's mouth in a particular context, and in so doing the utterance acquires sociolinguistic meaning; it takes on, as it were, illocutionary force and enters pragmatics.

Now interrogatives are not necessarily questions, and utterances are used to express some of our feelings, intentions, beliefs. At this point we take in something of Wilkins' categories of communicative function, as we have particular interlocutors in mind. Finally, we need to take up the layer of meaning exemplified by the positional significance of the INTERROGATE in the interactional process of the consultation, that is, the contextual meaning of an utterance. I am suggesting here that utterances derive some of their value from what precedes them and what follows them; indeed, it is one of the considerable contributions of discourse analysis to the understanding of meaning that we are prepared to admit that, given a view of language as coherent patternings of utterances, we often have to amend perceived value on receipt of more data, or only then really understand. To examine this layer of meaning we are still within pragmatics, and we have to trace how any utterance ties in, cohesively and coherently, to the text and discourse of which it is a part. This useful distinction of Widdowson's, between the grammatical relationship of cohesion within a text and the rhetorical coherence of a discourse, is central to this last layer of meaning. Many structuralist language teaching manuals offer evidence of cohesion bought at the price of coherence, and all of us, we would like to think, can cohere without constantly having recourse to the formal devices of cohesion. (As an aside, it is clear from the work of Labov into discourse rules, and the work of the ethnomethodologists into conversational talk, that it is this layer which will provide applied discourse analysis with the focus for understanding human interaction.)

On the basis of this so far somewhat rough layering of meaning, it would seem sensible to opt for 'communicative' as the defining label for our syllabuses, in that it means what the other terms individually say. We are concerned with enabling learners to impart cognitive and affective information about themselves and their beliefs in the company of present or absent interlocutors.

The extracts that we were examining were remarkable also, however, for the way in which the items in the respective lists differed in size and type. We shall return to this in the final section of this paper, but it might again be worthwhile at this stage to propose an interim clearing-up operation, without precluding the later more tentative discussion. Given the rapid growth of the communicative following (referred to among my colleagues in Germany as the pragmalinguistischer Ansatz, which makes me think that we are leading a battalion rather than worrying about the clanking noises in the engine), such a taxonomy as I shall propose may cause us as syllabus writers to look to our lists.

Language seen as communication fulfills a number of important functions, among which we could cite the following (Jakobson has his own list, as has Halliday):

1. Language as a means of communicating (seeking and giving) ideas
2. Language as a means of social coordination
3. Language as a means of social control
4. Language as a means of expressing wants, beliefs, and desires[3]

These functions overlap, and they are realisable by a variety of verbal and nonverbal means. We can always try to focus on one of these functions at a time in relation to an utterance, but to do so even within a specified context is to see a value which is open to denial. (For example, is It's warm in there an illustration of function 1 or function 3? The answer must be that it can be both or either.) We need, it appears, to mediate between functions and utterances by referring to an interlevel of speech acts, much in the way adopted by Corder (1973). We might take a function like the use of language as a means of social control, and then ask the question: 'how do we exercise social control through language?' We might receive a plausible reply: 'through the way we order, command, prohibit, threaten, warn'. If we were then to examine the 'how' and ask what we mean when we say 'by the way we do X', then we are led to the formal realisations of these various 'social-control-acts' in the verbal and nonverbal codes of the language in question, with the proviso that we cannot associate a syntactic structure uniquely with such an act.

Thus, we can say that the utterance 'I'll fix you' can be seen to realise an act termed 'threat', and 'threatening' is associated with the function of language we have called social control. We still need, however, to narrow down the 'can be seen' by situating the utterance as belonging to a specific social event. It has to come from a particular person in a particular setting with an identified interlocutor. It is only when we have this social data that we can begin to interpret the utterance by identifying the act it realises and the function it reflects. We can only say 'begin' since we have to come to terms with the situational presuppositions that imbue the utterance; we have to be clear that the interlocutors are obeying Grice's Cooperative Principle; we have to set the utterance against the cultural presuppositions of the particular social group (and here those like ourselves concerned with interethnic communication take a deep breath), the individual presuppositions which allow me not to be insulted by being called a 'lexicalist', and ultimately the occasional presuppositions to which I have to appeal in order to understand that in the context of my middle-class living room, reference to a fleck on the wall is construable as an admonition. 4 To this has to be added, of course, the ethnomethodological caveat that this presuppositional awareness is not static but dynamic, that is, as the discourse proceeds we alter the basis of our capacity to understand, and indeed, are compelled to reinterpret what we have felt we have successfully negotiated earlier. This is what Venneman (1973) calls the 'presuppositional pool'.

> Each participant of a discourse is operating within his own
> presuppositional pool. His pool grows as the discourse pro-
> ceeds. Each utterance made by another participant adds
> information to the pool; in particular each statement that is
> not challenged becomes presuppositional for the remainder
> of the discourse.

I am conscious that in an attempt to clarify some of the miscategorisations present in current 'item-banks' for communicative syllabuses, 5 I have too crudely sketched the relationship between form and function. I have, however, tried to point out from time to time areas of uncertainty and problem, and in the final section of this paper I would like to take up some of them as they relate especially to the application of discourse analysis to the construction of syllabuses for language learning.

4. I shall try here to interrelate descriptive and pedagogical questions, not only to sustain the interdependence of thought and practice alluded to in the introduction to the paper, but also because many of the knotty problems first emerge clearly when one is trying to put the concepts of discourse into production.

Central to most of the current 'item-banks' for communicative syllabus design is the Austin/Searle concept of the speech act. As we have seen, the usual procedure is to cite such acts with a performative label and to associate with them a number of different surface structure construction types in the following way:

Suggestion: 'Why don't you . . . ?'
           'I suggest that . . .'
           'We could . . .'
           'Let's . . .'
           'How about . . .'
           'Can't we . . .'

The first problem with this procedure is that it raises the central difficulty of the analysis of discourse, namely, the relationships to be established between function and form. How are the acts identified, and how are the realisations named?

Austin (1962) suggested that in saying something we are performing some kind of action, and this action will have locutionary, illocutionary, and possibly perlocutionary force. I have already referred earlier to the first two, the third is a nonlinguistic sequel to the locutionary and illocutionary acts; i. e. through 'warning' someone becomes perlocutionarily alarmed. Now the first question of the syllabus designer is: how many of these illocutionary acts are to be recognised? Austin suggests that there might be 10, 000 acts, so pruning is going to be necessary. Some help can be derived from Searle (1968) and his suggestion that there may be some 'basic illocutionary acts to which all or most of the others are reducible'. He indicates, for example, that 'asking questions' might be seen as a special case of 'requesting'. This opens up possibilities for applied linguistic processes of selection and grading in that a general syllabus might look to Austin's original sets of verdictives, exercitives, commissives, behabitives, and expositives (in rather the same way as earlier I made the point that one could link acts to functions) as an organisational starting point. It will, of course, be a starting point only in that, although with a structural syllabus it was difficult to motivate leaving out a grammatical structure, with such a general communicative syllabus one could make a strong case in the context of an anti-authoritarian educational philosophy for avoiding situations where pupils were asked to perform exercitives. [6] A more specific syllabus, say in EOP or EAP, [7] would have less difficulty in that scanning the raw data serving as input to the materials design would throw up limitations and selections.

Both these suggestions run foul of an allied problem which is the indeterminacy associated with relating any utterance to its underlying performative. As Kempson (1975) suggests, is I've got a headache a warning, a request, or an apology? This indeterminacy is one of her prime reasons for placing illocutionary force into pragmatics; the indeterminacy cannot be resolved without taking into account the speech event and the situational presuppositions I referred to earlier. Their unpredictability certainly underlines this impossibility of illocutionary definition without reference to specific context. Austin's suggestion was that the illocutionary force was a matter of speaker's intention, but this clearly produces the objection that my promise may be read as someone else's threat. Part of Kempson's problem, then, derives from the location of the interpretive source, with the speaker or with the hearer. Searle would argue that the illocutionary force derives from the listener's interpretation; pragmatic meaning is in the responses of the addressee, and his felicity conditions are set up to make this clear. Interestingly, in terms of what I suggested at the outset of this paper was the multi-disciplinary input to discourse analysis, Searle's position is supported by the ethnomethodologists who argue that the only evidence we have for inspection is hearer response, and that this both defines the 'taken' meaning of what has gone before and, in Venneman's terms, establishes presuppositions for the interpretation of what will follow.

The designer of language learning materials cannot, therefore, hope to explain illocution in the precise way that he can explain grammatical form; he can only conventionalize on the basis of par excellence examples at first selected on the grounds of their probability of this or that illocutionary interpretation in this or that event. As a support he can have recourse to Searle's conditions to assist the sensitising of the learner to the illocution in question, but his 'expression rules' are still different in kind to the traditional rules of grammar. In a world, however, where it is now possible to conceive of variable grammatical rules, the probabilities associated with interpreting illocution may worry us rather less. What the materials writer clearly must ensure is that utterances occur not as isolates but in conversations and in connected texts, where the interconnections are coherent, not merely cohesive. He has, in short, to draw on awareness of the social distribution of rights and privileges, such as Labov (1972) makes use of in his rules for hearing commands. The knotty problem here, especially with foreign learners, is that our making use of Labov's conditions derives from our experience of particular cases; we can always be wrong. A good deal of sociological research is wary of determining norms in particular cases; interaction makes its own rules. We should therefore be cautious in asserting particular illocutionary forces, unless we are able to constrain the presuppositions sufficiently to make one reading most likely. It is no accident, therefore, that those of us who are concerned

with the analysis of discourse and its application to language learning
have chosen just such settings. Johns' work in seminars and our
work in doctor-patient communication are cases in point, as is the
work of Allen and Widdowson (1973) with written texts.

We are, in fact, faced with what Wootton (1975) called the 'ethnomethodologists paradox', whereby the difficulties I have been citing
on rule-governed interpretation of illocutionary force are balanced
(outweighed?) by the fact that talk is experienced as an ordered phenomenon. In Garfinkel's terms:

> . . . if meaning is bound up with occasions of use, and if
> even then utterances are glosses which do not relate in any
> rule-bound way to the contexts in which they occur, how do
> we go about analysing natural language phenomena?

The ethnomethodologists provide two types of answer: the first is to
focus on the interpretive procedures we employ to try to make sense
of what we confront--in other words, to investigate our questioning
and paraphrasing; and the second is to suggest 'machineries' or rules
for connected discourse, which though not invariant, would be open
to evaluation on grounds of explicitness and adequacy in the normal
way.

Both of these responses can find correlates in applied discourse
analysis, and both depend from the outset on asserting that unique
identification of pragmatic value is a chimera (particularly, as it
were, from outside in). We may for didactic reasons grade our
introduction of indeterminacy, much as we have been known to deal
in grammatical 'rules of thumb', but eventually (and with ESP
learners, often quite soon) they must provide their own interpretations. The applied answer to the first response is to take a leaf out
of the ethnomethodologists' book and encourage glossing as a teaching/
learning procedure. We should organise the grading of language data
on a cline of the increasing questionability of meaning, and change our
methodological tactics accordingly. In the context of the doctor-
patient interview, we can suggest illocutionary values in the context
of describing doctors' purposes, but if we do not produce learners
who are sensitive to patients' response as a checking device to the
reading of their intentions, then communicative teaching has little
social value.

We have to be careful, however, that in the necessary didactic
procedure of highlighting par excellence examples we do not forget to
train the transferable skills of what we hear and read. Just as learners are encouraged to find grammatical rules, they should be encouraged to look for the pragmatic clues on which to establish procedures for interpreting discourse (Candlin, Bruton, and Leather 1976,

forthcoming). In a real sense learners have to become analysts of discourse themselves, and we have to use what means we can in terms of existing discoursal awareness from their mother tongue and the provision of a workable model of analysis to make this possible. We can devise procedures whereby the learner is led to an understanding of the referential meaning, encouraged to see the semantic identity of various surface forms, and then, if necessary, by a technique of making the communicative act overt with a performative we can establish the non-isomorphic relationship of sentences to acts. We still have to tackle the sociolinguistic problems of featuring these pragmatic alternatives in respect of varying encounters. I suspect that it is in this last step that we shall have the greatest pedagogical difficulty, and it is significant that the teaching materials exemplified in section 3 are as yet only very crudely beginning this task. Those of us working with spoken discourse and its application to language learning feel that we are experiencing here a degree of explanatory difficulty not so tractable as the applied discourse analysis of academic written texts where the sociolinguistic conventions on variant selection seem more stylised and constrained.

The applied implications of the second response, that of 'rules for discourse', is that an item-bank of speech acts, such as that exemplified by 'suggestion' from the Wilkins list in section 3, cannot serve any more than sentences as the direct endpoint of a communicative syllabus. Just as we expect learners to be able to make grammatically well-formed sentences and to be aware of intrasentential semantic identity, and to recognise and produce pragmatically equivalent utterances, so we must give them an ability to 'manage' the interaction. 'Suggestion' is itself to be used to expound moves in discourse, such as those briefly exemplified by Johns and by Candlin, Bruton, and Leather in section 3. Indeed, some discourse analysts (see Stubbs 1973) would make the point that 'it is not possible to "code" utterances as isolated units--as acts, moves (within a hierarchy of act, move, exchange, transaction) and then at a later stage look for recurrent patterns on the grounds that coding in this way involves knowledge of how utterances are sequentially placed'. I take this to mean that in order to interpret whatever act (say 'suggestion') fills the INTERROGATE position (and what acts typically do has to be determined), and to recognise it as expounding an INTERROGATE we must have knowledge of the coherence of the consultation. Insofar as this is not present, as with many patients, the coherence cannot be presumed; the sentence may be processed, the suggestion recognised without the INTERROGATE being perceived, and its meaning in relation to the history-taking process is not seen.

Both for the description of discourse and the devising of pedagogic procedures for developing communicative ability, there are thus reasons why it is necessary to establish clearly sizes of communicative unit within a hierarchy. It is here that there is much descriptive uncertainty, but it is a matter of common sense to realise that utterances are chained in sequences and that, provided we can refer to a general set of conditions on the issuing of particular acts, we interpret individual act values in specific cases partly on the interpretation of the previous utterances and partly on our knowledge extra to the particular interchange in question. Within the context of a particular type of oral discourse, say doctor-patient communication, we can indicate to the learner, using such a hierarchical model, how the exchanges typically pattern and give par excellence examples of realising utterances. We can also enumerate and classify the less probabilistically patterned techniques of, say, clarification and confirmation requests, and pedagogically use these as a means through which the learner can establish that shared knowledge which is necessary to prevent misfires. At a more micro level, we can take advantage of descriptive accounts of consultations and formulate rules for GREETing babes in arms which differ from those considered appropriate for elderly grandmothers who have been at Casualty before. All these pedagogic procedures are far removed from the practising of grammatical structure; by a process of examining the coherence of talk we develop not only ways of interpreting referential, sociolinguistic, and contextual meaning, but we isolate strategies of communication which can form the basis of the process of 'gradual approximation', in Widdowson's terms, to the transfer to authentic interaction.

As a postscript, a forestalling and a warning are added. It is argued that we have no account of the rules of use as we have accounts of sentence grammar, and as a result we have no basis on which to establish the type of communicative language learning syllabuses that I have been advocating. My linguistic reaction is to wonder whether the question is linguistically proper in that it implies a categorialness in sentence grammars that is being undermined, and that I am to infer from it that the equivalent account will do both for syntax and pragmatics. I think that they are different things and that the accounts we give differ as our focus on what we see as language differs. As to the pedagogic caveat, I would say this: if you look at language pragmatically, then you are centrally concerned with interpretation. You can make suggestions as to interpretations on the basis of your own experience and you can present this to learners as a starting-point for what you hope will be a consensus. The learners are themselves analysts of language, however, and they will derive their own rules of behaviour from the approximations to the authentic that you have been able to present them, and from their experience.

The warning concerns the social function of communicative language learning. With sentence meaning we were protected from having social influence; in pragmatics we hope to understand social inter-action, and in communicative language teaching we are involved in manipulating behaviour; as we are about to begin work in psychiatric training we are more than a little worried about norms.

NOTES

1. For a comprehensive treatment of these contributions to the understanding of discourse, see Coulthard (1975) and Candlin (1976, forthcoming). Some of the areas are examined later in the paper, where I consider existing problems of description in discourse analysis and their effect on syllabus design.

2. A comprehensive bibliography on 'The Communicative Teaching of English' is available from the English Teaching Information Centre Library of the British Council, 10 Spring Gardens, London SW1A 2BN, England.

3. This list is, I think, general enough to do for now, so long as we do not pretend that we can uniquely characterise utterances as being any single function of the four.

4. I am grateful to Manjit Singh for this subcategorisation of 'situational presupposition' and, in general, for his persuasive argu-ments against referring to presupposition without tying participant presupposition to that of logic and linguistics.

5. See especially the valuable work of the Bundesarbeitsgemein-schaft Englisch an Gesamtschulen at the Hessisches Institut für Lehrerfortbildung, Reinhardswaldschule 3501 Fuldatal, Germany, Tagungsprotokolle 1-10 (1972-1976 continuing) and the 1975 Council of Europe publication, The Threshold Level, Strasbourg.

6. This approach is explicitly adopted in current syllabus pro-posals for German comprehensive schools. See the Bundesarbeits-gemeinschaft für Englisch an Gesamtschulen, 9th Protokoll, 1976.

7. EAP = English for academic (study) purposes; EOP = English for occupational (job) purposes.

REFERENCES

Austin, J. L. 1962. How to do things with words. Oxford, Claren-don.
Candlin, C. N. 1976. Sociolinguistic analysis and language teaching materials. Language Teaching and Linguistic Abstracts 9.4 (forthcoming).

Candlin, C. N., C. J. Bruton, and J. H. Leather. 1974. English language skills for overseas doctors and medical staff. Reports I-IV. Lancaster, University of Lancaster.

_____. 1976a. Sociolinguistic variables in data-based course design. Mimeo. University of Lancaster.

_____. 1976b. Doctors in casualty: Specialist course design from a data-base. IRAL 1976.3 (forthcoming).

_____. 1976. Doctor speech functions in casualty consultations: Predictable structures of discourse in a regulated setting. Proceedings of the 3rd International Congress of Applied Linguistics.

Candlin, C. N., J. M. Kirkwood, and H. Moore. 1975. Developing study skills in English. In: English for academic purposes. ETIC occasional paper. The British Council.

Corder, S. P. 1973. Introducing applied linguistics. Penguin.

Coulthard, R. M. 1975. Discourse analysis in English: A short review of the literature. Language Teaching and Linguistic Abstracts 8.2, April. Cambridge University Press.

Jespersen, Otto. 1924. The philosophy of grammar. London, Allen and Unwin.

Kempson, R. 1975. Presupposition and the delimitation of semantics. Cambridge University Press.

Leech, G. N. and J. Svartvik. 1975. A communicative grammar of English. Longman.

Labov, W. 1972. Rules for ritual insults. In: Studies in social interaction. Edited by D. Sudnow. New York, The Free Press.

Searle, J. 1969. Speech acts. Cambridge University Press.

Selinker, L., L. Trimble, and R. Vroman. 1972. Working papers in science and technology. Seattle, Office of Engineering Research, College of Engineering, University of Washington.

Silva, C. 1975. Recent theories of language acquisition in relation to a semantic approach in foreign language teaching. ELT Journal XXIX.4.

Sinclair, J. and R. M. Coulthard. 1975. Towards an analysis of discourse. Oxford University Press.

Singh, M. 1975. Presuppositions, semantic relations and discourse analysis: A pragmatic approach to the study of dramatic dialogue with special reference to the theatre of the absurd. Master's thesis. Lancaster, University of Lancaster.

Stanley, J. 1975. Towards a theory of teaching English for special purposes including units of practical work. Master's thesis. Lancaster, University of Lancaster.

Venneman, T. 1973. Topics, sentence accent, ellipses. A proposal for their formal treatment. Mimeo. LAUT.

Widdowson, H. 1973. Directions in the teaching of discourse. In: Theoretical linguistic models in applied linguistics. Edited by S. P. Corder and E. Roulet. Paris, Didier.

_____. 1975. Linguistic insights and language teaching principles. In: Forum Linguisticum. Contributions to applied linguistics 1. II.

_____ and P. Allen. 1974. Focus on physical science. Cambridge University Press.

Wootton, A. 1975. Dilemmas of discourse: Controversies about the sociological interpretation of language. London, Allen and Unwin.

LEARNING TO READ BETWEEN TWO AND FIVE: SOME OBSERVATIONS ON NORMAL HEARING AND DEAF CHILDREN

RAGNHILD SÖDERBERGH

University of Stockholm

Abstract. This study has been based on data from ten preschool children in the Stockholm area, learning to read in their homes by a whole-word method. Three of the children are normal hearing (H), five severely hearing impaired (Hi), and two totally deaf (D). The three H children were 2.4, 2.9, and 1.10 at the start of the reading instruction; data from reading diaries covers 4 years 7 months, 1 year 1/2 month, and 10-1/2 months, respectively. For the Hi and D children the data covers a period of two years; the five Hi children ranged in age from 2.1 to 3.1 at the start, whereas the two D children were 4.0 and 4.11.

For comparison, additional data has been taken from a study of fifteen children in Novi Sad (normal hearing) taught by the same method, five in their homes, ten in kindergarten. The children ranged in age from 1.8 to 3.4 at the start, and the report covers an instruction period of nine months.

The childred read single words, sentences made up from single words previously learned, and stories. The single words were presented on reading cards, one word on each card.

Reading single words. Four of the children played with the cards, pretending them to be what was denoted by the words written on them.

Favourite cards were those with personal names and those with words denoting things near and dear to the child. Favourite words were easily learned words. As to word-classes, nouns--and with some children, interjections--were relatively easier than verbs and adjectives. The most difficult words were the so-called functors:

257

pronouns, certain adverbs, prepositions, and conjunctions, i. e. words without a direct reference to a concrete reality experienced by the child.

Reading errors were often semantically founded: semantically related earlier learned words were mixed up, such as stänger-öppnar 'shuts'-'opens', ögon-öron 'eyes'-'ears'. For the last case, graphic similarity adds to, and is perhaps the primary cause of, confusion. When a child was on the verge of breaking the code and tried to read words he had never seen before, reading was very often successful if the word belonged to the child's spoken vocabulary. If not, even structurally easy words may be impossible to read.

The children, being shown a new word, often tried to relate it to their own experience by talking about the things denoted by the word, or just by making a sentence containing the word presented. This last method was very common when a child was confronted with a functor. Less common single words inspired the children to talk about language itself, to metalanguage.

Reading sentences. Observations were similar to those recorded for single words, with one major difference: words differing only in grammatical endings, such as docka 'doll', dockan 'the doll', dockor 'dolls', were easily confused on account of graphic and semantic similarity when read as single words; read in sentences, however, they turned out correctly because the child was aided by the symbol of his spoken language.

Reading stories. Here also the children were helped in their reading if the words were known to them in spoken language. When reading stories the child often made 'corrections' of the text to make it conform more readily with his own norms (his own spoken language). Talk about words increased when the child read stories, and metalanguage became more common. The child also discussed the relation between fiction and reality.

In the beginning of the reading instruction, the child's knowledge of spoken language and his experience of reality helped him to make sense of written language. After some time of reading stories, however, the written language itself adds to his linguistic and factual knowledge. Reading inspires action and makes him expectant and prepared for a new experience in life.

This study has been based on data from ten preschool children in the Stockholm area, learning to read in their homes. Three of the children are normal hearing (H), five are severely hearing impaired (Hi), and two are totally deaf (D).

Subject	Date of birth	Start of instruction	Date of last notes in reading diary
H			
Astrid	May 27, 1963	end of Sept., 1965	May 22, 1970
Susanna	Apr. 2, 1971	Jan. 16, 1974	Jan. 31, 1976
Helena	May 10, 1973	Mar. 14, 1975	Feb. 1, 1976
Hi			
Jenny	Mar. 9, 1971	Jan. 15, 1974	Feb. 11, 1976
Klara	Dec. 10, 1970	Jan. 15, 1974	Feb. 16, 1976
Martin	Dec. 25, 1971	Jan. 15, 1974	Feb. 28, 1976
Ia	Sept. 18, 1971	Jan. 15, 1974	Nov. 12, 1975
Lotta	July 2, 1971	Jan. 15, 1974	Feb. 11, 1976
D			
Anna	Jan. 2, 1970	Jan. 15, 1974	Feb. 12, 1976
Stefan	Feb. 14, 1969	Jan. 15, 1974	Feb. 28, 1976

Additional data has been taken from a report by Mirjana Jocić and Svenka Savić, Novi Sad where fifteen children (normal hearing) were taught to read, five in their homes, ten in kindergarten (Jocić and Savić 1973). The children were between 1.8 and 3.4 when the experiment started, and they had been instructed for nine months when the report was written.

Method of instruction. The method used is a whole-word method. (Some of the parents, however, have tried to combine this with efforts to try to make the child break the code.) Astrid was instructed by the Glenn Doman method. Words are written on cards, one word on each card. To begin, the letters should be red and 12.5 cm high. The cards are presented to the child at a maximum rate of one a day.

The first word is mother. When the child says 'mother' as soon as you show that card, you go to the next card, which reads father. When you are sure that the child can discriminate the mother card from the father card, you proceed to nouns denoting parts of the body (hand, nose, ear, etc.). These words are written with 10 cm high red letters. Then you go on to what Doman calls the vocabulary of the home: words denoting the child's toys and other personal belongings, words denoting well-known things in the house, etc. The child should be able to see and touch the thing at the same time as the 'teacher' pronounces the word and shows the card to him.

The domestic vocabulary also includes some verbs denoting simple actions familiar to the child. To begin with, the teacher may illustrate a verb by performing the action at the same time as he pronounces the corresponding word and shows the card. The domestic vocabulary should be written in red letters 7.5 cm high. The 'teacher' should always be careful not to go on presenting new words without making sure that the child recognizes the old ones.

Then a book is provided. It should be very simple and short, containing not more than 150 different words. The letters should be 3/4 cm high. The 'teacher' copies the book, rewriting it in black letters 2.5 cm high. Then each word is written on a card, in 5 cm high black letters. These cards are presented to the child one by one in the same way as before. When the child knows all the words, they are put together to form the sentences of the book. The cards are put on the floor side by side; and the child now learns to read sentences, one sentence a day. When the child can read all the sentences of the book in this way, he is given the handwritten copy of the book and is taught to read the sentences from this copy: reading left to right, from the top of the page to the bottom. When the child is thoroughly familiar with this handwritten copy, the printed book is presented to him. And now he will be able to read this fluently, in spite of the fact that the letters are only 3/4 cm high.

You go on with other books; and now it is not necessary to have an intermediate handwritten copy. All words new to the child are written down on cards and shown to him. When the child knows these words, he gets the new book, and so on.

The instruction of Astrid was carried out as a reading experiment. Its aim was purely linguistic: to find out how a small child instructed in this way finally--all by himself--succeeds in learning to read. Learning to read has many aspects, one of which is the breaking of the code. In the case of Astrid it was possible to show how the child, by storing words in her memory, reflecting on them, and comparing them, succeeds in breaking the code without anybody trying to teach her. The breaking of the code was completed in fourteen months; this process has been described in Söderbergh (1971).

The Astrid experiment also showed that the way a child learns to read is closely related to the child's oral linguistic development. The findings were confirmed by observations made on five more children, one-and-a-half to three years old, who were shown reading-cards by their parents (Söderbergh 1975b). These observations led to the construction of reading material of the Glenn Doman type, but based upon what is known about children's linguistic development between one-and-a-half and four. The reading material (Söderbergh 1973a) was worked out on the basis of the preliminary results of Project Child Language Syntax;[1] it consists of 208 reading cards and a booklet of instructions. The booklet gives information about the child's early linguistic development and a plan of instruction, where the parents are told how to show single cards, how to put cards together into sentences, and how to make up stories. The booklet also contains some stories composed of the words in the material. [2]

This reading material was used by the mother of Susanna and Helena (the girls are sisters) and initially also by the parents of the hearing impaired and deaf children. As the reading material was not constructed to meet the special needs of deaf children, the parents in collaboration with me tried to devise special strategies for each individual child in order to obtain the best results (see Söderbergh 1976).

The reading experiment in Novi Sad was inspired by Söderbergh (1971). The children were taught a basic vocabulary of 50 words. Then they were taught to read sentences and finally their reading vocabulary was extended so as to permit the reading of a special book, based on the fairy tale of Peter and the wolf.

Collection of data. Astrid's reading was observed for 4 years and 8 months, notes being taken in the reading sessions of all she said and did which seemed relevant to the task of describing a child's reading acquisition and reading habits. A few tape recordings were also made, showing her way of reading aloud at different stages.

Reading diaries were also kept by Susanna's and Helena's mother during her reading sessions with the girls, and I have permission to use these diaries here.

For the hearing impaired and deaf children, no regular diaries were kept. The parents had more than enough to do with all the special training that a deaf child should have. Occasional notes were taken, however. I also interviewed the parents at regular intervals. During the two years that have elapsed since I was first brought into contact with these parents, I met five times with them in 1974, to discuss the children's progress. Since December, 1974, to this date I have visited the children in their homes, each child two to five times.

The observations made on these reading children have been placed under three headings: (1) Reading single words, (2) Reading sentences, and (3) Reading stories.

1. Reading single words. Only one of the children, Helena, was reported to have any trouble in distinguishing between the reading card and what was written on the card. One month before the instruction proper began, her mother had shown to Helena (then one year and nine months old), the card with _mamma_ 'mummy' written on it, telling her that the card said 'mummy'. On asking the girl what the card

said, she inevitably got the answer kort 'card'. Then the mother postponed the start of the reading instruction, and when one month later (March 14, 1975) she showed the card to Helena, with the girl's own name written on it, Helena immediately got it right.

The card as a symbol of the thing designed. In one of my visits to Anna (D, 5.1), I brought with me some toy furniture and two dolls. The girl, remembering that her playmates Anne and Lena had a double-bunk bed, took the bunk bed from the heap of toys, picked up the reading cards marked Anne and Lena, and put them on the bed, the card Anne on the upper bunk, the card Lena on the lower bunk. Martin (Hi, 4.2), when he does not succeed very well in drawing something, gives up and instead writes the object's name. Thus, after unsuccessfully trying to draw a cow, he preferred to write ko 'cow'. Astrid (H, 2.6), having no doll's pram, took the card dockvagn 'doll's pram', pushing it on the floor. Susanna (H) by the age of 2.10 excelled in this kind of play: putting the card mössa 'cap' above the card Susannas 'Susanna's', fot 'foot' below pappas 'daddy's', putting the card Susanna to bed, saying 'Susanna must lie in her bed'. Then she put together all cards standing for parts of the body and for clothes, forming a figure that she called Susanna (cap above hair, shoes below feet). Similarly, Astrid (H, 2.6) said that she was very frightened by the word hemskt 'frightful' on a reading card.

Favourite words, easy words, and difficult words. Favourite words with most of the children were names denoting members of the family, friends, pets, etc. Helen (H), although only 1.10, during the first week of reading learned seven names (including mummy, daddy, and granny) without ever confusing them. Jenny's (Hi, 2.10) first twenty words were all Christian names, and Klara (Hi, 3.3-3.5), who during the first two reading months learned 65 different words, clearly preferred names. It may be noted that Klara's family has many friends.

Next in popularity were words denoting things near and dear to the child. Astrid (H, 2.5) preferred kudde 'pillow'. Martin (Hi, 3.10), who is very fond of clothes, was reported to be very clever at learning even 'difficult' words for clothes, such as overall and pyjamas (as they are English loanwords in Swedish, spelling and pronunciation do not follow the general rules and they may in this sense be considered difficult for a Swede). Ia (Hi, 2.8), in spite of her handicap, could even be taught to say trappa 'stairs' because she was fond of climbing stairs.

It can be seen that favourite words are words which are closely linked with the child's pleasant experiences. Asking the parents what

words are difficult and what words are easy, one gets the impression
that verbs might be a bit more difficult than nouns (the Novi Sad children; Susanna, H, 2.10-3.4). Susanna (2.10-3.7) also had some
difficulty in learning adjectives, whereas interjections were favourite
words with her. This may be compared with Pačesová (1968:214).
Pačesová shows that during the period of the first fifty words, interjections and nouns are the most frequent; during the period of the
first one hundred words, nouns, interjections, and verbs (in this
order) hold the lead; and during the period of the first five hundred
words, nouns, verbs, interjections, and adjectives (in this order)
are the most common.

Verbs were a problem with Susanna, however, because of the way
they were first presented to her. On the third day of reading Susanna
received two new cards, äter 'is eating' and fort 'quickly'. As soon
as she had been taught to read äter, this was put together with all the
names of persons she knew to form the two-word sentences mamma/
pappa/mormor/Susanna/Helena/äter 'mummy/daddy/granny, etc. is
eating'; and as she was very fond of reading these sentences, she
also got fort 'quickly', and immediately fort was used to make three-
word sentences out of the sentences she had just read: mamma etc.
äter fort 'mummy etc. is eating quickly'. On the following day glass
'ice cream' and smörgås 'sandwich' were added, only to be used
immediately in four-word sentences like mamma etc. äter glass/
smörgås fort 'mummy etc. is eating ice cream/sandwich quickly'.
Within the next five days a variety of words were presented, among
them the verb åker 'goes by' and bil 'car'. These two words were
at once used to form sentences like mamma åker bil fort 'mummy
goes by car quickly'. As the girl was obviously much more fond of
reading sentences than individual words, most of the time was devoted to the reading of sentences. A few days later Susanna's mother,
when reviewing the cards the girl had been shown during the first two
weeks of reading, complains that her daughter does not seem to know
the verbs at all, only the nouns. She cannot understand why. What
has happened is obviously that Susanna, making acquaintance with new
words mainly in sentences without having acquired each individual
word, has worked out a strategy to make the reading of sentences a
bit easier. Presented with sentences such as:

mamma/pappa/mormor/äter glass/smörgås fort
'mummy/daddy/granny is eating ice cream/sandwich quickly'

mamma åker bil/tåg fort
'mummy goes by car/train quickly'

where the nouns in subject position are well known, the verbs and
nouns in predicate-object position almost new to her, and fort
'quickly' present in all sentences in the same position, her principal
task is to identify the verbs and the nouns acting as objects. The
verbs that have been presented to the girl before her mother's complaint are dricker 'is drinking', äter 'is eating', åker 'is going by',
köper 'is buying'; the nouns acting as objects to these verbs are
mjölk 'milk', glass 'ice cream', smörgås 'sandwich', bil 'car', and
tåg 'train'. Quite obviously, the verbs are rather difficult to distinguish from one another, as they are graphically rather similar,
all of them ending in -er, åker and äter containing å/ä, k/t in first
and second position, dricker, åker, and köper all containing the
letter k, etc. The nouns in object position are not so easily confused,
however, and so the child concentrates her efforts on them. And as
soon as she knows the nouns the task becomes easy: the semantic
content of the noun acting as object makes the verb predictable:

> mummy - ice cream
> daddy - car
> granny - train, etc.

Thus, she can read sentences quite well without learning the verbs
properly.

In the case of Susanna's sister Helena, there are no problems
whatever with the verbs. Their mother writes in her diary that she
is amazed to find how easily Helena learns the verbs. Since Helena
is only 1.10 at the beginning, however, her mother does not think it
worthwhile starting to let her read sentences, so she is allowed to
read single words for six months before starting with sentences.
Accordingly, she learns the verbs one by one, in exactly the same
way as she and Susanna learned the first nouns.

In the Astrid experiment, it was noted that the girl very easily
learned words with a heavy semantic load, such as nouns, adjectives,
and main verbs, the so-called 'contentives', whereas she had some
difficulty in acquiring words carrying a small semantic load, such as
conjunctions, prepositions, some adverbs and pronouns, auxiliaries,
etc., the so-called 'functors' (Söderbergh 1971:29). The functors,
being purely linguistic, cannot be linked with anything in the child's
immediate experience of life, they lack reference, they are 'abstract'.
They are also acquired relatively late in the child's spoken language.
The Novi Sad children had the same difficulty in learning functors.
Susanna and Helena also had some difficulty in learning functors, and
so had the hearing impaired and deaf children.

Reading errors and no readings. In the Astrid experiment, I noticed that when a new word was presented to the girl she often looked upon it as an entity, mistaking it for an already learned word that had certain graphic characteristics in common with the new word--as when mugg was taken to be mun. Such a misreading was called 'misidentification'.

All the children in this study made such misidentifications: glad 'happy' was read as glass 'ice cream' (Susanna H, 3.7), alla 'all' as nalle 'teddy' (Helena H, 2.5), vänner 'friends' as väntar 'waits' (Jenny Hi, 4.3), hund 'dog' as under 'below' (Klara Hi, 4.2), Ia as lampa 'lamp' (Ia Hi, 3.4), titta 'look' as Lotta (Lotta Hi, 3.6), kranar 'taps' as Klara (Martin Hi, 3.3), sönder 'broken' as Sören (Anna D, 5.1), Skansen as ska 'shall' (Stefan D, 6.4).

Often when the children mixed up two words learned earlier, there was not only a graphic but also a semantic similarity between the words, as when ögon 'eyes' was supposed to be öron 'ears' (Susanna H, 3.0), sitter 'sits' to be sätter 'make sit' (Susanna H, 3.4).

Sometimes words learned earlier may be mixed up only on the basis of semantic similarity: stänger-öppnar 'shuts'-'opens', kör-åker 'drives (a car)'/'goes by (car)', ledsen-sönder 'sad'-'broken' (Susanna H, 2.11). In the last example, it is the context of reality that is the same for the two words: Susanna evidently is very sad when something has been broken. The above-mentioned misidentifications are also due to the fact that the mixed-up words occur in the same syntactic positions: mamma stänger/öppnar dörren 'mummy shuts/opens the door', mormor kör/åker bil 'granny drives a/goes by car', Susanna/bilen är ledsen/sönder 'Susanna/the car is sad/broken'. Such misidentifications are typical of Susanna, who learns many of the new words by reading sentences, or rather sentence patterns, like mummy/daddy/Susanna/Helena etc. opens/shuts the door. Her sister Helena, on the other hand, who has an opportunity to learn the words one by one before they are put together to form sentences, makes reading errors that are purely semantic: kudde-säng 'pillow'-'bed', ledsen-gråter 'sad'-'weeps'. Susanna also seems to have some difficulty in learning words that occur in the same syntactic positions: inte 'not', mycket 'much', bra 'good, well', själv 'myself, yourself etc.', e.g. pappa läser mycket/inte/ bra/själv 'daddy reads much etc.'. In a few cases words that have the same syntactic distribution are also graphically similar, which makes them hard to learn. Thus Susanna (2.11) has difficulty in learning kramar and matar 'hugs', 'feeds'. Helena shows no sign of making misreadings on the basis of syntactical distribution.

The Novi Sad group also confused words on the basis of semantic similarity: šešir-kapa 'hat'-'cap', spava-krevet 'sleeps'-'bed', strašan-opasan 'terrible'-'dangerous'. In the last example there is also a question of graphic similarity.

Close graphic and semantic similarity may cause confusion when two or more words differ only in grammatical ending. The Novi Sad children are reported in the beginning not to have noticed suffixes: idem-ide was said to be 'the same thing'. Susanna (H, 3.2), seeing the cards docka 'doll', dockan 'the doll', dockans 'the doll's', dockor 'dolls', dockorna 'the dolls', just said 'many dolls' and counted to nine! In the same context Stefan (D, 5.1) indicated 'five dolls'. When shown one of the forms with grammatical endings, the children tend to read it as the basic form. In the case of Helena (H, 2.5), the reading of genitives was inhibited because she did not yet use these forms in her spoken language. On the whole, however, the children gradually showed an increasing interest in words differing only in grammatical endings and often compared them very closely, musing over them and putting a hand over the ending to make the basic form. Indeed, as has been shown in Söderbergh (1971), this is the way the child starts to break the code.

Sometimes when trying to read a word that has been shown to him earlier, a child may say a synonymous word. Lotta (Hi, 4.7) replaced hund 'dog' by the more colloquial vovve, and the names of her brother Bo and her sister Cecilia by the forms usually used by the family: Bosse, Cissi. Lotta made more interesting misreading, however, when reading mamma 'mummy' for Ragna (her mother's Christian name). When corrected by her mother, who took a pencil and wrote mamma, saying 'this reads mamma', Lotta answered 'Yes, Ragna-mamma'.

When she is starting to break the code after six months of reading, Susanna (H, 3.3) suddenly reads the old and well-known smörgås 'sandwich' as macka (a more colloquial word with the same meaning). Her mother thinks that it is either a kind of protest or a way of testing an hypothesis about the reading system: is the reading system alphabetic (letter-to-sound) or ideographic?

The two deaf children do not make any mistakes of this kind. Their language is sign language, a language with few synonyms. On the contrary, they acquire synonyms through written language, and both Anna (now 6.2) and Stefan (now 7) are very busy trying to find out about synonyms in written language, and enjoy doing so.

Trying to read graphically unknown words. Reading is a creative process where the child brings to bear his total knowledge of language--semantics, syntactics, morphemics, and phonemics. When it comes to reading words that the child has never seen before, this fact becomes more obvious.[3]

When a child is on the verge of breaking the code or has just
broken it, his success in reading graphically unknown words correctly
depends on whether these words are part of his spoken language or
not. If a word that is graphically new to a child belongs to his spoken
vocabulary or is at least known to him in the spoken language, he will
probably be able to read the word. If the child does not know the
word, however, he may not be able to read it even if it may seem
very easy from a structural point of view. At the age of 3.5 Astrid
was unable to read tamburen 'the cloak-room' or humör 'temper',
but she could read plötsligt 'suddenly'; at 3.6 she made several vain
attempts to read takåsen 'the ridge of the roof'; in fact, she sounded
it out correctly: tak-å-s-e-n, but could not make the synthesis; but
biblioteket 'the library'--well known to her from the spoken language
--was a success (bi-bli-oket, bi-bli-o-tek-et, biblioteket). By 3.5
she also succeeded in reading the difficult mattläggare 'man who puts
linoleum on floors', because she had just met one: 'That was the one
who put down granny's carpet. He is a mattläggare'.

Facing the task of reading a word that is completely unknown to
him in the spoken language, the child tends to change the unknown
word into a known one or into a combination of known morphemes,
that is, he wants the word to make sense semantically or to sound
plausible according to his knowledge of phonotactic (graphotactic)
structure. Thus, tamburen is changed to tramp-buren ('the step-
cage'), humör to hundmor ('dog-mother'), Jerusalem to Jerusahem
(hem = 'home').

Trying to relate written language to reality and to earlier linguistic
experience. When a single word from the text is presented to a child,
the child often tries to relate this word to reality by placing it in context.

Personal names are often put in a context of reality. Klara (Hi,
4.0), reading personal names, makes the following comments: Lisen:
Lisen mamma Ami 'Lisen mummy Ami', Manne: Lisens pappa 'Lisen's
daddy', Jossi: Jossi hund 'Jossi dog'. Ia (Hi, 3.4), reading mormor
'granny' says 'mormor bor i Finland' 'granny lives in Finland'.

Anna (D, 5.1), told that one of the dolls I had brought with me is
called Jonas, becomes very interested; seeing the written name, she
signs to her mother 'same as --' and mother fills in: 'grandpa'.
In the same way, the Novi Sad kindergarten group, shown the word
grandpa, immediately made comments like 'My grandpa is in
Zrenjanin', 'My grandpa is in the house with grandma'.

Astrid (H, 3.1), reading the surname Larsson, says: Den lilla
bebens pappa som bor härborta, han heter Larsson, å hennes morfar
han e lite barskallig 'The little baby's father living down there, he is
called Larsson, and her (the baby's) grandfather is a bit bald'.

Not only names but also verbs may be put into the context of reality in a similar way. Astrid (H, 3.3), reading såld 'sold', comments: Det kanske är min vagn som har blitt såld. Att jag inte behövde den 'Perhaps it is my pram that has been sold. For I did not need it'.

When the children were shown words other than nouns and verbs, they sometimes placed them in well-known linguistic contexts: this was often a strategy they used to tackle difficult words, e.g. functors.

Susanna (H, 3.0), being shown här 'here', said 'Dockan är här' 'The doll is here'; Stefan (D, 6.10) put färdig 'ready, finished' in the context 'I have finished'; Astrid (H, 2.9), being shown ner 'down', remarked: 'Precis som ta ner skynket' 'As in "take the curtain down"'. Astrid (3.4), looking at the word böj 'bend', suddenly remembered how I had tried to teach her to start the swing by bending and stretching her legs, saying 'swing-bend, swing-bend' rhythmically. She said: Detta böj e nog gung-böj, till när man gungar 'I think this bend is swing-bend to when you swing'.

The children, gradually gaining literary experience, also referred to written linguistic contexts. Susanna (H, 2.10) was particularly fond of och 'and', kissed the card, and said that och was written in her book, Four Lions Have Dinner. Astrid (H, 2.10), being shown bara 'only', said that she had read bara before, then immediately recited: Små kaniner bara äter och äter och äter 'Little rabbits only eat and eat and eat'. Three days later, being shown ju 'but', she said 'Jag fryser ju.' Det var Karo som sa det i Totos bok '"But I am cold!" Karo said so in Toto's book'.

Metalanguage. The reading of words also made the children aware of language and prompted them to talk about the meanings of words, to make explicit their linguistic systems. In the Novi Sad group one child did not know the meaning of a word: 'What is that nevaljalog?' Mother answered: 'A person who is not good, who does not obey', and the child retorted: 'It is the same as when I pluck your flowers and daddy gives me a spanking'. Astrid (2.10) reading såg 'saw', said: Precis som tittade, tittade e såg 'Exactly like looked, looked is saw'.

2. Reading sentences. Only five of the Swedish children were taught for a long period to read single sentences (i.e. sentences that were not part of a story), consisting of words learned previously.

Susanna (H), starting her reading at 2.9, was taught almost immediately to read sentences, because her oral linguistic development had advanced so far that she was more interested in sentences than in separate words. As Susanna had not learned the words properly before they were put together to form sentences, this caused a lot of confusion.

Helena (H), being only 1.10 when she started to read, was allowed to acquire a large reading vocabulary before she began to read sentences at the age of 2.4. Her mother's reading diary shows that Helena was unusually clever. After two or three months she was reading sentences consisting of nine to eleven words without hesitation, and enjoyed doing so.

After two months of reading, Jenny (Hi, 3.0) and Klara (Hi, 3.3) could read two- and three-word sentences, and Ia (Hi, 2.4) could read two-word sentences. Jenny's reading vocabulary was 70 words, Klara's 50, and Ia's 40, when they started to read sentences. By this time Jenny's spoken language was the most advanced; she could make three- to four-word sentences. Klara could speak in two- to three-word sentences and Ia in two-word sentences.

Lotta (Hi, 2.8) had learned only about ten words after two months; Martin's (Hi, 2.3) language was very poor, so his mother introduced written words to him very slowly; Stefan (D, 5.1) and Anna (D, 4.2) had also learned only a few words. Individual methods were found for all these children, as none of them seemed particularly interested in reading sentences composed of the ready-made reading cards (Söderbergh 1976).

The sentence as a symbol of the event described. During her first month of reading, Susanna (H, 3.10) read dockan sover 'the doll is sleeping'. She looked at the two reading cards, said that the doll must have a quilt, took a third reading card and put it (text turned down!) on top of the card saying dockan, leaving half of it uncovered.

Favourite sentences; easy and difficult sentences. The favourite sentences were those that dealt with the inner circle, family and friends. If the sentences were affective or indelicate, it was even better. Klara (Hi, 3.3) wanted all the family to be angry or to pass water. Anna (D, 5.1), not being regularly taught to read sentences, nevertheless had no difficulty in reading (by using sign language) 'Malin throws the puzzle', when her sister Malin had been naughty and had thrown her puzzle on the floor. Stefan (D, 5.5) did not want to read sentences, but learned one sentence immediately: 'Stefan and Annika are good' (Annika was one of his best friends). Susanna (H, 3.0) was particularly fond of the sentence 'Susanna hides (her) sandwich'. By the age of 3.0, Susanna was given seven different sentences to read, all made up of well-known words. She did not succeed in reading four of these sentences:

han har ett tåg 'he has a train'

jag sitter här 'I am sitting here'
du är färdig 'you are ready'
hon går hem/bort/långt 'she goes home/away/far'

The following three sentences, however, were a success:

Christian sätter en docka i båten 'Christian is putting a doll
   into the boat'
mormor köper två bilar 'granny buys two cars'
Susanna sover på pappas kudde 'Susanna is sleeping on daddy's
   pillow'

In the last three sentences something interesting is told to the
child; in the first four, the information given is very thin. But above
all, the four short sentences that the girl did not succeed in reading
begin with personal pronouns, whereas the last three sentences start
with names of members of the family. When Susanna is 3.7, her
mother finds out that she can read almost any sentence made up of
known words only if it starts with an interjection. The syntax of the
sentence also seems to be important. Helena (H, 2.7) had no difficulty in reading nu är hunden mätt och glad 'now the dog is satisfied
--i. e. not hungry--and happy', but two days later it was impossible
for her to read är hunden mätt nu? 'is the dog satisfied now?'.
When Helena was 2.5, her mother wanted to test how clever she
was in reading long sentences. Helena then read the following sentence without hesitation: Oj titta pappa Helena mamma Christian
Susanna mormor och Cecilia åker tåg 'Oh look daddy Helena mummy
Christian Susanna granny and Cecilia go by train'. From this
Helena's mother draws the conclusion that the length of a sentence is
not important to the child. The only thing to be said to this argument
is that it is not the length as such, but the number and complexity of
constituents, that matters. Moreover, this sentence starts with two
interjections followed by the names of six family members.

The reading of sentences as a source of confusion between words.
We have already mentioned that reading sentences consisting of words
that are graphically new to the child may cause confusion. I shall
give two more examples of this. Susanna's first two-word sentence
tack mamma 'thank you mummy' was learned in a context of play.
First, Susanna (2.9) was shown the reading card tack. Her mother
then gave things to her and she was to say tack mamma. Then her
mother put the two reading cards together to form the sentence tack
mamma, reading it to her daughter. By that time the card mamma
was already familiar to her, but tack was new. The next day, when

the mother showed tack to Susanna, asking her what the card said, she answered: Tack mamma.

Helena was not taught to read sentences until she was 2.4. When she was only 2.2, however, her mother wanted to see, just for fun, if she could read a sentence. Mother then showed her a new verb, äter 'is eating' and immediately combined it with the familiar Helena: Helena äter. On the following day, when Helena was asked to read äter, she said: Lena äter. Her mother then decided to defer letting her read sentences.

The same context-bound reading behavior is shown by Jenny, when she tries at the age of 4.3 to read a letter from her mother. Then the combination förfärligt mycket 'frightfully much' is read as förfärligt törstig 'frightfully thirsty', which she had learned in her favourite book, where a little boy was frightfully thirsty. The Novi Sad team Savić and Jocić also noted that their children 'often recognized words by the fact that they were learned simultaneously (on the same day, in the same situational context).' One of their children said rano 'early' when shown ujutro 'in the morning' because one sentence in the story they read began: 'Rano ujutro . . .' In this case the semantic similarity between the two words may also cause confusion.

Reading errors and no readings. The same reading errors are to be found when children read sentences as when they read single words, with one important exception. Different grammatical forms of the same word, which are confused when read individually, are almost never confused when read in sentences. Then the linguistic context helps the child to choose the right form on account of his knowledge of spoken language. This has been noticed both with the Swedish hearing children and with the Novi Sad children. The hearing impaired and deaf children, however, generally have no grammatical morphemes in their language (spoken language or sign language) which can put them on the right track. On the contrary, these children obtain their first knowledge about grammatical endings from written language. Klara's parents report that at 4.0 she succeeded in acquiring the genitive by means of reading, and that she is now using it in her spoken language.

Metalanguage. Reading sentences may also inspire children to remarks about language. The Novi Sad group reports that a child reading the sentence Srdjan viće 'Srdjan is shouting' makes the following comment: 'Can you say: the flower is crying? Yes you can. Can you say: the flower is dancing? Can you say: the flower is pushing the baby-carriage? No you can't'.

Reading inspiring action. In the hearing impaired and deaf children, reading seemed to inspire action. This is probably due to the way they were taught to read: the parents often wrote down the children's daily experiences and actions and read these diaries with the children.

Ia (Hi, 3.4) had just read the sentence Ia äter glass 'Ia is eating ice cream'; then she added och soppa 'and soup', which her mother wrote down and asked her to read. After reading this long sentence, Ia immediately rushed to the kitchen, shouting that mother must make coffee. Martin (Hi, 3.4) was absentmindedly sucking his sock. Then I wrote the sentence Martin äter strumpa 'Martin is eating his sock'. Martin read it, and then began frantically chewing his sock--it was impossible to stop him. On the same day, Martin had borrowed a blue pencil. He then was shown the following syntagms: en blå penna 'a blue pencil', blå om munnen 'blue mouth'. Having read them, he went looking for blue things, showing them to me: a blue toy animal, a blue car, etc.

Stefan (D, 6.4) had two dolls and a bathtub to play with. I wrote the sentence Klara ska bada 'Klara shall have a bath'. Stefan then rather elaborately put the other doll, Jonas, into the bathtub, looking askance at me to see what my reaction would be.

3. Reading stories. All the children have read stories; some of them, such as Jenny (Hi, now 5 years old), have also read a number of children's books. Little Helen (H, now 2.10) has read stories in the instruction book. The data from Astrid are especially rich, as they have been collected over a period of more than four and one-half years, from the age of 2.4 to nearly 7.

When children reach the age of about 3, learning single written words does not seem to interest them much. Instead, they want to read sentences. Susanna's mother started with sentences almost from the beginning. Susanna was 2.9 when her reading instruction began and she showed a remarkable preference for sentences. We have seen, however, that not all sentences are of interest to a child. And even a sentence that may at first evoke interest becomes tedious if it is repeated too often. The two hundred cards in the reading material do not permit the variation necessary to retain a child's interest over a long time. When Susanna was 3.9, she was allowed to read stories from the instruction book, and immediately she made progress again. Her mother writes in the diary: 'Susanna read about teddy and the doll and she was very clever indeed'.

Reading errors. The tendency already noted not to read or to misread words that do not belong to the child's spoken language is very strong when a child reads stories. When Jenny (Hi, 4.8) got a new book, she read all the words she knew but murmured something where there were words she did not know. 4 Sometimes she suggested graphically similar familiar words instead of those that were unknown to her.

Astrid (3. 8–3. 11) did not succeed in reading the graphically unknown såras 'be wounded', luden 'shaggy', and farstu(trappa) 'front doorsteps', because såras, luden, and farstu were completely unknown to her in her spoken language. But the word examen 'examination', which was also graphically new to her, was not a bit difficult, in spite of the rather uncommon letter x, owing to the fact that it was a familiar word from her spoken language. The girl even explained to me why she could read such a difficult word: 'Because you have passed an examination, so that is why I know it. '

About four months after Astrid had broken the code, a new type of 'reading error' occurred: she changed the form of the written word to make it conform with her own spoken form or what she considered to be the correct form, i. e. her own linguistic competence: Kristin (name) was changed to Kerstin (March 1967), glädes 'becomes glad' to glädjes (March 1967), vikingaskepp 'viking's ship' to vikingsskepp (April 1967). That her readings were not errors but corrections of the text is shown by the fact that during the same period she often openly criticised the text when the forms did not correspond to her norms. In April, 1967, reading väckarklocka, she said 'It is called väckaklocka'. When I told her that väckarklocka was correct, she retorted 'But väckaklocka is better'. In the same month, reading skridskor 'skates', she said 'It is silly to say skridskor' (the word is pronounced skrisskor). In May, she objected to skuld 'debt' and said it ought to be skull, which is how the word is pronounced colloquially.

The Novi Sad children were observed changing the text according to their own semantic and syntactic competence. In a sentence beginning rano ujutru Peca 'early in the morning Peter', a child added je ustao 'got up'.

Astrid's reading from April, 1967, onwards is rich in syntactical changes or corrections. I am going to give only one or two examples. En eld vi gör literally 'a fire we make' is changed to en eld gör vi (poetical word order changed to normal). In an enumeration of things, where the items mentioned were separated by commas, Astrid put in and instead of the commas. In June, 1967, she read an unusually difficult sentence, where subject and predicate were separated by two subordinate clauses: Och alla som inte är i arken när vattnet kommer ska drunkna 'And all who are not in the ark when the water comes will be drowned'. At the end of the second subordinate clause she lost track and changed när vattnet kommer ska drunkna to när vattnet

kommer att drunkna 'when the water will be drowned' (Swedish
kommer att means 'shall/will/is going to').

All these examples show that reading is a creative process. That
it is also a process where a young reader may be keenly aware of
what she is doing is evident from the following example. On February
11, 1967, Astrid read aloud a book about a girl called Sara. The
following sentence appeared: 'Det är faktiskt en blåmes' sa Sara
tyst för sig själv '"It really is a bluetit"', said Sara silently to herself'. Astrid started to read the sentence in a normal voice but
stopped before Sara--and then reread Sara's retort, in a whisper.
The semantic message about Sara's way of speaking (said . . .
silently) governed the girl's way of reading what Sara had said.

Trying to relate language to reality and to earlier linguistic
experience. When she read stories Astrid often talked about the
words she met. Sometimes she referred to people she had heard
using a certain word. In November, 1966, reading jäntan 'the lass'
she said: 'Sometimes I am a little lass; granny says so'. At other
times she remembered conversations where the word had been used.
On Easter Day, 1967, Astrid and I went to church. When we arrived,
the choir was singing. Astrid asked why. I told her they were only
rehearsing. A few weeks later she read a book where the word rehearse was used. Then she said 'rehearse singing to the organ in
the church of Kummelby'. She also cited songs or stories we had
told her when she found words in her books that she had also met in
those songs and stories. Often she referred also to her own previous
reading, as when in May, 1967, she found the word vansinnig 'mad'
in one of her books and immediately cited a whole sentence from one
of her earlier books where that word had been used: 'She would be
mad, said Lotta'.

Metalanguage. Metalanguage is very common in connection with
story reading. Jenny's mother recently told me that Jenny (Hi, 4.11)
often asks her about words and the meaning of words, and for the
most part she asks these questions during the reading sessions.
Astrid, reading books from 1967 onwards, often asked about the
meanings of new words. In the spring of 1967 (she was then nearly
four years old), she often wanted to know if a certain word was
frightful, e.g. listiga 'cunning', used about the snake in the garden
of Eden; or she asked if the thing denoted was dangerous, e.g.
lakritspipa 'liquorice pipe'. In the spring she also frequently paid
attention to homonymous words. Reading the sentence Vi har en
massa får här i Bullerbyn och dom får lammungar 'We have a lot of
sheep here at Bullerbyn and they get lambkins', she laughed: Får
och får Mamma! 'Sheep (får) and get (får) Mummy!' The meaning of

names was also very interesting at that time. Reading about a nasty man who was called <u>Snäll</u> 'kind', she objected to his name and said he ought to have been called <u>Stygg</u> 'nasty' instead. She also began to notice the way an author addresses his readers. One of her books began: 'Now you must listen attentively. I will tell you . . .' Reading it, she broke off, saying: 'They are talking to <u>me</u>'. The book then went on: 'Do you know where your food comes from? The good sandwich you have just eaten'. Astrid commented: 'I had a sandwich for breakfast and that is not long ago. So it is a good thing that the book says <u>just</u>'.

Thus, by reading and asking questions in connection with reading, the child gradually refines his linguistic system and increases his vocabulary. This is especially important for the deaf child, whose linguistic capacity will be very limited if he has access to spoken language only. Jenny's mother has told me that Jenny (Hi, 4.11) can read all the words in her spoken vocabulary, and that every increase of her vocabulary now comes through written language.

Reading fiction as an enjoyment. Children who read early soon get their favourite books. Jenny (Hi, 4.11) takes a pile of books and reads them almost every day. So does Martin (Hi, 4.2). Favourite books are read again and again. Anna's (D, 6.2) chief interest is said to be reading. A favourite book of Astrid's was <u>The Children's Bible</u> by Anne de Vries. I noticed that the girl often stopped her oral reading of the Bible after having finished a very dramatic passage, and then she went over this passage again, silently. On October 21, 1967, at the age of four and a half, the girl had read about the crucifixion. She went back and reread the passage telling how Jesus asks St. John to take care of his mother Mary and to be like a son to her ('When Jesus therefore saw his mother, and the disciple standing by, whom he loved, he saith unto his mother, Woman, behold thy son! Then saith he to the disciple, Behold thy mother! And from that hour that disciple took her unto his own home.') Astrid then said: <u>Det här var en fin liten dikt. Mittemellan det hemska var det en fin liten dikt</u> 'This is a fine little poem. In the middle of all the frightful things there is a fine little poem'.

Fiction and reality. The problem of fiction and its relation to reality was very keen for Astrid as early as December, 1965, when at the age of 2.7 she had read her first book. This book was a home-made one, dealing with herself and her family. A passage in the book related that her father, who lived in Denmark, would come and spend his Christmas holidays with us. But Father became ill and was taken to the hospital, so he could not come. The girl did not make any comment on this passage until two months after she had read the book for the first time. Then she suddenly said: 'My big book is wrong when it says that Father came on that day he was in the hospital. I am going to check it. When I become a big girl I am going to write all of it correctly.'

At the age of 3.9 she read the Dutch author Ninke van Hichtum's book about Mother Afke's ten children. Then she asked: 'Did these people really exist?' 'Possibly,' I said. 'Yes,' she replied, 'for if so, we will meet them in Heaven and then they can teach us to speak Dutch.'

Reading may also be a preparation for reality. At the age of four, Astrid read a book where she learned a lot about horses and stables. When, a year later, she was going by horse and carriage with some children she had never seen before, the coachman drove to the stable instead of going back to the starting-point. There he let the children off. Astrid told me afterwards about the adventure, saying: 'The horse ran into a dark room, and at first I was dreadfully afraid. But then I saw that it must be a stable, and everything was all right.' Reading about certain things may also make the later real life experience much more intense and rich than it would probably have been without the literary anticipation. Thus, Astrid's first sunset, experienced in August, 1967, was a sheer delight; and the first time she saw cows grazing she was in a rapture, stopped, and shouted in a joyful voice: 'Oh, this must be a pasture!' The sunsets and pastures of literature had finally come to life.

Reading inspiring action. The hearing impaired and deaf children have been inspired to an intense linguistic activity through reading. They ask their parents to write down words that are difficult for them to grasp in the spoken language and they inquire about the meaning of written words that are new to them. All of them also try to write. Anna (D, now six years old) collects cards showing words that she has learned because they mean much to her. Stefan (now seven years old), who is totally deaf, collects written words, takes them to the teacher who instructs him in sign language, and asks the teacher to show the signs corresponding to those written words.

For me, it has been interesting to experience the extent to which Astrid's reading has inspired her nonverbal life. She often introduced scenes from her books into her games, building houses after having read The New House, constructing roads for her cars after having read The New Road. From the age of 5 to 10, one of her favourite games was to take a book and make a play out of it, all her dolls and toy animals being the actors. She could pass a whole rainy day in that way without having a dull moment. Favourite books were those with many family members, such as Ninke van Hichtum's

<u>Mother Afke's Ten Children</u> or Laura Fitinghoff's <u>The Children from the Frostmo Mountains.</u>

From this and other studies we see that it is possible to start a two-year-old child reading by closely associating the words and sentences read with his actual experience of reality and by adjusting the written material to his factual knowledge of language.

Through reading he will then begin to add to his knowledge of both language and reality. His linguistic knowledge will automatically grow through reading in the same way that a child's spoken language develops through listening, and this development will be all the greater if the child has become accustomed to asking other people when problems arise. His knowledge of reality will also grow insofar as what he reads gives adequate information. In any case, whatever information he gets will make him prepared, expectant, wide-awake, ready to check his second-hand picture of reality against reality itself. Just as a person who goes to Rome well prepared through previous reading will have a wonderful time exploring the classical monuments, the medieval churches, the renaissance buildings, whereas his neighbour who goes there without any preparation or knowledge at all will only see rows of houses and ruins--in the same way, a child accustomed to reading will gain an enhanced awareness of reality, allowing him to see more and experience more. But he will also develop an early critical attitude towards written messages, an attitude that is reflected in two and one-half-year-old Astrid's complaint about her first book: 'My big book is wrong . . . I am going to check it. When I become a big girl, I am going to write all of it correctly.'

NOTES

1. Project Child Language Syntax at the University of Stockholm in 1970. See Söderbergh (1973b).

2. The instruction gives great freedom to the parents (teachers), telling them to pay attention to what is interesting to each individual child. They are also told to link the presentation of the cards closely with reality--to show the things when reading the nouns, to illustrate the action when reading the verbs, etc. Several games are also suggested and the parents are invited to invent new games with their own children.

3. The reading of graphically unknown single words is illustrated only by examples from Astrid. This is due to the fact that all the other Swedish children were shown cards for the purpose of learning how to read. Thus, the parents always told the children immediately what was written on a card when showing it to them for the first time. With Astrid, however, the aim was to find out about the learning

process, and therefore I always asked her first what was written on a new card before telling her. By writing down her suggestions I obtained useful information about her reading strategies which made it possible for me to find out how she broke the code.

4. According to her mother, Jenny's reading vocabulary at that time completely covered her spoken vocabulary. The new words she learned were introduced by means of the written language.

REFERENCES

Bloom, Lois. 1970. Language development: Form and function in emerging grammars. Cambridge, The MIT Press.

Carroll, John B. 1972. The case for ideographic writing. In: Language by ear and by eye. Edited by James F. Kavanagh and Ignatius G. Mattingly. Cambridge, The MIT Press.

Conrad, R. 1972. Speech and reading. In: Language by ear and by eye. Edited by James F. Kavanagh and Ignatius G. Mattingly. Cambridge, The MIT Press.

Doman, G. 1964. How to teach your baby to read. The gentle revolution. New York, Random House.

Gibson, Eleonor J. and Harry Levin. 1975. The psychology of reading. Cambridge, The MIT Press.

Gough, Philip B. 1972. One second of reading. In: Language by ear and by eye. Edited by James F. Kavanagh and Ignatius G. Mattingly. Cambridge, The MIT Press.

Jocić, Mirjana and Svenka Savić. 1973. Acquisition of reading ability in early childhood. Several questions of theory and practice. Paper read at the 3rd congress of Yugoslav pedagogues, Ohrid, 1973. Xerox.

Lange, Sven and Kenneth Larsson. 1973. Syntactical development of a Swedish girl Embla, between 20 and 42 months of age. Part I. Age 20-25 months. Stockholm, University of Stockholm, Department of Scandinavian Languages, Report 1.

Lotz, John. 1972. How language is conveyed by script. In: Language by ear and by eye. Edited by James F. Kavanagh and Ignatius G. Mattingly. Cambridge, The MIT Press.

Martin, Samuel E. 1972. Nonalphabetic writing systems: Some observations. In: Language by ear and by eye. Edited by James F. Kavanagh and Ignatius G. Mattingly. Cambridge, The MIT Press.

Pačesová, Jaroslava. 1968. The development of vocabulary in the child. Brno, University J. E. Purkyně.

Söderbergh, Ragnhild. 1971. Reading in early childhood. A linguistic study of a Swedish preschool child's gradual acquisition of reading ability. Stockholm, Almqvist and Wiksell. Reprinted 1976. Washington, D. C., Georgetown University Press.

_____. 1973a. Läspaket. Stockholm, Skriptor.

_____. 1973b. Project Child Language Syntax and Project Early Reading. Stockholm University, Department of Scandinavian Languages, Report 2.

_____. 1975a. Language acquisition and reading. Paper read at the 3rd International Child Language Symposium, London, 1975. Stockholm, University of Stockholm, Department of Scandinavian Languages. (P)reprint 7.

_____. 1975b. Reading and stages of language acquisition. Prepared for the IXth International Congress of Anthropological and Ethnological Sciences, Chicago, 1973. Stockholm, University of Stockholm, Department of Scandinavian Languages. (P)reprint 9.

_____. 1975c. Review of: Language by ear and by eye. In: Journal of Child Language, 2:1.

_____. 1976. Learning to read: Breaking the code or acquiring functional literacy? In: Georgetown University Papers Number 13. Washington, D. C., Georgetown University Press (forthcoming).

Wolff, J. G. 1973. Language, brain and hearing. London, Methuen and Co.